THE REALMS
OF HEALING

Other Books by Stanley Krippner

Shamlet (1971)
Dream Telepathy (with Montague Ullman
  and Alan Vaughan; 1973)
Galaxies of Life (edited with Daniel Rubin; 1973)
The Kirlian Aura (edited with Daniel Rubin; 1974)
The Energies of Consciousness (edited with Daniel
  Rubin; 1975)
Song of the Siren (1975)
Future Science (edited with John White; 1977)

By Alberto Villoldo

*Multi-cultural Assessment Tools for Early
  Education* (1976)

THE REALMS
OF HEALING

STANLEY KRIPPNER
ALBERTO VILLOLDO

INTRODUCTION BY
EVAN HARRIS WALKER

CELESTIAL ARTS
Millbrae, California

Copyright © 1976 by Stanley Krippner and Alberto Villoldo
Celestial Arts
231 Adrian Road
Millbrae, California 94030

First Printing, May 1976
Made in the United States of America

Library of Congress Cataloging in Publication Data

Krippner, Stanley   1932–
    The realms of healing.

    Includes index.

I. Villoldo, Alberto, 1949–   joint author.
II. Title.

                        75-7858

ISBN 0-89087-112-4-pbk.
    3 4 5 6 7 8—81 80 79

Contents

Acknowledgments

The authors wish to thank Carol Guion, R. D. Mattuck, Ken Kimell, Alan Brandt, Jimmy Munro, Rhea A. White, Henry Dakin, Reneé Hendrick, Eugenio Barbera, JoAnn Bakula, Tom Helsabeck, Donald Westerbeke, Carmen Marinho, A. Elaine McLaughlin, and Olga Worrall for reading and commenting on various portions of this book. In addition, Hadley Smith and Helen Manetti are to be commended for typing the book's manuscript. Special thanks also to Margot Rivero, without whose help many parts of this book would not have been possible.

The authors would also like to acknowledge the financial support of the Erickson Educational Foundation for financial grants which enabled them to obtain the information from Brazil and Czechoslovakia presented in this book.

Introduction

It is often said that a new age—the Age of Aquarius—is upon us. This era supposedly supplants the Age of Pisces, the events of which were to prepare us for major changes in our world.

One need not look far to conceive of a better world. We can hope for the end of war, famine, and want. We can envision the healing of the sick and distressed. We can aspire to a world in which each person will have a burning desire to help others live in happiness and harmony with nature.

But what is to trigger such a change? Will humanity embrace a new messiah? Will we suddenly seek remorse for our errors? Will we flock to a great political leader or a new politics? Not quite. Tools cut poorly when they become dull. The old device must have a new edge. We cannot expect this new age to bring change unless it is based on a solution to the unresolved problem that lies at the heart of the era drawing to a close.

What is the unresolved problem that lies at the heart of the Age of Pisces? Two events produced a monumental conflict. Jesus was believed to have healed people, to have performed miracles, and to have been resurrected after death—all to demonstrate the existence of a personal God. On the other hand, science and its accompanying technology brought knowledge of the basic workings of reality to people. This technology allowed them to control their destiny to a degree never before possible—although neither values, morals, purpose, God, nor the significance of life existed in that technology. These two colossal events took place, yet in the end we still do not know who we are. This is the central quest, the pivotal issue, the unfinished business of the Piscean Age.

Sadly, the reality of miracles, of healing, of any significant entity that could be called God, is not thought to be compatible with the reality of science. We are told that miracles were natural events misinterpreted by a superstitious and illiterate people. Healings were psychosomatic in origin, we are told, and the resurrection of Jesus was most likely a political plot. Who can know now, anyway? Yet, without deeper meaning in life, without something of value to dedicate one's life to, the advances of our science and technology are hollow.

Do healing and miracles still occur? In this book the question of unusual forms of healing is looked at again. We need to understand these things, to look again for the miraculous. In fact, truth and reality will not be completely discovered until we know if these miracles exist and how they occur. The evidence and the understanding must come together. If there are new facts, they must come into accord with the scientific method.

If we discover that psychic healing is real and employs techniques that are novel to orthodox medicine, we will have found new paths to health. And if in understanding these phenomena we alter our basic picture of the universe, we will win a new future. Indeed, this new knowledge may indicate that all people have in their consciousness a quality as real and fundamental as space and time, matter and energy. It may demonstrate that consciousness not only can be quantified and understood, but can be shown to affect matter—and can be shown, moreover, to interconnect a part of each person's conscious existence into a universal and transcendent consciousness. In other worlds, if the scientific knowledge about consciousness teaches us about collective will and God, we will have won a new age.

That new age will not find people drifting aimlessly, but will put individuals in real contact with the infinite sea of consciousness. Indeed, to understand these things will be to see God walk on this earth.

Evan Harris Walker, Ph.D.

Dedication

TO OUR PARENTS:
Carroll and Ruth Krippner
Pedro and Elena Villoldo

Chapter One

The Case Against
"Psychic Surgery"

On February 28, 1975, Judge Daniel H. Hanscom declared "psychic surgery" to be "pure and unmitigated fakery." He stated that "operations by psychic surgeons, psychic healers, spiritual or spirit healers, and magnetic healers are simply phony" and ordered several travel agencies to stop promoting "psychic healing" trips to the Philippines. Hanscom, an administrative law judge, acted in response to an action instigated by the Federal Trade Commission against the travel agencies which had featured visits to the "psychic surgeons" as part of their tours to the Philippines.

On March 17, 1975, *Time* magazine reviewed William A. Nolen's book, *Healing: A Doctor in Search of a Miracle,* praising the celebrated surgeon's attempt to "debunk faith healing." The *Time* reviewer wrote, "The result of his two years of research is a book that should serve as a warning to any patient who prefers spirits to medicine."

Time presented a summary of Nolen's visit to the Philippines, stating:

> Nolen . . . has no use for the psychic surgeons who "operate" in the Philippines often on desperate patients who have spent plenty of money to get there. He watched several of these sleight of hand artists scratch their patients with deftly

concealed mica flecks to give the impression that they had
made incisions by sheer psychic energy. Nolen also discovered that the healers simulated blood with betel nut juice,
and quickly disposed of all tissues supposedly removed during their operations to prevent laboratory analysis.

Citing Nolen's first hand experience with the "psychic surgeons," *Time* noted that:

> . . . Nolen, who had not revealed his identity, tested
> Filipino healers by undergoing surgery himself for high
> blood pressure. Before the operation began, he noticed his
> "surgeon" palming a reddish-yellow object. During the op-
> eration, he watched the psychic double up his hands so that
> it would look as if they were inside Nolen's body. Nolen,
> who knows a little anatomy, was not fooled: the surgeon's
> hands never even penetrated his skin. Nolen, who has re-
> moved enough tumors to know what one looks like, recog-
> nized the tissue as a lump of fat, probably from a chicken.

In April, 1975, the *National Enquirer* ran a banner head-
line, "Fake Psychic Healers!" The story told how an *Enquirer* reporter had visited the Philippines, had observed a
"psychic surgeon" at work, and had left convinced that she
was fraudulent after the "tumor" she appeared to remove
was scientifically analyzed and proved to be a section from
a tropical plant.

At first glance, the case against "psychic surgery," the
most controversial type of "psychic healing," would appear to be closed.* The most powerful elements of American society had spoken: the Federal Trade Commission, an
administrative law judge, a distinguished surgeon, the nation's most popular news magazine, and the newspaper
with the highest circulation in the land.

---

*The authors have used quotation marks whenever a traditional word (such as
energy, healing, surgery) is used in an untraditional way. Someday more refined
language will be invented. In the meantime, ordinary terms must be borrowed for
the sake of communicating information about extraordinary phenomena.

Judge Hanscom's Decision

But one needs to take a closer look at the evidence. Judge Hanscom's decision was based on hearings held between September 9th and 24th, 1974. Of the 48 witnesses who testified, 33 were called by the complaint counsel and 15 by the travel agencies that were charged with "promoting, offering for sale and selling package tours to the Philippines so that customers could undergo 'psychic surgery. . . .'" The transcript of the hearing states:

> According to the complaint, respondents engaged in written, oral and visual repiesentations which had the tendency and capacity to lead members of the public to believe that "psychic surgery" performed in the Philippines is an actual surgical operation, that the body is opened, and that disease-causing material is thereby removed.

There were 134 exhibits received by Judge Hanscom during the hearing, 131 being introduced by the complaint counsels. Among the exhibits was a film which Hanscom described as recording

> . . . a series of "operations" on individuals, each of whom is shown lying on a table surrounded by onlookers. The "psychic surgeon" or "faith healer" appears to have his hands, surrounded by blood, in a depression in one part or another of the patient's body, and appears to have opened or to be opening it with his bare hands, without anesthesia or surgical instruments of any sort, and to be removing tissue or other material from inside. During the "operation," the "psychic surgeon" or "faith healer" from time to time holds up to the view of the onlookers what appears to be tissue or material removed from the body. Thereafter, the abdomen, or other part of the anatomy which appears on the film to have been opened, is wiped clean by the "psychic surgeon" or "faith healer," or his attendants. No marks of any incision are seen, and there is no scar. The patient arises and walks away.

Following the witnesses' testimony, Judge Hanscom concluded, "The illusion of opening the human body with the bare hands, and the removal of diseased tissue or material therefrom, is created by a variety of crooked devices, mainly clever sleight of hand." Hanscom's opinion was that "psychic surgeons" are "skilled sleight of hand artists, and additionally employ a variety of tricks, devices and methods of deception, including the use of small animal parts, to convey the deceptive impression that . . . material is being removed from the body."

The Witnesses

Hanscom's decision was influenced by Donald F. Wright and Carol Wright, two Americans who initially were impressed by the Filipino "healers." However, they reported that they soon discovered that none of the Americans they brought to the Philippines were assisted by the "operations." They also began to observe objects falling from the "healers'" hands before the "operation." One day, Carol Wright inspected a "tumor" that had been produced during a "psychic surgery" session. She reported:

> . . . I took the membrane and pulled it back and found that
> . . . it appeared very much like a tumor, but it was . . . just
> a flat piece of membrane that had been stuffed with cotton
> and blood clots to look like a round tumor.

Eventually, one of the "psychic surgeons" reportedly took the Wrights into his confidence and taught them how to buy animal parts at a market, where to hide them, and how to make it look as if the animal part emerged from a sick person's body during an "operation." The Wrights testified that they observed several "psychic surgeons" performing sleight of hand, among them: Terte, Marcello, Virgilio Gutierrez, Jr., Tony Rumbo, Tony Alcantara, Romeo

Bugarin, Juanito Flores, Alex Orbito, Tony Santiago, José Mercado, Felicia Irtal, Rosita Bascos, and Rudy and Placido Palitayan. Judge Hanscom noted:

> The Wrights considered these healers to be the "major psychic surgeons" in the Philippines. . . . They concluded that the techniques used by the "psychic surgeons" were all essentially similar and all were fake.

Hanscom's decision also mentions the testimony of Robert Gurtler, a professional magician, who observed seven of the Filipino "healers" and detected sleight of hand techniques. Among the procedures used were capsules filled with blood, concealed animal tissue, and—in the case of a "healer" named Juan Blance—a preliminary cutting of the skin with a concealed razor blade so that when the "healer" pointed his finger at the patient's skin, it would "open" and begin to bleed.

A third witness, Larry Allen, filmed Tony Agpaoa and noticed his assistants enter the operating room with two shopping bags. Mr. Allen looked into the bags, reporting that they were filled with capsules and animal tissue. This testimony about "psychic surgery" provided Hanscom with "additional compelling evidence of its wholly fraudulent nature." Hanscom also cited instances in which analyses were made of material produced during the "operations":

1. Erna Hansen saved garments which were stained with blood during "psychic surgery." Later, an American criminologist examined them and concluded they were stained with hog blood.

2. Phyllis Douglass was treated by Tony Agpaoa for breast cancer. Her husband brought back a portion of the tissue "removed" by Agpaoa; a pathologist examined it and concluded it came from the bowel of a small animal.

3. William Chambers was afflicted with amyotrophic lateral sclerosis and was given three years more to live. Shortly after receiving this prognosis, Chambers joined a travel agency tour to the Philippines. Chambers' treatment consisted of "psychic surgery" with frequent intensive massage of the legs. Upon returning home in 1973, Chambers entered the hospital. It was the opinion of his physician that Chambers' condition had been worsened by his trip to the Philippines and by the massage. In 1974, he entered the hospital again and died. His physician stated that the Philippine "psychic surgery" tour "resulted in Mr. Chambers' death when he was still expected to have approximately two years to live."

Other Witnesses

The entire transcript of the hearing covers 2,388 pages. The decision runs only 75 pages and completely ignores all testimony supportive of the Filipino "healers'" claims.

One of those appearing at the hearings was a California biologist and business executive, Donald Westerbeke, who suffered hearing and vision problems after a skiing accident in 1972. A team of physicians examined Westerbeke, decided he had a tumor in his pituitary gland, and advised an operation. While making plans to enter the hospital, Westerbeke saw a film depicting Tony Agpaoa's "psychic surgery." A few days later, Westerbeke talked with Agpaoa's wife on the telephone, was assured that "psychic surgery" could be done on the brain, and was directed to a San Francisco travel agency.

After a conversation with Agpaoa, and after witnessing several operations, Westerbeke found himself on a table in a Manila hotel. He later recalled the "operation":

> . . . two cotton pads were put over my eyes and we were on the way. I felt my forehead being stroked with what seemed to be an application of oil and grease, and then a pulsing or

vibration movement of Tony's hands. . . . Suddenly, there was a movement of hands on my forehead—sort of a "pushing it all back in" movement—and Tony said, "We are finished."

Westerbeke tried to bring the material back to the United States for analysis, but Agpaoa's assistant reportedly had thrown it away.

On the following day, Agpaoa performed a second "operation" to improve Westerbeke's vision. Upon returning home, Westerbeke felt that he had lost the symptoms the physicians had attributed to the tumor.

The authors visited Donald Westerbeke in 1974, 1975, and 1976. He stated that although no conclusive medical tests had been attempted to see if the tumor was still there, he had not had a recurrence of his ailments. Further, he had returned to the Philippines several times to visit other "healers" and to compare the various approaches used. Westerbeke also noted that many of the "psychic surgeons" resorted to fraud much of the time, and some used fakery all the time. Nevertheless, Westerbeke stated his conviction that some of the "operations" could not be explained away as sleight of hand.

One of the authors (S. K.) went to the Philippines in 1974 and observed several of the "healers." He asked his guide, Hiram Ramos, a clinical psychologist, to take him to the "healers" who were least likely to use sleight of hand. One of the "healers" that Ramos knew was Josephina Sison who, for many years, had operated a small chapel in the province of Pangasinan on the island of Luzon. When Sison was asked to do "psychic surgery," she made a quick diagnosis and the following procedure was reported by Krippner:

I unbuttoned my shirt, spreading it out so far that nothing could be secreted in the folds. I also loosened my pants, lying down on the wooden table with my head on a Bible. Sison bowed her head in prayer and folded her hands. As she opened her hands, I could see that the fingers were wide apart. As the hands came down on my abdominal area, small red drops of fluid began to appear. Soon, streams of red fluid trickled down my sides. The fluid appeared to come from the part of my skin which came into direct contact with Sison's hands. There were no clotlike objects and she later took this to mean that the ailment was not serious.

After wiping her hands and my abdomen with cotton, Sison tore a fresh piece of cotton from a roll and dipped it in coconut oil. Earlier, she had claimed that coconut oil was used by "psychic surgeons" for "healing" because "it helps direct the power of the Holy Spirit." Sison pressed the wad of cotton, which measured about one inch by half an inch, to the right side of my abdomen. While I watched, the cotton appeared to vanish into the skin until only a small tuft remained. As Sison gave this a pat, it also disappeared. Still standing at the right side of my body, Sison moved her hands to the left side of my abdomen. I looked at her hands carefully and they seemed to be empty. Again, the fingers were not pressed together and the palms were open.

As Sison brought her fingers to my side, a piece of cotton appeared to protrude from my skin. She began to pull it up and I could see that it was streaked with red. I moved my body to get a better look. Sison stopped pulling, removing her hand from the cotton. And for that moment, the cotton appeared to be sticking halfway out of my body. Then she finished removing the cotton and I could see traces of red fluid on either side of it—but no coconut oil. She told me that the fluid was "impure blood" and that the coconut oil remained in my body to complete the "healing" process.

Could Sison's effects have been the result of legerdemain? For this possibility to be considered, one would have to conjecture that small capsules of red fluid had been palmed by Sison before she touches a person's skin. The empty capsules would have had to accumulate somewhere—in the drawer of the table, on the floor, in her pockets, up her sleeves. However, Krippner, an amateur magician, reported:

When I gave Sison a donation for her work, I noticed that she opened a drawer. It was quite empty, as she had run out of cotton, and I could see no capsules, empty or full. As for her clothing, she wore a shortsleeved smock devoid of pockets. The capsule hypothesis, therefore, could not be reasonably maintained unless it were determined where the containers were hidden before and after the red fluid appeared. Also, I had observed her hands so closely, and from so many different angles, that the palming procedure appeared highly unlikely.

The cotton phenomenon would also be difficult to ascribe to legerdemain. Sison would have had to "palm" a piece of cotton after it appeared to enter the body. To produce the red streak on the cotton, which I noted after it had appeared to emerge from my abdomen, Sison would have had either to substitute cotton or break a capsule of red fluid on the same piece of cotton after it seemed to emerge from the skin. And what about the time when I appeared to see the cotton protrude from my flesh even when Sison was not touching it? This could have only been explained in terms of a hypnotic effect, and I simply did not feel that anyone was overtly or covertly making an attempt to alter my perceptions of the external world.

When Mary Jane Ledyard, a clinical psychologist, heard this account, she altered her travel plans to Asia so that she and her friend could visit the Philippines. They made contact with Dr. Ramos, and spent several hours with Josephina Sison. Dr. Ledyard took special care to observe Sison's hands and the location of the cotton. Nevertheless, after witnessing several "operations," she brought back similar impressions.

Although both observations were made by psychologists,

it must be pointed out that the observations were not controlled. This would have involved buying the cotton oneself, inspecting Sison's hands in detail at several points during the "operation," and stopping the procedure several
times so that the cotton could be photographed and
examined while it appeared to protrude from the body.
Until this is done by a team of critical scientists, physicians,
and magicians, the possibility exists that these first person
accounts were deliberately exaggerated, unconsciously fal-
sified (due to poor memory and the speed at which the
"operations" took place), or the result of extremely sophisticated sleight of hand by Sison.

The Decision Re-examined

In the meantime, Judge Hanscom's decision needs to be
re-examined. It is not surprising that he ordered the travel
agencies to stop promoting trips to the Philippines for the
purpose of "psychic healing." The transcript contains evidence that some of the advertising on the part of the tours
was irresponsible. It is also obvious that many people were
not helped at all by the tours and that a few might have been
harmed.

However, Hanscom went beyond a justifiable curb on
the travel agencies. He stated, in no uncertain terms, that
all the "psychic surgeons" were "fakes" and that there
was "compelling evidence" of the "wholly fraudulent nature" of these procedures which "are simply phony" and
represent "pure and unmitigated fakery." Hanscom's opinion becomes invalid if even one "operation" by one
"psychic surgeon" can withstand the scrutiny of critical
observation. And in the report's 2,388 pages, there are several such accounts that Hanscom simply refused to deal
with when writing his opinion.

William James, the founder of American psychology, investigated several self-styled "psychics" and "mediums,"
noting that most of them were obviously fraudulent or en-

gaging in self-deception. However, James wisely observed that one only has to see one white crow to prove that not all crows are black. James eventually found a person who submitted to scientific tests and satisfied his criteria, and scientists may eventually find the "one white crow" in the Philippines who will prove that the procedures are not "wholly fraudulent."

In the meantime, the question of fraud can be raised not only with the Filipino "healers," but with some of those who have investigated them. Donald F. Wright and Carol Wright, who testified before Judge Hanscom that they had uncovered fakery among the "psychic surgeons," have come under attack by many of the "healers" for making untrue statements which were motivated by personality clashes with some of the "healers." These charges may or may not be true, but it is known that in 1974 the Wrights wrote a series of articles for a Filipino magazine, *Women's Home Companion,* in which they not only praised the integrity of the "psychic surgeons" but indicated that they had "healing powers" themselves. In their fourteenth article for the magazine, the Wrights wrote:

> . . . the older woman, pushing the younger one ahead of her as they approached us, spoke: "My daughter has a cyst here on her breastbone. We came here to see if she could be healed." The thin young woman nervously fingered the cyst which stood out prominently above her neckline. . . . The young woman . . . gathered her courage and finally blurted out, "Please! Will you heal me?" With a sigh of resignation at having been pounced upon even during lunchtime, Don laid his fork on his plate and placed his hand on the girl's forehead. "Do you believe that God can heal you?" he asked. "Yes," she said quietly, and closed her eyes. He prayed silently, directing healing energy into her body. After perhaps a minute, he said, "There you are! Now where is the cyst?" Nervously, her searching fingers probed again for the unwanted lump, and it was not to be found.
>
> By this time her mother . . . began examining the area where the cyst had been. "It's gone, it's gone," she

exclaimed, and insisted that I also feel the girl's breastbone. True, there was precious little between skin and bone on the thin girl's chest. . . . Don looked at me quizzically, shrugging his shoulders, and picked up his fork to finish his lunch.

What happened to the Wrights between the time they wrote this article and the time they testified before Judge Hanscom that "psychic surgery" was entirely "fake"? Does this include their own work with the alleged cyst? If not, how do they explain all the phenomena in which they participated directly?

Until these issues are resolved, the Wrights simply cannot be regarded as reliable witnesses.

A Doctor in Search of a Best Seller?

One would be likely to ascribe considerable reliability to William Nolen, author of the best-selling books, *The Making of a Surgeon* and *A Surgeon's World*. In 1974, Nolen published another book, *Healing: A Doctor in Search of a Miracle*. In the third section, he admits he hoped to be "the first one to write on 'psychic surgery' . . . ." However, he discovered that two books had been written previously— one by Tom Valentine and one by Harold Sherman. Although both Valentine and Sherman had been impressed by the Filipino healers, both reported instances of fraud as well. And Nolen ignored a 1968 report by D. Scott Rogo and Raymond Bayless which revealed fraudulent procedures including the surreptitious stretching of an animal skin over a patient's stomach so that tissue and blood could be pulled from under the skin at critical moments.

Nevertheless, Nolen arrived in the Philippines and recorded his immediate reactions:

> First, it is a very hot country. . . . Also humid. Very humid. In fact, I'd suggest that if you're thinking of visiting the Philippines—that is, if after you've had your head

examined you still want to go—you lock yourself in a sauna
for two weeks instead; weatherwise, you'll know exactly
what it's like to visit the Philippines . . . and you'll have
saved yourself about $2,000.

Nolen, in his book, proceeds to describe his visits to various "healers," describing how each of them used
legerdemain—palming an animal eye for an "eye operation," using betel nut juice to simulate blood, scratching
the body with a hidden piece of mica to resemble a "psychic opening," etc.

When Nolen visited Josephina Sison, he observed her
work with three patients. One of them

. . . complained of a pain in her left cheek, and for this
problem Josephina performed what I later learned is her
specialty: she took a wad of cotton, shoved it into the left
cheek and pulled it out of the patient's left nostril. . . . All I
could think of was my own experience with the cinder.

Nolen's reference is to a childhood incident in which a
neighbor boy took a cinder in his right hand, apparently
stuffed it into his right ear, and then pulled it out of his left
ear. When Nolen tried this himself, the cinder became
stuck and a physician had to dislodge it. Nolen observes:

I am easily deceived by magicians. I say this with some
pride because it has been demonstrated that the more intelligent you are, the more likely you are to be blind to sleight
of hand. I don't know why this is so, but perhaps it has
something to do with the ability to suspend one's critical
faculties at will, a characteristic also found with greatest
frequency among the more intelligent people.

When Nolen says that this phenomenon "has been demonstrated," he gives the reader no reference to any per-
tinent psychological study. Actually, no such experiment
has ever been done, although it would be a worthwhile
project. Nolen makes the statement in an apparent effort to

indicate to the reader why he cannot explain Sison's
cotton-stuffing "specialty." But this is simply not enough.
Nolen has accused Sison of fraud and it is his responsibility
to back up this accusation with a reasonable explanation of
how the purported fakery is perpetrated.

The crux of Nolen's diatribe against the Filipino "healers" occurs in Chapter 20 of his book. There is a lengthy
account of an interview with a "Dr. Luis Martinez," described as "a practicing clinical psychologist" who knows
most of the "healers" personally. Martinez is quoted to the
effect that:

1. There are about 20 "healers" altogether.
2. Tony Agpaoa operates in Manila; he is afraid to go back
    to his former office in Baguio City for fear he will be
    assessed for back taxes.
3. "Psychic surgery" began about 30 years ago.
4. Many of the "healers" manufacture "blood" from betel
    nuts. Nolen recalled seeing a bucket of betel nuts in
    Josephina Sison's laundry room. Therefore, Sison is in-
    criminated as using sleight of hand.
5. When tissue from an "operation" is taken to a labora-
    tory, it turns out to be animal tissue.

Martinez concludes by observing, "This 'psychic surgery'
business is getting out of hand; it may be bringing money to
our country, but it is also giving us a bad reputation with
respectable people from abroad. Something needs to be
done. I hope you can do it."

The uninformed reader of Nolen's book will not realize
that there are dozens of Filipino "healers" rather than
"about 20," that Agpaoa *did* return to Baguio City, that
"psychic surgery" in the Philippines can be dated back to
precolonization times, and that observers of Sison's "operations" have failed to observe containers for the betel nut
juice or other fluid which appears during the "operations."
In regard to the material examined in the laboratory, it is
quite true that it often turns out to be animal tissue or animal

blood. However, exceptions have been reported. Lyall Watson, a biologist, has written of one "operation" in his book, *The Romeo Error:*

> I took blood samples from a friend before, during, and after a simple operation on a cyst on her arm, and supervised their typing in Manila City. They were all the same blood.

In his book, *Psychic Surgery*, Valentine reports taking two genuine gallstones to a laboratory in the Philippines and remarked that the stones had been removed by a "psychic surgeon." When the laboratory report came back, it carried the flat statement that the stones were not organic. This event points out the importance of preconception and belief even on the part of those who do laboratory analysis.*

Finally, there is no such person as "Dr. Louis Martinez" in Manila. Apparently, Nolen used "Martinez" as a pseudonym for Dr. Hiram Ramos, a clinical psychologist who does know most of the Filipino "healers." Why should Nolen use a pseudonym for a professional person whose information is vital to Nolen's argument? Perhaps Nolen did this to protect himself. When Donald Westerbeke, on a return visit to the Philippines in 1975, brought Ramos a copy of Nolen's book. Ramos recalled seeing Nolen but denied making the statements ascribed to him by Nolen.

The Strange Case of Neal Cook

Nolen admits using pseudonyms in his book and this practice is certainly understandable when Nolen refers to patients. However, a close inspection of one of these cases is extremely disquieting.

---

*The authors have had no contact with Valentine and do not know whether or not he is a reliable observer. However, Raymond Bayless and D. Scott Rogo, two writers, have told one of the authors (S. K.) that the part of Valentine's book of which they have previous knowledge (specifically an interview with Bayless) is "hopelessly biased." Therefore, the reader should take this opinion into account when evaluating the Valentine material.

In Chapter 21 of his book, Nolen details the story of one "Neal Cook"—who has "a degree in both business administration and biology." Cook is described as "a successful, intelligent, pleasant person. . . ." In 1972, Cook developed vision problems, had a thorough physical examination, and was told he had a tumor in his pituitary gland. At that point, Cook saw a film of Tony Agpaoa's "psychic surgery." A few days later, Cook spoke with Agpaoa's wife on the telephone, was assured that "psychic surgery" could be done on the brain, and was directed to a San Francisco travel agency.

After a conversation with Agpaoa, and after witnessing several operations, Cook found himself on a table in a Manila hotel. Cook is reported to have told Nolen:

> As he began the operation, he put cotton pads over my eyes, and from then on, all I could feel was the power of his hands. He pushed and shoved and I could feel him, but it didn't really hurt at all. . . . Tony showed me the tissue he'd removed. It was grayish white, about two inches long and shaped like a worm. I told him I'd like to have it so I could get it examined back in the States, and he said he'd have his assistant take care of it. Unfortunately, when the assistant was cleaning up for the next case, he threw the specimen out with some pieces of cotton.

Thus far, one would suspect that "Neal Cook" is a pseudonym for Donald Westerbeke as the details of the two cases correspond closely. However, Nolen continues the story, stating that "in December of 1973, his tumor became so large that he could no longer ignore his loss of vision." Cook reportedly returned to Agpaoa for another "operation." According to Nolen, "This time, however, even Neal Cook had to admit that there was no improvement." He returned to the United States, had an operation, and made a complete recovery. Nolen concludes:

> He never speaks of his Philippine experience any more. He has, in fact, become an active supporter of a charitable

foundation devoted to funding research into the cause and treatment of tumors.

In evaluating the strange case of "Neal Cook," it is apparent that either Cook is Westerbeke or he is not. Nolen did visit Westerbeke for several days and became familiar with his story. So if, in reality, "Cook" is a pseudonym for Westerbeke, Nolen certainly appears to distort the facts.

If, on the other hand, "Cook" is another person who coincidentally bears a relationship to Westerbeke, Nolen has done Westerbeke a disservice. By writing an account in which the tumor begins to cause problems again, Nolen has planted this possibility in Westerbeke's mind, thus activating any doubt about the "operation" that Westerbeke might have. This could have been avoided had Nolen had the courtesy to write Westerbeke a letter stating, "Neal Cook is *not* your story, even though there are several similarities." Westerbeke never received such a letter from Nolen. In the meantime, Nolen's behavior in the "Neal Cook" case as well as in the "Dr. Luis Martinez" conversation raises doubt about other examples used by this celebrated surgeon to debunk "psychic healing."

Those Fake "Operations"

What about the *National Enquirer's* claim to have uncovered "fake psychic healers" in the Philippines? The newspaper's reporter, Steve Tinney, travelled to a small village, located 150 miles north of Manila. In the presence of Thomas Hausen, a physician from West Germany, and two Filipino physicians, Augustus Damian, Jr., and Leopoldo Lazatin, Tinney examined Josephina Sison, a "healer" who worked with sick people daily in her small chapel. The *Enquirer* reported:

> First with Dr. Hausen, then with two Filipino doctors, Tinney watched Josephina "open up" patients using only her

hands, remove bloody lumps, cysts, and tumors—then apparently restore their bodies to wholeness with no trace of a scar.

Tinney examined the psychic before the "operations." She was wearing a sleeveless blouse and had no rings or jewelry which could conceal phony body tissue.

After witnessing one of her surgical sessions, Dr. Hausen declared: "This woman certainly isn't a hoax. It's a medical mystery how she performs the operations, but she does it."

The Filipino physicians were equally dumfounded. "What I've seen today defies all the medical training I've had," said Dr. Augustus Damian, Jr. "This isn't a hoax, but I can't explain it either. . . ."

And Dr. Leopoldo Lazatin said: "I just can't figure this out. She doesn't appear to be a fake."

The *Enquirer* article described how Sison began rubbing a patient's leg. Then, "Josephina's hands seemed buried up to the knuckles in the woman's flesh and she plucked out several dark objects she said were blood clots." Sison stroked her hand over the leg and the apparently open wound disappeared. The woman told Tinney, "My leg pains are gone and I can work in the fields again."

Dr. Hausen had sent a specimen from a previous Sison "operation" to West Germany for analysis. The institute reported that the human "tumor" was actually part of a plant. Hausen also sent a "growth" to West Germany which apparently had been removed from his wife sometime earlier by another Filipino "healer," Rudi Himenes. The laboratory report identified the "growth" as animal tissue. A "blood stain" resulting from the "operation" turned out to be red dye. The *Enquirer* quoted Hausen as stating:

> I still can't believe that I was tricked. . . . I'm a medical man—trained to observe surgical procedures. I'm not easily impressed or fooled. . . . If I was fooled, I just don't know how they did it.

Hausen's wife commented on Himenes, noting that he was

dressed in such a way that he could not have concealed anything on his person. The *Enquirer* concluded:

> But she, like thousands of other persons, was hoaxed. So were the three doctors who watched Josephina . . . at work. And reporter Tinney. . . . But how the "psychic surgeons" manage their fraud and why patients like Mrs. Hausen, the physician's wife, actually feel better after these operations, are questions which may never be answered.

A careful reading of the account will reveal that the *Enquirer* convicted Sison of fraud on the basis of logic, rather than evidence. The assumptions explicit in the article would follow a sequence along these lines:

1. For "psychic surgery" to be genuine, material must be produced by the "healer" under conditions that are inexplicable to modern medicine.
2. If the material produced by the "healer" is found to be animal tissue, plant segments, or anything other than human tissue, "psychic surgery" is not genuine.

There are also a number of implicit assumptions in the *Enquirer* article, assumptions that the writers may have made without realizing it:

1. Laboratory reports are accurate and free from error.
2. The material sent to the laboratory is inevitably the same material produced by the "healer"; there is no chance for a substitution.
3. The material produced by the "healer" could not possibly have been human tissue at the time of the "operation," only to change into animal tissue or plant segments before arriving at the laboratory.
4. If the material produced by the "healer" is not human tissue, it could not have been in the patient's body before the operation.
5. The material produced by the "healer" could not

have been "teleported" by psychic procedures
from another area at the time of the "operation."
6. The material produced by the "healer" could not
have been "materialized" by psychic procedures
at the time of the "operation."

If any of these implicit assumptions is incorrect, the *National Enquirer's* "fakery" charge falls apart. It is true that to question these assumptions raises serious questions about laboratory procedures, the structure of the human organism, and the nature of reality. But one can at least consider the possibilities that:

1. A mistake was made at the West German laboratory, or a deliberate error was made once someone found out the material was produced by a nonmedical "healer."
2. A person who opposed the work of the Filipino "healers" simply substituted animal and plant material before the package was sent to West Germany.
3. Due to some unknown mechanism characteristic of "psychic surgery," the material produced by the "healer" during the "operation" was actually human tissue but changed through some type of paranormal metamorphosis into animal or plant material by the time it arrived in West Germany.
4. Due to some unknown mechanism characteristic of "psychic surgery," diseased human tissue must change into animal or plant material before it can be removed by a "healer" during an "operation."
5. The "healer" does not remove anything from the body at all; some unknown psychic procedure enables animal material to be "teleported" from a nearby butcher shop—or plant material to be "teleported" from a garden or forest—during the "operation."
6. The "healer" does not remove anything from the

body at all; some unknown psychic procedure enables animal or plant matter to "materialize" during the "operation."

In the case of the last two possibilities, it could be claimed that animal and plant material are easier to "teleport" or "materialize" than human tissue. Far-fetched? Unlikely? Outrageous? Of course! But a careful investigator must consider all the possibilities, especially when fraud has not been observed.

In other words, the *Enquirer* would have done a greater service to its readers, and a more responsible piece of journalism, if it had merely stated the facts: A newspaper reporter and three physicians observed a Filipino "healer" produce some provocative phenomena after which several sick people said they felt better. Laboratory analysis of some of the material produced by the "healer" indicated that it was animal or plant material. There are several ways of explaining these incidents, one of which is trickery. However, if fraud was involved, it was not apparent to the observers. Thus, more investigation is needed of the "healer" and the problem remains unsolved until more facts are available.

Unfortunately, the *Enquirer* did not present the material this way; it charged fraud even though no trickery was observed. And it avoided describing the ways in which fakery could be perpetrated by stating that these were "questions which may never be answered."

Rules of the Game

The explicit and implicit assumptions of the *Enquirer* reporter have been examined. But some other assumptions also need to be stated. The patient—and probably the "healer"—would view the situation this way:

1. For "psychic surgery" to be genuine, the sick person must feel better following the "operation,"

with a remission of the symptoms that were present before the "operation."
2. This improvement in the ill person's condition
must be long-lasting rather than temporary. If that
person submits to a medical examination, the results will verify the ill person's subjective feeling
of well-being.

From the indisposed person's point of view, the most important consideration is the "cure." It matters little if the
material produced by the "healer" is human tissue, animal
tissue, a plant leaf, or a billiard ball, just so long as the sick
person's condition improves.

With some sick people, of course, the charges of fakery
brought against the "healers" who helped them will destroy
their confidence in the "operation." This relates to an additional assumption some of these people may hold:

> Not only must I feel better after the "operation," and not
> only must the effects be long-lasting and verifiable by a
> medical examination, but any material produced by the
> "healer" during the "operation" must be shown to be
> human tissue rather than anything else.

In this case, it is apparent how one's assumptions can affect
the course of one's improvement following a visit to a
"psychic surgeon" or other "healer."

Scientists interested in studying psychic phenomena hold
still a different set of assumptions. To them, improvement
following "psychic surgery" is not the critical issue. They
are interested in phenomena which cannot be easily explained by the prevailing scientific models of the universe.
Therefore, they would propose that:

> For "psychic surgery" to be genuine, the material produced
> by the "healer" during an "operation" must be material
> that could not have been produced by any ordinary method.
> Precautions need to be made that the "healer" is not using

sleight of hand, that the subject is not using trickery, and that none of the onlookers are engaged in fraud.

In other words, for "psychic surgery" to be genuine, material needs to appear in an unorthodox way and to be objectively recorded. It makes no difference whether the material is human tissue or animal tissue, if the fluid which appears is blood or vegetable dye, or if the body is actually "opened" or merely appears to "open." The critical fact to be established is the appearance of a material object during the "operation" which cannot be explained by any mechanism known to orthodox science.

In summary, it is apparent that one must check out one's assumptions before one makes a decision. The evidence that one accepts as valid and the perceptions that are considered to be real, depend to a large degree upon the "rules of the game" that society and individuals alike play by as they create their reality. It is also apparent that the case against "psychic surgery" is not yet closed but deserves a fair analysis as do the other phenomena in the realms of "psychic healing."

Chapter Two

Paranormal Healing
In the Laboratory

"Psychic healing" and "paranormal healing" are terms used to describe the alleviation of physical ailments when there appears to be no adequate medical, physiological, or psychological explanation for the healing. It is one example of a variety of events categorized as "psi phenomena"—interactions between organisms and their environment (including other organisms) which cannot be explained by currently held scientific models of the universe.

There are four major categories of psi phenomena: telepathy, clairvoyance, precognition, and psychokinesis. Telepathy refers to instances in which information appears to be transferred from a "sender" to a "receiver" by some means other than the known senses. In clairvoyance, the "receiver" obtains information about distant objects or events without the assistance of the known senses. Information about future events is classified as precognition, if that information could not be inferred from what is already known. In psychokinesis, an organism is apparently able to manipulate external objects at a distance by means other than the known forces and channels.

If a "psychic healer" were able to repair a broken bone by concentrating on the ailing person, one would investigate the possibility of psychokinesis. If the "healer" were able to diagnose the tumorous condition of a stranger merely by holding a slip of paper containing that person's name, one would suspect clairvoyance. If the "healer" were to predict an accident that then actually occurred, one might term the prediction a case of precognition. And if the "healer" were able to identify a personal problem which was troubling a person the "healer" had never met, one might infer that telepathy could be implicated. Needless to say, each of these examples would have to be examined to rule out coincidence, sensory clues, faulty memory, inaccurate observation, or deliberate falsification of facts.

In addition, it is often difficult to decide whether something is an example of one psi ability or another—what seems to be telepathy may actually be clairvoyance. For this reason, most psi experiments have utilized decks of cards, dice, and other simple test materials which can be controlled so tightly that it is easier to draw conclusions than it would be in a real-life situation.

But "psychic healing" is such a complex process that it cannot be investigated through card-guessing or by attempts to influence the fall of dice. This is one reason why parapsychologists have done so little work in this particular area. "Psychic healing" is a difficult area to investigate for yet another reason: many physical ailments actually have a partial or completely psychosomatic basis. Thus, the belief that a treatment is going to be effective may be sufficient to produce a cure. If this were to happen, no paranormal element would have to be conjectured to explain the phenomenon. Therefore, experiments in "psychic healing" characteristically center upon one aspect of the total "healing" process—an aspect which can be manipulated in such a way as to determine whether "psychic healing" is occurring.

The Grad Experiments

Bernard Grad, at McGill University, worked with a Hungarian-born "healer," Colonel Oskar Estebany, who had a long history of treating both animals and people by laying his hands on the afflicted areas. In one of Grad's experiments, mice received small, surgically inflicted wounds on their skins, and the rate of healing of the wounds was objectively measured daily. The mice were divided into an "experimental group" and a "control group." Each mouse in the experimental group was put into a paper bag by an investigator, and Estebany held the bag and its contained mouse in his hands while doing the healing. Mice in the control group were put in paper bags for equivalent periods of time but not held by Estebany. The results showed that the wounds healed more rapidly in the case of the mice which received the healing treatment. The difference in rate of healing was statistically significant.*

The paper bags were used to prevent any physical handling factors or warmth factors from affecting the results. In an attempt to eliminate this possibility even more completely, Grad designed an experiment in which seeds were "wounded" by being heated in an oven at a temperature that would kill some of them and adversely affect those that survived. These seeds were then planted in pots and watered with a sterile saline solution (salty water). The saline solution came in sealed jars. Some of the jars were held in Estebany's hands, then put aside so as to lose any heat they might have accumulated during the treatment. Later, the seeds in the experimental group were watered with this

---

*To indicate whether or not an effect was actually obtained, statistics are used. Statistical tests use the known mathematical properties of numbers to enable one to decide when a difference is probably due to chance and when a difference is so large that chance seems unlikely. If the outcome of a particular test could have happened by chance only five or fewer times in a hundred trials, one begins to doubt that this is a chance happening. The term "statistically significant" is used whenever the outcome of an experiment could not be explained through coincidence as determined by mathematical techniques.

solution. Seeds in the control group were watered with saline solution from jars that Estebany had not held. The person who watered the plants did not know which water had received Estebany's treatment. A different person (also ignorant as to which seeds had been experimentally treated) measured the number of seeds which actually sprouted and the heights to which the seeds grew in a certain period of time, as well as the final weight of the plants at the end of the experiment. The results indicated that for seeds watered with the treated solution, more seeds sprouted, the seedlings grew faster, and the plants weighed significantly more at the end of the experiment.*

The Smith Experiments

While engaging in her doctoral research, M. Justa Smith discovered that the activity level of trypsin was increased by a magnetic field. Trypsin is an enzyme produced by the pancreas to assist in the digestion of proteins; it can be damaged by ultraviolet radiation. Smith put all of this information to use in another study of the "psychic healing" abilities of Colonel Estebany.

She divided solutions of trypsin into four portions. One was treated by Estebany who put his hands around a covered glass flask containing the enzyme for a maximum of 75 minutes. Another sample was exposed to ultraviolet light at a wave length determined to be the most damaging for enzymes, and was then treated by Estebany. The third sample was exposed to a high magnetic field for three hours. The final sample was used as a control and was untreated.

---

*Grad's work inspired G. H. Elguin and Brenia Onetti-Bächler, at the University of Chile, to work with three groups of cancerous mice. The tumors of one group decreased significantly when they were concentrated upon with the intent of reducing the cancer. Tumors in a control group did not change, nor did they change in a third group which was concentrated upon with the intent of enlarging the tumors.

The most striking finding of Smith's study was that the effect of Estebany's treatment of the undamaged sample was similar to that of the enzyme's exposure to a high magnetic field. The effect of Estebany on the damaged sample was similar but not as dramatic.

Smith repeated the study with three other "healers" and three individuals who did not claim to have "healing powers." In no instance were the effects significant. Another experiment with Estebany also yielded non-significant results. However, arrangements were made with a local physician for Estebany to attempt healing with 24 of the physician's patients. Estebany said he would not help two of the 24, suggesting that they see a psychotherapist. Of the remaining number, 21 stated that they "felt much better" following Estebany's treatment. Smith pointed out that there was no way to determine how much of each patient's improvement mirrored placebo effects, but noted, "I don't believe too many physicians have that kind of batting average!"

Smith's next study involved three additional "psychic healers." Trypsin was used again, and the results resembled those obtained by Estebany in that the activity level increased significantly in the case of the samples worked with by the "healers." Work was also done with two other enzymes: nicotinamide-adenine dinucleotide (NAD) and amylase-amylose. NAD removes hydrogen from carbohydrates to prepare them for the action of other enzymes. In a pure solution without the necessary biochemical checks and balances, this action takes place very quickly, but in a living body it is vital that it should be more carefully controlled. After the NAD in Smith's flask had been exposed to "psychic healing" influences, its action on carbohydrates was significantly decreased. If there had been no retardation of this kind, it is theoretically possible, according to Smith, that "healers" could produce a runaway cancer while trying to repair a minor wound.

The other enzyme, amylase-amylose, is involved in the breakdown of glycogen that is stored in the liver and muscles, then released into the bloodstream as glucose if it is needed. If there is too much amylase-amylose activity, the concentration of sugar in the blood soars and the organism becomes diabetic. If amylase-amylose underreacts, blood sugar falls and the organism suffers in a different way. For an optimal effect on people, there should be no change in the reactivity of amylase-amylose following "psychic healing." In Smith's experiments, there was no change.

In other words, the "healers'" effects on the three types of enzymes studied were exactly what one would predict if they were functioning in the body to combat illness. Smith concluded that "human thought can generate a force that heals. And this force is marvelously selective in its effects on specific body processes."

The Krieger Experiments

Dolores Krieger was stimulated by Grad's and Smith's work to experiment with hemoglobin, the respiratory pigment in red corpuscles. Krieger noted that hemoglobin "is an iron-containing protein and, as do all the proteins, it is able to act either as an acid or a base, depending on the medium in which it is. This ability . . . would appear to make it an appropriate vehicle for the 'balancing of the positive and negative currents' of the life energies during the healing process as postulated by the Eastern literature."

Krieger's first study involved the effects on hemoglobin of healing through a "laying-on" of hands; again, Colonel Estebany was the "healer." There were 19 subjects in the group who received the "healing," and nine in the control group. It was noted that the hemoglobin values increased over the six-day period of the experiment in the "healing" group but not in the control group. It was further discovered that the difference in the "healing" group was greater for those subjects who meditated than for those who did not.

In her second study, Krieger utilized 33 persons in the

control group and 43 indisposed persons in a group which worked with Estebany. Each of the 43 persons was treated by a "laying-on" of hands daily for 14 days. Krieger again found increased hemoglobin values for the experimental group.

Krieger's third study utilized 46 subjects in the experimental group and 29 in the control group. A "color meter" was used to determine hemoglobin values as it was felt to be an extremely objective method of observing the change in red blood corpuscles. Once again, the hemoglobin values of the experimental group showed a greater change than did those in the control group.

After one year, follow-up questionnaires were sent to members of the experimental group and were returned by 70 per cent. Questionnaire responses stated that 90 per cent of those answering had normal histories for blood pressure, body temperature, and pulse rate over the year. Seventy-five per cent of the questionnaire responses listed appetite as "good" while the rest listed appetite as "fair"; no one used the third alternative of "poor." Only one person answering the questionnaire cited the use of tobacco.

Estebany himself showed no hemoglobin change during the study. Further, the temperature of his hands did not change. Krieger concludes that:

> ...If one conceives of the healthy individual as an open system of "streaming energy" in constant flux . . ., then it is not difficult to visualize the ill person as one in whom this system has closed in, so to speak, upon oneself. The role of the "healer" then would be concerned with helping the ill person to reestablish this vital, flowing, open system, to restore, as it were, unimpeded communication with one's environment.

Once this "opening" is instigated by the "healer," according to Krieger, the ill person can continue to improve over the course of time, providing that no additional blockages occur.

The Dean Experiments

Douglas Dean, a former president of the Parapsychological Association and a Research Fellow of the Humanistic Psychology Institute, became interested in the results of a pilot study conducted by another HPI Research Fellow, J. Schoneberg Setzer. Dr. Setzer grew radishes with ordinary water as well as with water that had been placed in church sanctuaries during Sunday services. It was found that the church water produced larger radishes than the purely secular water on one Sunday, but inferior radishes the next Sunday. Setzer's later work revealed a 14-day cycle which coincided with the lunar period. Dean adds:

> . . . the effect itself seems to be genuine, because another series of experiments was done by a leading spectroscopist at a major chemical company in the United States. He measured the concentration of hydroxyl ions and the amount of hydrogen bonding in the two kinds of water and found the same kind of 14-day oscillation; in fact, on Sundays near the full moon there was a decrease of hydrogen bonding compared with regular water, but on Sundays near the new moon, the hydrogen bonding was in excess. Perhaps therefore, this work initiated by Setzer falls into the category of subtle astrophysical effects. Even so . . ., it suggests that very subtle and weak forces can have chemical effects.

Dean also reviewed the work of Bernard Grad with Oskar Estebany. Grad concluded that Estebany's hands must have altered the water in some way and proceeded to test the idea. Grad passed infra-red (IR) light through samples of saline solution from the "treated" and the "untreated" bottles using a Beckman DK-2 IR spectrophotometer. This instrument measures the percent transmission of IR light which appears in colors just as visible light does, but is described in numbers instead of such names as red, orange, and yellow. The instrument measures the per cent transmission for each of the wave lengths from 400 to 3,000 millimicrons; 400 to 750 is the visible range and 750 to 3,000 is infra-red.

The per cent transmission for the "untreated" saline and the "treated" saline were the same from 400 to 2,800 millimicrons at which point they diverged. For the "untreated" saline there was about an 80 per cent transmission of IR light but for the "treated" saline, 63 per cent transmission. Dean noted:

> This result at this IR bond suggests a change in the oxygen-hydrogen bond distance (0.95 Å) or in the amount of hydrogen bonds which are the bonding of one water molecule with the water molecules around it.

Dean asked Grad to send him six bottles of saline solution, some handled by a "healer" and some that were not handled by a "healer." Dean and a colleague again noticed the divergence from 2,800 to 3,000 millimicrons, confirming Grad's work. Using special instruments, they found another divergence at 3,600 and at 4,400 millimicrons; these differences were still apparent when Dean re-examined the bottles three years later.

In 1974, Grad gave Dean four bottles of distilled water; Dean was not told which bottles had been treated by "healers" (one of whom was the noted "healer," Olga Worrall). Dean took the bottles to a chemistry laboratory which observed less than average oxygen-hydrogen bonding in two bottles of water. These were the two bottles "treated" by the "healers." Dean commented, "It was as if the healers had heated the water up and broken some hydrogen bonds . . . ."

The four bottles were then sent to the University of Delaware for "heat of dilution" measurement. Again, the two "treated" bottles showed a definite "heat of dilution" effect. These bottles again showed less bonding, even when a completely different measurement technique was employed.

The Watkins Experiments

The studies by Bernard Grad were the first systematic attempts to study "psychic healing." M. Justa Smith moved a step forward by examining enzyme changes during "healing." Dolores Krieger was the first to work with people and to measure their hemoglobin values before and after attempted "psychic healing." Dean and his associates were interested in molecular changes in the water used in "laying-on" of hands experiments.

The studies by Grad, Smith, Krieger, and Dean were impressive. However, as long as one attempts a "laying-on" of hands with sprouts, animals, water, or people, the possibility exists that the effect is due, at least in part, to the "healer's" bodily heat or to the electrodynamic fields which surround the "healer's" body.

Graham and Anita Watkins designed an experiment in which 12 volunteers worked on animals, part of the time at a distance. The task given these individuals, most of whom did not profess to have any "paranormal healing" abilities, was to arouse mice more quickly from anesthesia than would be expected under ordinary circumstances.

Pairs of mice were rendered unconscious with ether at the same time. These pairs were closely matched; they were of the same sex, of the same size, and had been litter mates. After both mice were unconscious, they were placed in plastic containers. One mouse was placed before one of the 12 volunteers; the volunteer was asked to "awaken" the animal. The other mouse served as a control; therefore, the numbers of mice in the experimental group was the same as the number in the control group.

Tests were conducted under various circumstances. In some cases, the volunteer and the mouse were in one room while the control mouse was in another room. In some cases, the volunteer and both mice were in the same room. In some instances, both mice were in the same room with the volunteer looking through a window. And in some cases, the volunteer was blindfolded. In no instance was the volunteer allowed to do a "laying-on" of hands with the unconscious mouse.

The overall results of this study were statistically significant; the animals assigned to the volunteers required an average of 13 per cent less time to revive as did the control animals. There were no clearcut differences among the various conditions. However, when the mice were viewed through a window, the unblindfolded volunteers did significantly better than the blindfolded volunteers.

Watkins and Watkins found three subjects who did exceptionally well in reviving the mice, so much so that in 24 attempts their mice revived significantly more quickly than did the control mice. An additional subject also produced significant results; in that instance, the control mice revived more quickly.

Roger Wells and Judith Klein, two of Watkins and Watkins colleagues at the Foundation for Research and the Nature of Man, reported significant results following an attempt to repeat the experiment themselves with an additional finding. Once a mouse revives more quickly than expected by chance, the location of that mouse is recorded. Future mice placed in the same location are more likely to revive quickly than mice placed in other locations—even though the subject does not know about the former inhabitants of that spot. This "lingering effect" suggests that some spots are better than others as locations for "healing," or that a residue of "healing power" remains there to help the next mouse revive.

The Goodrich Experiment

Joyce Goodrich's doctoral dissertation for the Union Graduate School centered on the "psychic healing" procedures devised by Lawrence LeShan. Having written several papers in psychical research and having intensively studied all varieties of psi phenomena, LeShan decided that "paranormal healing" offered the greatest potential for the application of parapsychological phenomena. After interviewing and observing dozens of "healers," LeShan arrived at a theory on the operation of "psychic healing." He began to apply this theory first by learning "psychic healing" himself, then by teaching others.*

LeShan felt that most instances of "psychic healing" occur when the "healer" is in an altered state of consciousness—one in which the "healer" seems to "merge" with the patient or "healee."** This merging is done with an attitude of love and concern on the part of the "healer." At an unconscious level, the healee's self-repair mechanisms are stimulated to function in an accelerated manner. LeShan suggested that this stimulation can be brought about telepathically, especially when the "healer" and healee are separated by distance.

The typical training seminar led by LeShan would begin with a theoretical discussion of "Sensory Reality" and "Clairvoyant Reality." LeShan's theory states that a "healer" shifts from "Sensory" to "Clairvoyant Reality" during a "healing" session. To facilitate this shift, LeShan would teach students a series of exercises designed to:

1. Strengthen their sense of self so they would not be confused when shifting from one state of consciousness to another.
2. Develop alternate ways of conceptualizing reality.
3. Develop the ability to enter the altered state of consciousness associated with "Clairvoyant Reality."
4. Attempt "healing" other students in the seminar. LeShan refers to distant "healing" as Type One and "laying-on" of hands as Type Two. He stres-

---

*A doctoral dissertation was written by Shirley Winston at the Union Graduate School on the topic of variables in communication between LeShan's "healers" and their healees; the best "healings" seemed to occur when the "healer" and healee met but did not communicate verbally.

**The term "healee" will be used throught this book to refer to ill people who go to "psychic healers" for assistance. Because the type of aid they receive is not understood at this time, the word "healee" is preferable to the term "patient."

ses Type One "healing" and, in the seminars, the
healee is told simply to be receptive, not to "do"
anything, and not to "try" cooperating. The
"healer" attempts to enter "Clairvoyant Reality"
and merge with the healee.
5. Persons with medical problems are then brought
   in for attempted "healings."

Joyce Goodrich became one of LeShan's students and conducted her study in an attempt to discern whether "healing"
at a distance actually worked. In the experiment, "healers"
were assigned to healees with whom they did a face-to-face
healing. Then "healers" attempted, at various intervals, to
"merge" with the healees from a distance of several miles.
The healees kept a journal, carefully assessing their "healing" experiences.

The results of this study were statistically significant.
Independent judges were able to identify correctly the
times that the "healers" were at work merely from examining the journals kept by the healees. LeShan has described
the state of consciousness experienced by these "healers"
in his book, *The Medium, the Mystic, and the Physicist*:

> It is essential that there be a deeply intense caring and a
> viewing of the healee and oneself as one, as being united in a
> universe . . . in which this unity is possible. . . . This is a
> perfectly valid set of beliefs about reality. Since at this mo-
> ment of intense knowing on the part of the healer it was
> valid and the healee was an integral and central part of the
> system, the healee knew it too.

LeShan has stated that "psychic healing" is a basic human
potential—something that many people can develop. On
the other hand, healing without preparation is not advised;
like other human abilities, "psychic healing" is best developed within a framework of training and discipline.

Kirlian Photography Studies

Two Soviet scientists, Semyon and Valentina Kirlian spent several decades at Kazakh State University developing electrophotographic techniques which utilized neither a lens nor a camera. Instead, they placed objects directly on film and produced a corona emission around the object by means of an electrical discharge. Soviet investigators began to use this technique for detecting flaws in metal surfaces and for detecting mineral traces in soil. It was soon discovered that photographic prints of living organisms could be made by selecting a low amperage current and by controlling the output of the high voltage power supply (such as a Tesla coil or a Oudin coil). The pictures had to be taken in a darkroom or by enclosing the film and object to be photographed in an opaque envelope.

In the Kirlian photographs, one sees an image of the object's surface as well as a surrounding corona or "aura" which represents a discharge of electrons from the object. There is very little emission from a dead leaf or from the fingertip of a corpse. The Kirlians felt that the electron discharge from a living organism was—to some extent—a measure of the life processes occurring within that organism.

One of the subjects in a Kirlian photography study was Alexei Krivorotov, the best known "psychic healer" in the U.S.S.R. Krivorotov's right index fingertip was photographed while he was in a state of rest. It was photographed again when he said that his hand was activated and in the condition needed for for the "healing" process to be effective. An interesting change could be seen; the long, diffuse flares seen in the original photograph had now congregated into a dense pattern of short flares. The original photograph was white and blue; the second photograph was marked by red and orange as well.

In the United States, a number of attempts were made to

replicate this effect. At the Jersey Society for Parapsychology, Douglas Dean took Kirlian photographs of the fingertip of a "psychic healer," Ethel DeLoach. As one examines the coronas, one can observe the appearance of orange flares as DeLoach enters the state of consciousness she associates with "healing." Once she returns to her ordinary state of consciousness, the flare pattern alters again, resembling the original photograph taken.

Another series of photographs was taken by Jonathan Cohen, at the Foundation for ParaSensory Investigation, with another "psychic healer," Maria Janis, a student of Lawrence LeShan. Cohen photographed Janis' right index fingertip while she was at rest, while she was concentrating on a healee who was several miles away, and after the attempted "healing" was completed. Another set of photographs was taken before, during, and after Janis' work with a healee who was in the same room—and just after Janis had removed her hands from the healee.

There was a marked degree of consistency for the attempts at both "distant healing" and "contact healing." During Janis' attempted "healing," the Kirlian photographs showed a more diffuse flare pattern. However, the pictures taken before and after the attempted "healing" looked very much alike.

Working with Olga Worrall and other "psychic healers," Thelma Moss, at the U.C.L.A. Neuropsychiatric Institute, obtained results similar to the Kirlians. In addition, Moss took photographs of the healees. At the time of the attempted "healing," the corona of the healees appeared to expand and become brighter. One could make the case that these results indicated an exchange of "healing power" between "healer" and healee, and that Kirlian photography was able to measure this "power." Any such conclusion would be premature. For all one knows, the healees merely pressed their fingers more firmly on the film while the attempted "healing" took place. And the differences observed with the "healers" may have been due to a change

Before attempted "healing"   During attempted "healing"

Kirlian photographs of right index fingertip of Alexei Krivorotov, the best-known "psychic healer" in the U.S.S.R. Note the change from diffuse to concentrated flare patterns during attempted "healing." (Courtesy V.G. Adamenko)

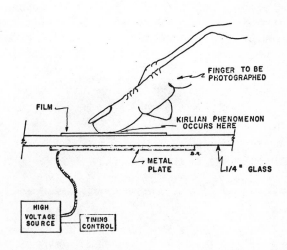

Electrode plate for Kirlian photography process using high voltage power source. (Courtesy G. Poock)

Three examples of the "phantom leaf" effect in Kirlian photography. This effect is observed when a portion of a leaf is cut away before it is placed on film for an electrophotograph to be taken. The apparent outline of the cut portion constitutes the "phantom."

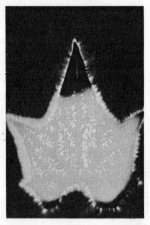

Soviet "phantom leaf"; cutaway portion is on left side. (Courtesy V.G. Adamenko)

Brazilian "phantom leaf"; cutaway portion is on bottom center. (Courtesy H.G. Andrade)

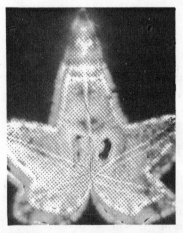

American "phantom leaf"; cutaway portion is on top center. (Courtesy R. Wagner)

in finger pressure on the film as well as finger placement, body heat, perspiration, etc. Moss has succeeded in ruling out many of these factors, but no firm conclusions can be made until the phenomenon is studied more thoroughly. For example, J.W. Robinson, in a 1976 report, noted that Kirlian photographs are influenced by the amount of water in an object.

In the meantime, Moss performed a series of experiments with gashed leaves. After a photograph was taken of a leaf which had been gashed in the center, Olga Worrall attempted to "heal" the leaf by holding her hand above it while another Kirlian photograph was taken. The resulting picture showed the leaf intact, even though the gash still appeared on the leaf. Worrall's performance was dubbed the "green thumb" effect.

Moss attempted a similar experiment with Barry Taff, a "psychic sensitive" who had considerable experience with telepathy, clairvoyance, and precognition—but none with "psychic healing." The leaf was gashed, photographed, and photographed again while Taff held his hand above it. In the resulting photograph, the gashed leaf has all but disappeared. Taff's efforts were referred to as the "brown thumb" effect.

It is clear that interesting results have been obtained by using Kirlian photography to investigate "psychic healing." It is also apparent that the Kirlian photography process must be more thoroughly understood before any firm conclusions can be drawn from these provocative results. In addition, it must be kept in mind that each Kirlian photography researcher uses a different type of apparatus; standardization and replication are also needed to make sense out of the studies.

Why We Need Science

Two people looking at the same scene often report seeing two different things. An Eskimo and a Bedouin could be

taken through the desert and asked to describe the scenery.
The Eskimo might report, "There was nothing but sand,"
while the Bedouin would describe carefully each type and
variant of sand. If the two were taken to the tundra, the
Bedouin might remark, "All I could see was snow." The
Eskimo, having a vocabulary which included several words
for "snow," might give an extensive report on the varieties
of snow in the landscape.

J. B. Watson originated "behaviorist psychology," so
named because it emphasized the study of overt behavior
rather than attitudes, values, experiences, and states of
consciousness. Watson once stated that his observations of
infant behavior had convinced him that, among infants,
loud sounds and falling elicited fear reactions while physical
restraint produced anger. In 1927, a study was published in
which movies about infants had been used. The films had
been shown to graduate students in psychology who were
asked to describe the babies' reactions when they were
exposed to loud sounds or physical restraint. The students,
all of whom had learned Watson's views, reported that the
infants reflected fear following the loud sounds and anger
when physically restrained. Then pictures were shown of
the infants' reactions only—not of the condition that produced the reaction. This time there was a wide variety of
responses from the students. In other words, what they
thought they saw was heavily influenced by their previous
learning experiences and the belief system that resulted.*

Some people have realized that past experiences, preconceptions, and prejudices can influence one's views of
reality and cloud one's judgment in regard to what is
"really" happening. A few individuals throughout history
have tried to determine what is real and what is misleading

---

*This study, originally published by Mandel Sherman in the *Journal for Com-
parative Psychology*, is discussed by Wayne Dennis in chapter one of *The Proper
Study of Man* (edited by James Fadiman). Dennis' chapter contains several other
examples of how one's belief system can influence one's perceptions of the world.

in our ideas about nature. These seekers of knowledge have been regarded as "scientists."

"Science" can be called the study of knowledge, of using observation and experimentation to determine facts about nature, rather than to accept without question what one's culture has determined reality to be. Observation and experimentation are part of the "scientific method"—an effort to systematize the process of acquiring knowledge in such a way as to minimize error. A. H. Maslow, one of the founders of "humanistic psychology," has outlined this process succinctly. First comes "knowing in the experiential sense; then the checks on the fallibilities of the senses and of experiential knowledge; then come the abstractions, the theories . . . ."

Scientists, through their use of the scientific method, attempt to produce a steady movement toward the acquisition of "facts" about reality. In his book, *Transpersonal Psychologies*, Charles T. Tart has pointed out that scientific method is based on four principles:

1. *Accurate observation.* If we observe something incompletely, we end up knowing so little about it that our conclusions will be distorted. On the other hand, we might observe a phenomenon completely but with strong preconceptions that prevent us from accurately understanding what we see.

2. *The repeatable nature of observations.* In science, an observation must be "public," in the sense that any properly trained observer can have the same experience with a phenomenon and reach the same conclusions. The original observer must describe the conditions under which he or she had the experience so completely that anyone else can set up a similar situation and make an identical observation. This replication by another observer is called "consensual validation." If one cannot

get any reasonable degree of agreement among different observers, one cannot build a science.

3. *The necessity to theorize logically.* Scientists are not content simply to observe; they want to know what their observations mean. Therefore, it is necessary to make conceptual links between observations and the ideas put forth to explain them. Often scientists observe a group of similar phenomena, then come up with a concept, or theory, which links these observations together and explains them logically. But before other scientists accept the theory, they examine the assumptions behind the theory. If they feel the assumptions are sound, they label the theory "logically valid."

4. *The testing of theory against predicted, observable consequences.* A theory may be logical but may have no relationship to reality. That is, it will not predict the next event in an observable sequence. Further observation becomes necessary to check the theory against events both in the laboratory and in real-life settings.

The repeated application of this method leads to a collection of "facts" that describe the universe in which we live. In *Transpersonal Psychologies*, Tart has applied these principles to "psychic energy" to demonstrate how scientists can examine unorthodox healing phenomena:

Suppose that . . .numerous observers report being able to experience certain kinds of tingling, pulsing, or warm sensations that can move readily about in the body, to which they give a generally agreed-upon name, "psychic energy." Suppose they further report that when they have been physically ill . . .with some kind of illness that affects one part of the body more than another, they find they can feel less of this psychic energy in the afflicted part of the body than in the rest of the body. Now, an observer/investigator might theorize that this hypothesized psychic energy is important in the general, healthy functioning of the body, and is an underlying basis of physical health. This is a simple theory consistent with the observed observations, namely that a deficiency of the psychic energy is associated with physical afflictions and spells out a possible underlying mechanism.

Now, it is a straightforward step to reason that if one could deliberately control this energy . . ., and one then deliberately created a deficiency of this energy in a certain part of the body . . ., that part of the body would be liable to come down with a physical affliction. Or, conversely, if a given part of the physical body was ill, and one deliberately "took" psychic energy from the rest of the body . . .and moved it into the ill part, the ill part should heal. Both of these are testable predictions.

Tart goes on to say that if proper experimental conditions were met, and if observations showed that the predicted effects were indeed produced, this would be a workable theory. The next steps would be to check out alternative theories to explain the same phenomena, to have independent investigators do the same experiment to see if their results are similar, and to explore the underlying neurological, endocrinal, and electrophysiological mechanisms behind the "psychic energy" in question.

It would be useful to apply the four principles of scientific method to the field of "psychic healing" to see what progress has been made in constructing a science from the anecdotal, clinical, and experimental reports that have accumulated over the centuries. In regard to the first principle, accurate observation, it is apparent that reports of unorthodox cures for bodily ailments have been recorded for thousands of years. It is only in recent years, however, that "paranormal healing" has been observed scientifically, and that experiments have been designed to study "healing" phenomena.

Tart's second principle emphasizes the repeatable nature of observation. Unfortunately, with the exception of the Kirlian photography studies, each investigator in this field has studied a different aspect of the realms of "psychic healing." What is needed is for other investigators to repeat the pioneering experiments by Grad, Smith, Krieger, Dean, Watkins and Watkins, and Goodrich. Eventually, the most productive lines of experimentation will become evident and more detailed work can be done.

Tart's third principle involves logical theorizing. Until more research data are available in "psychic healing," it is difficult to go very far in building a theory of how "psychic healing" happens. Although there is much speculation about a "psychic energy" being involved in "paranormal healing," there is absolutely no proof that "energy" has anything to do with the process. For all we know, telepathic communication between "healer" and healee may account for the effects observed. For example, telepathy could easily explain the results of the Goodrich study. As for the studies which appear to implicate psychokinesis, parapsychologists are still undecided as to whether or not psychokinetic effects involve "energy."

This is only one example of the questions involved in developing a theory of "paranormal healing." Tart's final principle is that a theory must be tested. Once a theory of "healing" has been stated, scientists can check it out against further observations. For example, it may be theorized that the healee must always cooperate with the "healer" in order for "psychic healing" to occur. But if a significant number of cases is found where the healee did not know about the "healing"—or even resisted it—that theory would have to be modified or discarded.

Science and Paradigms

Thomas Kuhn, a historian of science, introduced the idea that science functions under the control of "paradigms," a variety of intellectual achievements that solve puzzles posed by scientists, thus underlying the scientific enterprise enterprise and guiding its work. Stephen Toulmin adds that "one of the best indications that a new science has arrived at a clear definition of its intellectual goals, and has achieved a proper disciplinary status, is the eventual enthronement of an agreed set of fundamental concepts and selection criteria." Charles T. Tart has referred to a paradigm as a "super-theory" about the nature of reality. Its scope is sometimes so wide that it seems to account for most or all of the known phenomena in its field. Toulmin adds that a paradigm is a "population of presuppositions" which can act as a measure of the internal consistency of a science.*

Copernicus introduced the idea that the planets revolve around the sun. This paradigm still guides astronomy, but when it was introduced, it was opposed by people who held to the notion that the planets revolve around the earth. This opposition produced a "paradigm clash," as adherents to both points of view advanced their positions. Eventually, there was a "paradigm shift" as astronomers discovered many facts that could better be explained if they thought of the sun as being in the center of the solar system.

Historically, Kuhn has shown that paradigm clashes have been characterized by bitter emotional antagonisms. Indeed, Kuhn points out that a new and better paradigm is rarely advanced solely by a rational scientific debate centering on observations and experiments. What usually happens is that the staunch adherents of the old paradigm die off and are replaced in their positions by younger people.

A. H. Maslow has written that the first obligation of science is to confront all of reality as human beings experience it; scientific paradigms are based on assumptions about the nature of that reality. Sometimes these assumptions are supported by facts and sometimes merely by prejudices and biases. Thus, it is necessary for scientists to adopt paradigms that are open-ended, that allow for

---

*Kuhn and Toulmin use the term "paradigm" in slightly different ways, and for a full exposition of their points of view the reader is referred to Kuhn's *Structure of Scientific Revolutions*, second edition, and to Toulmin's *Human Understanding*.

changes in the paradigm if repeated observation and experimentation prove some of the assumptions underlying the paradigm to be incorrect.

There are many ways that scientists can gather information. Plato utilized reason to formulate his world-view but shunned testing his theories against reality, calling this "an impious undertaking." It was Plato's student, Aristotle, who pioneered scientific observation, as he meticulously catalogued plants, animals, and other natural phenomena. Another Greek philosopher, Democritus, conducted some of history's first experiments; his findings led to his writings on atomic theory. Plato had engaged in building "abstract theories"—ideas spun inside the mind without reference to experimental knowledge. Democritus had developed an "empirical theory," one based on observable events and experimental data. Abstract theories tend to be arrogant, dogmatic, and are usually presented as unchangeable truths. Empirical theories tend to be humble; they change as new information becomes available. A. H. Maslow wrote that if a theory "purports to interpret and organize our knowledge of reality, then it must of necessity be a changing thing." Our knowledge of reality keeps changing and our theories must change with that knowledge. Maslow continues, "There is a kind of mutual feedback involved here between theory and facts, a feedback which can be totally lacking in the . . . abstract theory. . . ."

In summary, it is quite possible that research results in "paranormal healing" will eventually result in a paradigm shift and necessitate a revision of our scientific world-view. However, scientists have barely taken the first steps in that direction. More laboratory experiments in "psychic healing" and more real life observations of "psychic healers" are needed before scientists formulate theories that will eventually explain "paranormal healing" phenomena so well that they will be accepted as fundamental aspects of the way the universe works.

Chapter Three

Three North American Healers: Rolling Thunder, Doña Pachita, and Olga Worrall

When an individual becomes ill, it is not unusual for several opinions to be offered as to how to restore the person's health. A student of the authors complained of feeling indisposed and having a fever. His paramour insisted he see a physician; a friend said the disease was "all in his mind" and that he should "think positive thoughts." Another friend insisted that the student had become "possessed by evil spirits" and that the best remedy was an exorcism. The student was very confused over the conflicting advice; while trying to decide whose suggestion to take, he recovered.

To an outsider, it was apparent that the three different pieces of advice were based on different world views, and upon "models" of illness consistent with those world views. Miriam Siegler and Humphry Osmond, in their book, *Models of Madness, Models of Medicine,* have defined a "model" as an arrangement of a theory, an ideology, or a point of view in such a manner that it can be compared with other theories, ideologies, or points of view. For Siegler and Osmond, comparability is the essence of model-making.

The indisposed student who received three pieces of advice was actually presented with representatives of three different—and comparable—models of illness. His paramour suggested a physician. If this approach had been followed, the physician would have determined the physical basis of the disease, and would have prescribed the proper medicines (or rest, surgery, or nursing care) for that disease. The treatment would have been directed toward the patient's body; health would be restored once the infection, inflammation, or other malfunction had come under control.

The well-meaning friend who suggested that the student "think positive thoughts" adopted a different model of illness. The cause of disease is negative thinking which, in turn, weakens the body's physiology, making it less resistant to germs and viruses. The best type of treatment would be psychological; it would consist of positive suggestions (e.g., hypnosis, prayer, meditation, counseling), coming from either the sick individual or from others. Once the person's self-concepts are positive, health will be restored. The importance of the body is not denied, it is just that thought patterns are the key to understanding sickness and health.

While the student's paramour held a world view which emphasized the "physical" aspects of visible reality, and one friend took the point of view that "psychological" determinants are the key to behavior, the third friend lived in a world which was largely "psychic." For this friend, sickness depended less on the body and the mind than on astrological patterns, the condition of the "etheric body," and the presence of benign or evil forces from the "spirit world." Treatment might consist of understanding one's astrological health cycle and one's "karmic" debts from a previous lifetime. It might involve impugning an evil "spirit" and asking for the aid of benevolent entities from the "spirit world." It might even consist of drinking magical potions—not for their medicinal or nutritional qualities but because of some "power" with which they are endowed.

The Placebo Effect

Frequently, adherents of one point of view do not discourage a patient from seeking help outside their particular model, thinking that it might serve as a useful placebo. Sigmund Freud realized the power of placebo effects, noting that "expectation colored by hope and faith is an effective force with which we will have to reckon . . . in *all* our attempts at treatment and cure." More recently, scientists have tested the usefulness of various medicines and treatments by giving some patients the substance being investigated and other patients a placebo—an inert substance that has no physiological effect of its own. Nevertheless, the expectancy of the patient can produce an effect with a placebo.

In one study of patients hospitalized with bleeding peptic ulcers, 70 per cent showed excellent results lasting over a period of one year when the physician gave them an injection of distilled water, telling them it was a new medicine that would cure them. L. H. Gliedman, Jerome D. Frank, and their associates have presented data from five separate studies involving 56 patients; an average of 55 per cent showed significant symptomatic improvement from the placebos. In some studies, patients have improved following the administration of a drug, but a similar group of patients improved just as much after taking a placebo. Jerome D. Frank, in his book *Persuasion and Healing,* admits the effectiveness of placebos but warns that the phenomenon is not simple; there are many aspects of the healer-patient relationship that may be involved. Frank concludes:

> Experimental studies of the effects of the administration of inert medications by physicians demonstrate that the allevi-

ation of anxiety and arousal of hope through this means
commonly produce considerable symptomatic relief and
may promote healing of some types of tissue damage. This
relief may be enduring. Although persons predisposed to
trust others and to accept socially defined symbols of healing are most likely to respond favorably, the response seems
to depend primarily on interactions between the patient's
momentary state and aspects of the immediate situation.
Important among these are the attention and interest of the
healer.

Sophisticated practitioners of various types of healing
know about the placebo effect, but sometimes disagree on
what part of the procedure constitutes the "active treatment" and what constitutes the "inert placebo." Someone
devoted exclusively to a physical, physiological model of
healing would view drugs and surgery as "active treatments" and everything else as placebos. A person exclusively devoted to a psychological, psychosomatic model
would view the messages from the "healer" to the
patient—as well as the patient's changing self-concept—as
the "active treatment." Medicine would be a harmless
placebo, something which would facilitate treatment because of the patient's expectations rather than because of
any properties of the medicine itself. A person who completely adhered to a psychic, paranormal model of healing
would see the status of one's "etheric body" as all-
important; medicine and suggestion, at best, can temporarily do away with symptoms of the disease but the healee
will likely fall ill again if evil "spirits" are not exorcised or if
other means are not taken to assist one's "spiritual purification." In addition, there are those who accept a physical
model for some ailments, and a psychological or even a
psychic model for others.

The first written reference to acupuncture dates back
some 2,500 years. It is only recently, however, that the
ancient Chinese practice has been taken seriously by West-

ern scientists. Few investigators deny that acupuncture assists a large proportion of the patients to whom it is administered. However, different models are proposed to explain acupuncture's efficacy.

Ronald Melzack, for example, presents a physiological model of acupuncture in his book, *The Puzzle of Pain*. In trying to understand how acupuncture controls physical discomfort, Melzack asserts that pain depends, in part, on the relative amounts of activity in the large A-beta fibers which are activated by non-painful stimuli, and the small c-fibers which are activated by painful stimuli. Increasing the activity of the A-beta fibers is thought to close a spinal "gate," preventing the further transmission of information from the c-fibers. Melzack suspects that acupuncture needles selectively stimulate the A-beta and that the high level of activity in the A-beta fibers closes the "gate" and thus inhibits pain. To explain how pain is alleviated in the face, ears, and other areas above Melzack's "gate," two other investigators, P. L. Man and C. H. Chen, have postulated a second "gate" located at a higher level of the nervous system.

A psychological model of acupuncture's effectiveness is presented by those who maintain that hypnotic-like effects and suggestion are involved. W. S. Kroger, in a 1972 article in the *Journal of the American Medical Association*, noted the similarities of acupuncture's effects to those produced by hypnosis. J. F. Chaves and T. X. Barber, writing in *Psychoenergetic Systems*, described how acupuncture-induced reduction in pain during operations could be due to several psychological concomitants of the procedure. These included a lowered anxiety level, a strong belief in the treatment's effectiveness, special preparation and indoctrination before the operation, and suggestions for pain relief provided by the acupuncture practitioners. Chaves and Barber also noted that acupuncture needles may distract patients' attention to pain and that drugs are often given along with acupuncture treatment. They further observed that many people overestimate the physiological aspects of pain; many bodily tissues are insensitive when they are cut.

A psychic model of acupuncture is held by such contemporary practitioners as Lok Yee-Kung of Hong Kong and J. R. Worsley of Great Britain, both of whom adhere to the traditional Chinese concepts. Both Lok and Worsley refer to the *Nei Ching* which holds that there are 12 "meridians"— channels of *ch'i* energy. These channels run vertically through the body maintaining a balance between the receptive, feminine *yin* force and the assertive, masculine *yang* force. *Yin* meridians are associated with such organs as the liver, kidneys, and spleen, while *yang* meridians are associated with such organs as the stomach, gallbladder, and intestines. Disease is thought to reflect the imbalance of *yin* and *yang* forces. The insertion of the needles in appropriate acupuncture points is thought to correct the imbalance, thus curing the disease. Thus, the acupuncturist works with the invisible *ch'i* energy rather than with the physical body.

It is only in recent years that scientific research has attempted to determine which model of acupuncture (or which combination of models) most accurately describes the process. For example, R. O. Becker has identified a "primitive data transmission and control system" in the body. Becker has stated, in an article written for *Psychoenergetic Systems*, that the prime function of this system is that of "sensing injury and effecting repair . . . ." Becker reported that this primitive data transmission system appears to be influenced by acupuncture treatment. Further, Becker has found electrical correlates on the skin for a large number of the ancient Chinese acupuncture points. Thus it may be possible to develop models that are not restrictive and which combine the most useful information from each model. These models would represent a broader or more holistic world view. And once the correct models for "paranormal healing" have been established, scientists may be forced to develop new paradigms of knowledge.

With Rolling Thunder in California and Kansas

The authors have visited several "healers" in various parts of the world, finding that each of them had a view of the world which influenced the model of "healing" they utilized. By understanding these world-views, one may also obtain glimpses of future paradigms in which science may at last find a common ground with the primitive shaman and the esoteric philosopher.

In 1970, one of the authors (S.K.) met an American Indian medicine man at a rock-and-roll concert:

In 1970, I visited Mickey Hart's ranch in Novato, California. One night, he played drums with the Grateful Dead at "The Family Dog," a well-known San Francisco dance hall. During a blues number, a husky, gray-haired man walked in. He was wearing a leather jacket and a beaded necklace. Most of the members of the audience took one look at his long hair and beads, dismissing him as an aging hippie. But I knew that he was Rolling Thunder, a medicine man for the Shoshone Indians and a close friend of Mickey Hart.

Hart and I took Rolling Thunder back to the ranch with us; the next morning we went to the top of the tallest hill on Hart's property where Rolling Thunder led us in a sunrise ceremony.

After lighting a fire and praying to the Four Winds, Rolling Thunder passed a peace pipe filled with a mixture of wood shavings and various herbs. We were each given a chance to send a prayer into the winds so it could be carried to the Great Spirit.

In 1971, I was back at Hart's ranch with Irving Oyle, a

friend of mine who is an osteopathic physician. When Rolling Thunder arrived, Hart and I brought the medicine man and the osteopath together. We were somewhat apprehensive because this was Rolling Thunder's first serious encounter with a physician. We sent them to Hart's recording studio where they could talk privately. After several hours, they walked through the door, arm in arm. Oyle reported, "We compared our practices. Rolling Thunder said that when a sick person comes to him, he makes a diagnosis, goes through a ritual, and gives that person some medicine that will restore health. I replied that when a patient comes to me, I make a diagnosis and go through the ritual of writing a prescription which will give the patient some medicine to restore health. In both cases, a great deal of magic is involved—the type of magic called 'faith in one's doctor.' "

Later that year, I planned the program for the Third Interdisciplinary Conference on the Voluntary Control of Internal States, sponsored by the Menninger Foundation and held at a country retreat in Kansas. To represent an American Indian's point of view, I had invited Rolling Thunder to the conference. He spent two days quietly evaluating the 80 scientists who participated in the meeting. When he was satisfied that they were sincere in their desire to learn about "the other world," he agreed to lead the group in the same morning ritual I had seen him perform at Mickey Hart's ranch. Once again I heard his invocation "to the East where the sun rises, to the North where the cold comes from, to the South where the light comes from, and to the West where the sun sets."

On the third day of the conference, Rolling Thunder agreed to discuss "psychic healing" with the scientists. He said, "When a baby is born, Indians have a way of knowing if he is supposed to be a medicine man." As this young Indian grows up, seven ceremonies await him. He learns that the love of all life is basic to his expertise as a "healer." Rolling Thunder remarked, "Many times I don't know what medicine I'm going to use until the 'doctoring' is going on; I sometimes can't remember what I've used. That's because it's not me doing the 'doctoring.' It's the Great Spirit working through me." Rolling Thunder also noted that the healee must have a proper attitude to get the most value out of a "healing" experience. He said, *"The people who are being 'doctored' must have cleared up their thinking so that they can accept the Great Spirit's work."* He also said, *"After the 'doctoring' is over, we feel good when the person gets better and appreciates what has been done."*

Rolling Thunder stated that one's health could be preserved by a balance maintained among *"energy centers"* of the body as well as keeping the *"energy channels"* free from clogging. He advised, *"If you can purify your mind, you don't need drugs and you don't need liquor. You can get high any time, just with your good feelings. And if you want to be even higher, you can go out on a hill; fast and pray until you see a vision. This will tell you your purpose in life."*

Rolling Thunder was given a chance to demonstrate his *"healing"* ability when one of my student assistants complained of a swollen ankle which had been injured during a game of touch football. Rolling Thunder asked me to find some raw meat and a pail of water. Once this was provided, Rolling Thunder prayed to the Four Winds, observing that *"from them we gain our strength as we breathe the air."* He lit a fire in the dining hall fireplace, noting that fire *"enables us to cook our meals, warm our bodies, and conduct our ceremonies."* He made a *"sacrifice"* of the raw hamburger and made some passes over the student with an eagle wing. (We later discovered that the eagle is Rolling Thunder's totem bird.) He then pressed his mouth to the young man's swollen ankle, held it there for a minute, and then spat a bilious fluid into the pail of water. He followed this procedure several times, and fanned the ankle with the eagle wing. He uttered a silent prayer and then asked me to *bury the content of the water pail. We observed that the swelling had gone down and that the discoloration was less noticeable. Rolling Thunder later remarked that this had been the first "doctoring" he had carried out before a group of professional people.*

Rolling Thunder had expressed his world-view during the sunrise ceremonies. He exhorted, "Great Spirit, creator of all things, I ask that this prayer be heard and carried on the wind. I pray that we can recognize and appreciate those things given by the Great Spirit and placed on the Mother Earth for us. I ask that we give thanks to the Father Sun which brings forth life on this land." In other words, Rolling Thunder saw the human being as an integral part of the universe. "Healing," therefore, had to be carried out with full knowledge of the forces outside of the body as well as those of the body itself.

From Rolling Thunder's point of view, the earth is a living organism. Like a person, the earth is more healthy at certain times than at other times. Just as people should treat their bodies with respect, they should treat the earth with respect. In Doug Boyd's biography of Rolling Thunder, the medicine man made the comment:

> Too many people don't know that when they harm the earth, they harm themselves, nor do they realize that when they harm themselves, they harm the earth. . . . Understanding begins with love and respect. It begins with respect for the Great Spirit, and the Great Spirit is the life that is in all things. . . . Such respect is not a feeling or an attitude only. It's a way of life. Such respect means that we never stop realizing and never neglect to carry out our obligation to ourselves and our environment.

Rolling Thunder's "healing" ceremonies grew out of this point of view. To him, a "healer" does not break or transcend natural laws, but makes use of them. The "life force" in all organisms is an important part of the "healing" process, but so are herbal medicines and the healee's mental attitude. Therefore, a case could be made that Rolling Thunder has practiced a brand of "doctoring" that is primarily psychic but which does not ignore the physical and psychological dimensions of the human being. This typifies the practice of other American Indian medicine men. Rolling Thunder has often mentioned "birth control" and other practices that medicine men have used over the centuries. These claims were verified by Janet W. Brown, writing in a 1975 issue of *Science*:

> Native Americans made wide use of anesthetics and narcotics, cathartics, emetics and febrifuges, as well as psychotherapy and drugless therapies like cupping, sucking, and enemas. Among the better known drugs of Native American origin are quinine, curare, and ipecac. Their skill in treating bone injuries has been widely praised by both early and modern writers. Less well known is the surgical prowess of some groups, including their ability to perform trephination. Most tribes practiced some kind of population control, and oral contraceptives were discovered and used centuries ago in some tribes. The Shoshone of Nevada, for instance, used *Lithospermum* ("stoneseed"), which, when used in varying concentrations and periods of time, could effect varying durations of sterility in the female.

With Rolling Thunder in Nevada

In 1974, the authors visited Rolling Thunder's home in Nevada. One of the authors (A.V.) recalled:

The drive from San Francisco to Carlin, Nevada, is a long one. Five of us were squeezed into a Volkswagen, with our sleeping bags and packs filling the trunk and what little floor space was left over. I was thinking about my previous meetings with Rolling Thunder and the many times I had heard him criticize the Bureau of Indian Affairs and the

*manner in which the European settlers and their descen-
dants had destroyed the natural environment. Rolling
Thunder had stated that the earth does not belong to anyone. When the Europeans came to the Western Hemisphere, the Indians were willing to share their knowledge
of natural medicine as well as the skills they had developed
in cultivating the land and in hunting. But the Europeans
were not interested in sharing the land, but in owning it–
not in cooperating with nature, but in mastering and exploit-
ing it. "Now the white man is realizing that he has made
the land barren and polluted the environment," Rolling
Thunder would say, "and he has also contaminated
his heart and left his spirit barren."*

*That evening we arrived at Rolling Thunder's home in
Carlin. He was out on a run with the railroad, where he was
working as a brakeman. We pitched camp in the large back
yard which extends into the distant foothills. We rolled out
our sleeping bags, enjoyed the Nevada sunset, and greeted
Rolling Thunder when he returned late that evening.*

*The next day was spent in conversation about Rolling
Thunder's current activities as both a medicine man and a
political leader. That evening, he declared that there were
so many lovely ladies with us that we could not pass up the
opportunity for a dance. During that time of year, there
was no rain in Nevada, as it was the dry season. Yet,
Indian tradition holds that before one initiates a dance
there should be a brief shower to settle the dust on the
dancing ground. After the dance, there should be a
stronger rain to wash away the tracks of the dancers.*

*At sunset, we climbed into three cars and headed for an
abandoned ranch in a valley a few miles away. On our way
to the valley, I gazed at the stars which were shining
brightly in the clear sky. Not a cloud was in sight. Suddenly, the driver slammed on the brakes and we focused our
attention on the road ahead of us. Three deer were standing by the side of the road. Recovering from their surprise
upon seeing our headlights, they took off in a trot, leaping
gracefully into the hills.*

Just a few seconds had elapsed, but when we looked into the sky again, we observed small, puffy clouds gathering in front of us. A few minutes later we turned the windshield wipers on. The shower stopped as we arrived at the dancing ground. There were no puddles, yet the water had settled the dust.

We danced for hours as Rolling Thunder's group played drums and sang Indian songs. Rolling Thunder taught us the Snake Dance which is often used in "healing" ceremonies. The sky was still clear as we finished our dance. But on the way to our cars, dark clouds gathered over the clearing. Thunder began to crack, there was lightning close by, and a heavy rain poured down as we ran the last few yards to our cars. Rolling Thunder observed, "It's not good to leave our prints behind. We don't want the white folks to think that a bunch of savages and hippies were doing some kind of pagan ceremony."

The next morning, Spotted Fawn (Rolling Thunder's wife) had breakfast waiting for us as we entered the house. After breakfast, we sat in the living room and talked. Rolling Thunder was speaking about disease. "Every time there is sickness, there is a reason for it. Everything has a cause—and at the same time it is going to be the cause of something else. The medicine man knows this and takes it into account when he is deciding whether to 'doctor' someone or not. Everything has its costs, and illness can sometimes be the necessary price that the person pays for something. This is why a medicine man can take up to three days to decide if he is going to 'doctor' someone or not. If we take away an illness or a pain when we are not supposed to, the price the person pays in the future might be even greater. The sick person's spirit knows this even if, on the surface, the person is not aware of it."

Rolling Thunder continued, "I am interested in helping to alleviate pain by using herbs and the waters and all the natural things around us. Every physical object in nature has a spiritual side; therefore, these objects can be spiritual helpers to the medicine man. The medicine man must know

*the laws of nature and understand the spiritual side of
things, then these objects can be helpers. This is why my
medicine cannot be duplicated. One fellow I 'doctored' had
my herbal mixture analyzed and discovered what plants
were in the mixture. He thought that he had discovered one
of the secrets of my medicine, and put together a similar
mixture. Well, that mixture did not work. He had duplicated the physical part of the mixture but did not know how
to handle the spiritual portion."*

*Rolling Thunder observed, "When I find a plant I have
never seen before, I can hold it in my hand and tell what its
uses are. It will communicate with me. It will sing its songs
and reveal its secrets. In the winter, when there are three
feet of snow on the ground, and I need a certain green plant
I can go outside and dig in a certain place. I will find the
plant, with green leaves on it, even if I have never been in
that place before. But a medicine man cannot do this for
show. These things can be done only when they are
needed."*

In retrospect, it was apparent that Rolling Thunder's path
could be described as one of action. The teachings of the
Great Spirit come our way through living them, not by
talking about them. When the medicine man lives these
laws, they respond to him. To an observer, it might seem as
if Rolling Thunder had caused the rains to come before and
after the dance. To Rolling Thunder, however, it was a
matter of aligning himself with the natural laws. In "healing," Rolling Thunder would look for the natural laws
which operated in the situation and, if he decided that "doctoring" was the proper step to take, would align himself
with those laws. In the foreword that he wrote for Stanley
Krippner's book, *Song of the Siren*, Rolling Thunder
stated:

> What scientists call psychic phenomena, the American In-
> dians would refer to as the "other world." These

phenomena are very important. In fact, they are the most important aspects of our lives. They have to do with life and death and sickness. They even have to do with the rise and fall of governments.

Everything in the universe rises and falls and travels in cycles. These cycles are energy patterns created in the universe itself, then in bodies of everyone living and everything that has life. I think that as scientists go more into explorations in this area, they will find that these energy patterns explain a lot. Scientists have done some . . . experiments on the life force in plants and animals; I think this is the deepest aspect of what you call psychic phenomena. The meaning of life itself seems to be what these scientists are working on at this time, and I think it's a real good thing.

When the authors visited Rolling Thunder's home in Nevada,* he expanded on this world view. Sitting underneath a stuffed eagle, and smoking a pipe filled with raw tobacco "that doesn't contain the poisons they put in commercially prepared tobacco," he observed:

Professors teach so much about the atom and of different sources of energy, but they have forgotten about the lightning—the source of life energy. They still have to discover just how lightning is formed and transferred to the earth—and about certain rocks that hold that energy, and that all life has some of that lightning in it. Everything that has life also has an electrical force. The flow of energy has to be in certain directions, and if it gets upset or unbalanced it can affect our bodies in such a way that we might become ill or even paralyzed. This energy flow in the human body is very important.

The human body is divided into two halves, plus and minus. Every energy body consists of two poles, positive and negative. We can control this energy just like we learn to control our physical bodies.

---

*Rolling Thunder is part Caucasian and was born a Cherokee. However, his practice as a medicine man has been among Indians in the West Shoshone Indian nation.

Rolling Thunder mentioned a case in which he touched a sick person's stomach and several pebbles appeared to emerge. Rolling Thunder did not feel that the stones had been in the person's stomach. Rather, they were symbolic of the disease, the sick person being especially "hard" and "dense"—thus liable to fall ill again unless a personality change occurred.

Rolling Thunder and "Exorcism"

Rolling Thunder recalled his visit with Irving Oyle, the osteopathic physician, and how he had agreed to serve on the advisory board for Oyle's clinic in Bolinas, California. The authors had heard that Rolling Thunder had performed an "exorcism" at the clinic and asked for some details. Rolling Thunder responded:

> There is great interest at this time in what is called "exorcism." We've been dealing with these forces or spirits for thousands of years and they are always present. We don't say that we hate these spirits. What we say is that they have a function and a place—but that place is not in someone's body. If the spirits are up to mischief, it becomes the task of a "healer" who specializes in those things to coax the spirits out.
>
> Sometimes the spirits are very persistent; they lie and play tricks. But when they meet someone they can't fool, they get angry. They may be tough and persistent but must be made to realize that they have to go.
>
> One of Dr. Oyle's associates tried to help a young woman who had tried to kill herself. He gave her mouth-to-mouth resuscitation but she died anyway. After that, the doctor was in very bad shape. He had been a good man, but after he had been "possessed" by whatever was bothering this woman, his personality and character completely changed. He himself knew and realized it, but was unable to do anything about it. Members of his family also realized this and

were becoming very afraid of him. They were even considering putting him away in a mental hospital.

So I happened to come along at that time. I was looking for a place to rest up and I went to Bolinas because this had been a sacred area of the Indians a long time ago. So I met with the doctors and they fixed a place out in the woods. I felt like I was in my own element and they were all very respectful people. They didn't throw a lot of questions at me—like why I used feathers in this ceremony and other things like that.

It went very well. It wasn't too tiring like some I've been through. The doctor did scream and shake all over when this thing that was "possessing" him came out. But it did come out. I could see that there was only one way to do it. When I'm challenged by these spirits and when they persist in wanting to bother people, this "exorcism" has to be done.

Rolling Thunder also told the authors about treating a young man who had been labeled a "hopeless schizophrenic" by a physician. After the man had set fire to his parents' home, he was taken to the hospital in a strait jacket. The parents contacted Rolling Thunder; they were told, "Your son will come home soon and I will come to see him."

A week later the young man was unexpectedly sent home for a visit. Rolling Thunder and his party arrived at a prearranged time, after rubbing a white herb on their faces for protection. Rolling Thunder spoke with the young man and asked for some raw meat. He burned herbs to purify the room, asked the man to stand on the meat, and pulled an eagle claw and feathers from his medicine bag. Rolling Thunder moved around the room slowly, chanting in an Indian dialect.

The young man cringed whenever the eagle feathers came near him. Finally, as Rolling Thunder passed the eagle feathers over the man's head, he screamed and flung himself to the floor, and as he writhed on the floor, Rolling

Thunder began to whimper, sniff, and growl like a dog. The young man's body stiffened, he screamed again, and began to shiver. Rolling Thunder's body also stiffened; he then coughed up a black substance which he expectorated into a can.

Five hours after the ritual began, the young man began to talk in a relaxed manner and said that he felt "totally relieved." This incident had taken place almost a year before the authors' visit; the man's illness had not returned.

Accompanying the authors to Carlin, Nevada, was Corinne Calvet, an actress. For several years, she had suffered from a gallbladder ailment and the accompanying pain. Rolling Thunder agreed to perform a "healing" ritual. He initiated the authors into the sweat-lodge purification ceremony so that they could assist with the "healing." Upon entering a hide structure, or "wickiup," water was poured over hot rocks. The participants cleansed themselves by chanting, praying, and sweating out their impurities. One of the authors (S.K.) noted:

The wickiup was constructed of saplings bent and tied together over which animal hides had been draped. A shallow pit had been dug in the center and filled with red-hot rocks. As the water contacted the rocks, an explosive hiss was followed by a wave of intense heat that enveloped our naked bodies. We took turns adding water and the heat increased until I thought my skin was on fire. With every breath, the fire extended to my lungs. I realized that I could not fight the heat. It was necessary to receive the heat and ride with it. I became one with the heat, one with the hot air, and allowed every breath I took to enhance the feeling of oneness. The feeling of unity extended to the group, to the elements, and to the universe itself. As the sweat poured from my body, I felt purged of anxiety, depression, and all the petty concerns that would prevent me from fully participating in the "healing" ceremony which was to follow.

Rolling Thunder with Corinne Calvet (left) and Stanley Krippner's stepdaughter Carie Harris (right) during the authors' visit to Rolling Thunder's home in Nevada. (Courtesy S. Krippner)

The inside of a shaman's hut in central Mexico, depicting various herbal medications and "power objects." (Courtesy A. Villoldo)

The eagle is one of Rolling Thunder's most powerful "healing" symbols and is portrayed in this painting by his son-in-law, Russell Jones. (Courtesy R. Jones)

The entire group made a circle around the fire, performing the Snake Dance while Rolling Thunder worked with Calvet. Again, he used raw meat, an eagle claw and feathers, and spit something into a pail after sucking on Calvet's skin. The following morning she reported a complete absence of pain. Two years later she noted that the discomfort had never returned.

Rolling Thunder told the authors what was required of a "healer."

> The place to start is learning how to control your thinking. If you find a harmful thought going through your head, learn how to put it out. Thoughts can be very powerful. Some people can learn how to see broken bones coming together and they can "doctor" in that way. They can see a person as beautiful and healthy, and will help them to recover from a sickness. This is the first step in becoming a "healer." But even after you learn all that and have perfect mental control, you still have to learn about your protections and the proper respect you have to pay the "spirit world." You need to realize that we all live many lifetimes and sometimes you will remember episodes from your previous lives. Also, it is sometimes necessary to visit the "spirit world" while you are "doctoring" someone. I guess this is what people call "astral projection," but it has to be done in just the right way or it can be dangerous.
>
> You have to know if it's meant for you to do these things in the first place. In the Indian world, we realize that each of us has a mission to fulfill in life. People should find out what work is meant for them. You start by finding out where you feel good in your own mind, then where you're most in accord with nature and with the people around you.
>
> Every medicine man has his own way. In the past there have been some jealousies. Some chiefs and some medicine men have worked against each other, listening to the talk of the white men, the missionaries, and the politicians—people who were trying to trick and deceive them. I see less of that nowadays.
>
> The spirit is returning to the Indians and is extending to young people across the country. Many of them are becom-

ing spiritual warriors. That doesn't mean they are going to make war. Being a spiritual warrior means becoming a complete person. It means having consideration for other people, and in finding spirituality through truth and beauty.

Many people who are looking for spiritual guidance look for things that will benefit themselves only. They need to break away from the "I want" way of thinking. They need to transcend their egos; they have to lose their greed before they can become spiritual warriors.

In his conversation with the authors, Rolling Thunder has stressed controlling one's thoughts, maintaining "one-pointedness of mind," and focusing attention as prerequisites to "healing." In addition, the medicine man must be able to leave the physical plane, making frequent excursions to the "other worlds" to fully understand health and "healing." All of these procedures are consistent with a world view in which the physical model can not explain the full range of phenomena experienced by a medicine man.

Doña Pachita's "Psychic Surgery"

In 1971, a medical student showed one of the authors (A. V.) an abdominal scar which he claimed was the result of a visit to a "psychic surgeon" two days previously. He had suffered severe pains, and a diagnosis of appendicitis had been made at a local hospital. The medical student had heard of doña Pachita's "psychic operations" and wanted to experience one first-hand. If nothing significant happened, he would still have had time to undergo conventional surgery at the hospital.

He reported that doña Pachita cut into his body with her hunting knife and removed the appendix, without the customary use of anesthetics or sterilization procedures. He claimed that the scar was originally three inches long, but had shrunk to half that size over the two-day period. After hearing this account, Villoldo wrote:

I examined the scar carefully, placing my thumbs on either side and pressing the skin together. When the body is opened in surgery, scar tissue forms through all the layers. This scar tissue remains as the new "connecting" tissue at the spot where the cut was made. When someone presses the skin, it feels rigid—not having the elasticity of normal skin. The surprising phenomenon about the medical student's purported "appendectomy" was that no scar tissue had been formed. There was only a superficial scab from the clotted blood. And yet this student, who had studied psychosomatic medicine for five years and was engaged in a clinical internship, claimed that he had lost all his symptoms of appendicitis. I insisted that he take me to meet doña Pachita!

Doña Pachita's home was located in the outskirts of Mexico City. To enter, one had to open a heavy steel door, then pass the piercing eyes of her pet falcon. The bird appeared to look every visitor over, seemingly expressing its approval or disapproval by ruffling its feathers, spreading its wings, and making strange gutteral sounds.

Pachita ("doña" is a term of respect in Spanish) proved to be a robust, jolly mestizo woman. Following his first visit to her home, Villoldo wrote:

Doña Pachita is about five feet high and almost equally wide. She received me warmly, taking me to the room where she diagnoses illnesses and prescribes her remedies. The small room was filled with cupboards crammed with herbal medicines. Opposite her desk there was an altar cluttered with bottles of sweet-smelling oils, burning candles, and a large painting of Cuahutémoc the "spirit guide" who supposedly works through Pachita when she performs "psychic operations."

Cuahutémoc was the last great Aztec prince. In the picture, he is portrayed standing on the top of a mountain, his right knee bent and his foot on a large rock. Feathered wings sprout from his shoulders and his face is half man and half eagle. Cuahutémoc, according to Pachita, was a spiritual as well as a political leader for the Aztecs. When he was about to be burned at the stake for refusing to convert to Roman Catholicism, he was given a final chance to save his life by accepting the Spanish God. According to the legend, he exclaimed, "What sort of God is this to whom thousands have been slaughtered in battle and who still thirsts for more blood?" The legend holds that as the flames enveloped Cuahutémoc's body, he was transformed into an eagle and flew into the sky.

I asked Pachita about the Aztec custom of sacrificing human beings by cutting out their hearts. She answered that this custom was done only at certain intervals such as when the Spaniards came and the Aztec priests thought their gods needed to be appeased. In addition, the victims accepted their sacrifice as a great honor. Years of preparation were required during which time the sacrificial victims conquered fear, elevated their consciousness, and prepared to rejoin their ancestors in the next life. How different this was, Pachita noted, from the contemporary belief that death is the worst thing that could happen to someone.

Doña Pachita told me that she had been aware of possessing paranormal powers since her youth. She said that she could predict events which later occurred as well as move objects at a distance. One night she dreamed about a "spirit guide." This "spirit" told her that she would develop as an instrument of the Divine Will. Different "spirits" would come to her, in her dreams as well as when she was awake, to teach her about medicinal plants and herbs, about "spiritual purification," and about "magnetic passes" used in healing.

Several of Pachita's healees were waiting for her in the living room of her house. I was told by one of them that it was not wise for too many healees to assemble at once because of police harassment. From time to time, police officers would break into Pachita's home, destroy her herbal preparations, and place her under arrest. Pachita

*would spend a few days in jail, point out to the authorities
that she has never had a casualty, and would be released.
Her typical statement in court was, "Do you really think
that I—an illiterate woman who cannot even read or
write—could do things the best doctors in the world can not
do?"*

*Doña Pachita told me that her "healing" procedures are
"spiritual" in nature but that herbal compresses and teas
are also used. Pachita remarked that these substances
"prepare the body to come into a state of health that is
strong enough to maintain the benefits of 'healing.'" One
of the healees in the waiting room was an adolescent girl
who had been diagnosed as having a brain tumor the size of
a golf ball. The tumor weakened one side of the girl's body
and was responsible for a partial paralysis. For a month,
Pachita had been meeting regularly with the girl to prepare
her for the "operation." They had lengthy talks about the
girl's childhood and family life as well as her health problems. During that period of time, the girl was receiving
herbal treatments. Pachita told me that the girl's "operation" had been scheduled for that evening; she invited me
to return and observe the procedure.*

The model of "healing" espoused by doña Pachita can be
seen to be psychic and paranormal in nature with some
attention given to the healee's physiology (through herbal
treatments) and psychodynamics (through discussion and
preparation sessions). Pachita's world view is similar to
that held by the Aztecs; of key importance is the focus on
an invisible world populated by "spirits," some of which
take an active interest in human affairs (as was the case
with the "spirit guides" who taught Pachita her skills and
who have guided her during her "operations"). Pachita's
procedures became apparent when Villoldo returned to her
home:

*I returned to doña Pachita's home after the sun had set.
Again, her pet falcon served as sentinel as a string of*

healees arrived. I observed that they represented a wide range of social-economic backgrounds; people with torn blankets around their shoulders were sitting by those wearing business suits and expensive dresses.

I was called into the "operating room," a small cubicle with two beds, a pile of clean sheets to one side, and a desk—the top of which was covered with several bottles of alcohol and wads of cotton. Pachita acknowledged me with a brief greeting, then returned to the preparations she and her two assistants were making. I stepped to the side, feeling a bit like an outsider who was intruding on one of humankind's oldest dramas: the struggle between life and death, health and illness.

Eventually I felt more at ease and observed the preparations as closely as I could, given the fact that the only source of illumination was a candle resting on the top of a table. One of Pachita's assistants was cutting strips of cotton about eight inches in width and 16 inches in length. The assistant then placed the strips in a basin filled with alcohol. The other assistant was placing sheets on the bed. Pachita then sat in the chair and began to take long, deep breaths; her entire body appeared to relax. As her breathing became deeper and slower, the seven of us in the room joined hands, forming a circle around the "healer." One of the assistants asked that we elevate our thoughts to the highest level we knew, asking God for guidance.

Pachita's body then began to convulse and jerk. We were told that she was turning her will over to the "spirit" of Cuahutémoc, the Aztec prince who died in 1525 and supposedly permeates her mind and utilizes her body as his instrument. A few seconds later, she opened her eyes, stood up and greeted us in a tone that was somewhat gruffer and harsher than before. From that point on, no one addressed her as "doña Pachita," but as "El Hermanito" or "The Little Brother"—Cuahutémoc's nickname. One by one each of us stepped forward to receive a blessing.

The first healee was the girl with the brain tumor.

Pachita took her by the hand and walked her to one of the beds. The girl reclined, and the "healer" sat in a chair at the head of the bed, asking the girl to breathe deeply. The girl was told that the "operation" would hurt a little but that she should trust God and pray. As the girl began to relax, Pachita reached into the basin, taking a strip of alcohol-moistened cotton, laying it on the girl's forehead.

Shortly afterwards, Pachita removed the cotton and placed her left hand over the girl's forehead. With her right hand, she stroked the girl's head and face. The "healer" asked the girl if she felt any pain; the girl responded that she did not. Pachita then reached for her bone-handled hunting knife. She brought the knife down directly on the girl's forehead, with the tip pointing just above the eyebrows. Pachita then appeared to push the blade into the skull.

Astounded, I moved closer to the bed and, by the dim candlelight, examined the girl. She was lying motionless, apparently oblivious to the knife that appeared to be sticking in her forehead. Meanwhile, Pachita stood at the head of the bed and seemed to insert her fingers into the girl's forehead, extracting what looked like a compact piece of tissue about the size of a ping-pong ball. Pachita referred to this object as the tumor. She withdrew the knife and held a piece of cotton over the healee's forehead for about a minute. Then she bandaged the girl's head and left to wash her hands. The "operation" had taken less than ten minutes.

The girl's mother and sister entered the "operating room" and the girl began to talk animatedly. She mentioned feeling some pain during the operation but that the discomfort had disappeared.

I was still standing near the healee, absolutely amazed. Did the "healer" really cut the girl's skin and enter the skull with the hunting knife? I knew that it was virtually impossible to enter the skull through the forehead with a sharp instrument, but I thought that I had seen this occur.

Could it have been sleight of hand?

Possibly. But at one point, the knife seemed to be sticking into the girl's head with no one touching it. How could this be explained?

Doña Pachita needed to be studied further, and Villoldo resolved to see her again.

Helen Kruger, in her book, *Other Healers, Other Cures*, refers to doña Pachita as a *curandera*, the Mexican term for a female "healer." Kruger has interviewed several people who have visited Pachita. One of them concluded that the dim light and super-charged tension that permeates Pachita's "operating room" were not conducive to critical observation. He suggested that Pachita might puncture a pillow filled with blood; indeed, there is a market nearby where chickens can be bought. Another visitor reported a different story:

> Gerry M. went under the *curandera's* knife for a "football knee" which doctors had told him required surgery. While he sweated profusely, Pachita sliced his knee open, reached in and "pulled at something"—presumably Gerry's torn cartilage—rubbed in grease, then bandaged it. Gerry says he felt no pain. Today the knee works fine and bears no scar so far as I was able to see.

Kruger, in her book, also relates that a physician, E. Stanton Maxey of the Miami Heart Institute, took several of his patients to see Pachita. These healees reportedly made considerable improvement following the "operation." Furthermore, the blood samples Maxey collected during the "operations" were certified to be human and coincided with the blood types of the healees.

On one of Villoldo's subsequent visits, he was accompanied by a surgeon, Eugenio Barbera, his wife, Luisa Barbera, his stepdaughter, Andrea, and her father. As a result of a childhood accident, Andrea suffered from a cataract in her right eye. Villoldo reported:

Doña Pachita received us with her usual good humor. When asked if she could help Andrea, Pachita looked into

*the girl's eyes and identified the condition as a cataract
without being told, even though the film which veiled the
cornea was almost imperceptible. She told us that Andrea
must wash her eyes with a certain herbal preparation and
should take daily doses of Kasdei, a medicine. But rather
than injecting Kasdei, as is ordinarily done, Andrea should
dissolve it in orange juice and drink it. Dr. Barbera said he
had never heard of the medicine but later that day, when we
looked it up in a pharmacological reference book, we discovered that it was a vitamin compound specifically recommended for corneal hernias. I was to observe this
phenomenon several times; the name of a medicine would
come to Pachita when she needed it, even though she could
not even spell the product's name.*

*I have also noticed Pachita's employment of astute psy-
chological principles. One example involved Andrea's
father whose receding hairline had been a cause of great
distress. He asked Pachita if she had any herbal remedies
for baldness, noting that he was very reluctant to enter into
conversations with women. If he could regain some of his
hair, he felt his shyness would disappear. The "healer"
began to chide him, pointing out that he was a personable
and interesting man and, being divorced, should have little
trouble making new acquaintances. Nevertheless, she continued, if he really wanted to grow back some of his hair,
she would help him.*

*Pachita described her formula. It involved mixing to-
gether five pounds of honey and an equal amount of rat
feces—which he could obtain easily from a medical or psychological laboratory. For an entire month, this concoction
was to be placed on his head each night before going to
sleep, and then washed out in the morning. "It smells terrible," she admitted, "but it will do the trick."*

*Andrea's father gasped, "You must be kidding!" With a
stern expression on her face, Pachita replied, "No, I don't
kid around; this is what you must do if you want to get rid of
your baldness." She walked away leaving the man gasping
incredulously.*

*For the next two weeks, Andrea's father debated whether
to mix Pachita's concoction or not. He bought the honey
but could not bring himself to obtain the rat feces. In addition, he explored every aspect of what it meant for him to be
bald. Finally he decided against putting the mixture on his
head. Through introspection, he had discovered the real
reason for his shyness—and it had nothing to do with his
baldness. In my opinion, doña Pachita had utilized a clever
psychotherapeutic strategy which had worked quite well.*

Accounts of doña Pachita's work indicate that she has
made frequent use of psychological procedures. With native people, she has prescribed herbal teas, but has prescribed medication to foreigners suffering from the same
ailment. She appears to have known what her healees expect and has given advice accordingly.

If the healees were Roman Catholic, they were encouraged to pray to their favorite saint. If the healees were
Indians, they were told to make peace with Mother Earth
and perform various devotional acts relating to nature.

For those who have expected a ritual, Pachita has performed accordingly—and has often given them a step-by-
step procedure to insure the effectiveness of the ceremony.
From time to time Pachita has confided that "psychic
surgery" is really unnecessary. However, it convinces the
healee that something is actually happening; this, in turn,
strengthens the healee's belief in the process and facilitates
the "healing."

The belief system of the healee is a critically important
part of the "healing" process. Its importance is illustrated
in the case of Anita,* a ballet dancer in her mid-thirties with
a back ailment that threatened the continuation of her successful career. One of the authors (A.V.) studied this case
in collaboration with Dr. Eugenio Barbera, who filed the
following account:

---

*A pseudonym.

When I first spoke to Anita about having an "operation" with doña Pachita, it took a great deal of effort to steer her away from her conviction that being operated on with a dirty knife would mean her death. The clinical diagnosis of her condition, which is not unusual among ballerinas, was luxation of intervertebral discs L-4 and L-5, increase in the lumbrosacral angle, and compression of posterior nerve roots. This produced a painful syndrome in the lower extremities, pavestesis (or numbness), and decrease of muscle strength in the toes. All this was impairing her career as a professional ballerina, and for the two years previous to her visit with doña Pachita, she restricted her activities to the teaching of dance.

Dr. Barbera, in his report, goes on to explain that Anita's psychodynamics played an important part in her encounter with the "healer." Anita had repeatedly turned down the options of orthopedic surgery and neurosurgery, claiming that these options might cripple her permanently. Barbera suspected that her fear of failure as a dancer became acute once she entered middle age; these fears were exacerbated by her back condition. These fears also prevented her from making an immediate commitment to "psychic surgery." Barbera continued:

> After much effort, I finally manged to convince Anita to see doña Pachita. The first time she visited Pachita, she only told the "healer" that she had a problem with her back. Anita was wearing a heavy fur coat, as it was winter and the examining room was cold. Pachita felt Anita's back through the outside of the coat, and told us that the last two vertebrae before the sacrum were "squished." This was correct. Pachita said that we needed to obtain two fresh vertebrae from a recently deceased woman to replace Anita's. If Anita was unable to obtain them, Pachita would do so.
>
> The ballerina left, somewhat frightened. Yet she initiated the process prescribed by the "healer"; it included taking a vegetable preparation, the contents of which were unknown to me. On a later visit, Pachita agreed to obtain the verte-

brae, and Anita agreed to bring a bottle of alcohol, a roll of cotton, and a bandage that was 12 inches wide.

We all arrived at Pachita's house on the evening of the "operation," feeling somewhat nervous. When the time came, we stepped into the poorly ventilated and semi-darkened "operation room."

The "operation" did not last more than fifteen minutes yet was truly impressive. Despite the semi-darkness, I seemed to observe Pachita opening the skin. I heard the sound that tissue makes when it is being cut, as well as the banging of the knife against the vertebrae. I did not see Pachita remove any vertebra, but I did see her—or so it appeared to me—insert a vertebra and then hammer it until it disappeared into that cavity in the spine filled with a liquid which appeared to be blood. Anita was then bandaged and told to rest and remain in bed for one month, getting up only to eat or go to the bathroom.

Later that evening, we returned to Anita's home. I looked underneath the bandages and was surprised to find nothing but superficial scratches, not the surgical cuts I had apparently observed a few hours earlier. To increase Anita's belief, though, I told her that there was actually a cut on her back. She had been instructed to drink one of Pachita's herbal preparations and, during the next few days, she began to feel progressively better.

Nevertheless, after looking for the scar, which by that time had vanished, she began to doubt that there ever had been such an "operation." Anita began to move around and go outside; she stopped taking care of herself and discontinued following Pachita's instructions.

The pain returned with even greater intensity. We performed a radiological examination which indicated that her spine was in the same condition—that is, the lumbrosacral angulations persisted as well as the luxation of L-4 and L-5. From this moment on, Anita lost all faith in her "healing" and continued the vicious circle of visiting orthopedists and neurosurgeons.

Anita's case demonstrates the role that one's belief system plays in "psychic healing." As long as Anita believed that the "operation" had been effective, she felt progressively better. But when she lost faith in the "healing," the pain returned. This is reminiscent of the cancer patient described by David Bresler and Richard Kroening in *Psychoenergetic Systems*. Although seriously ill, he begged to be administered a controversial drug, Krebiozen. After one day of treatment, his tumors were half their original size. Within ten days, all signs of the disease had vanished. But when the American Medical Association announced that the drug was worthless, the cancer reappeared and the patient died.

Pachita has stated that the main responsibility for improved health rests upon healees themselves. When they direct their thoughts in the direction of greater well-being, the "healer" is able to cooperate with the healee to effect a lasting change. When this is not the case, the feeling of being well tends to be transitory. The healee's belief system is not the only factor involved in "psychic healing." Yet it is one of the most critical, and doña Pachita has paid considerable attention to it.

Doña Pachita's Assistant

An important element in the case of Anita was the firsthand observation of a surgeon. Another physician, Gabriel Cousens, accompanied the surgeon's wife and one of the authors (A.V.) during a visit to Pachita in the summer of 1974. Villoldo reported:

We had been forewarned that doña Pachita was not receiving any visitors as she had been harassed recently by the Mexican Medical Association for practicing medicine without a license. We decided to take our chances and go anyway, following a period of silent meditation to put us in the most favorable state of mind possible.

We reached the steel gate and prepared to knock, when

*the door opened and her nephew let us in. The pet falcon
was more apprehensive than usual. We learned that the
police had broken into doña Pachita's home a few days
earlier, tearing up her "operating room," breaking vials of
herbal preparations, and destroying other medicinal substances. Pachita greeted us as we entered, perhaps delighted to see a familiar face after so much adversity.*

*An American couple from Texas had arrived for a "heal-
ing" session. Pachita turned to me and asked if I would
translate as she did not speak English, and the Americans
did not speak Spanish. It turned out that the woman, who
was quite obese, was suffering from a cancerous tumor in
the urinary bladder. Pachita agreed to "operate."*

*Later that evening we stepped into an improvised
"operating room" in Pachita's home. As Dr. Cousens and
I entered the room, Pachita handed me a pair of scissors. I
was to be one of her assistants, she explained; I began by
cutting the strips of cotton that were to be used during the
"operation." I placed them in a basin and another assistant poured alcohol on them. During the "operation,"
doña Pachita (who again took on the identity of El Hermanito) used only two instruments, the pair of scissors I
was holding and her hunting knife.*

*As the woman from Texas walked into the room, I began
to translate Pachita's instructions to her. She was to lie
down on the bed, pull her skirt down, and her blouse up. As
the woman bared her enormous abdomen, Pachita told
her to relax, breathe deeply, and elevate her thoughts to
God.*

*As Pachita began to massage the woman's abdomen, I
observed what I had noticed many times before—Pachita's
hands seemed to disappear into the healee's body. Since
the candlelight in the room was dim, it was impossible to
tell if Pachita's hands were actually "inside" the woman's
body or if they had been obscured by the woman's copious
skin.*

*Although there was little light in the room, the area
where Pachita's hands were working appeared to be much*

brighter than the surrounding area. It was just as if a reflector from the ceiling was trained upon the spot, even though I searched the room later and was unable to find such an object. I have observed this phenomenon whenever doña Pachita operates, just as if the area in which she works were iridescent. Doña Pachita has stated that she needs no light to operate by because El Hermanito can see in the dark.

Doña Pachita asked the healee if she felt any discomfort and the woman responded affirmatively. Pachita massaged that area until the pain disappeared, then asked for the pair of scissors that I had used earlier. The "healer" stretched the skin of the healee's abdomen with one hand; holding the pair of scissors in the other hand, she snipped the skin making a small cut. The woman sighed and began to moan.

Doña Pachita then took the knife and made an incision about eight inches in length, slightly below the woman's navel. I was sitting no more than two feet from the healee's abdomen. As Pachita cut, I could see what appeared to be various layers of skin emerge in much the same way that it appears in the medical surgery I have observed.

Pachita appeared to cut through the outer layers of skin, reach the layer of fat, and enter the abdominal cavity. A red liquid appeared to exude from the cut, yet it was not the profuse bleeding that characterizes abdominal surgery. As the red fluid seemed to trickle down the healee's side, I thought of the absence of antiseptic conditions in the room. At no time did I observe Pachita wash her hands, much less the hunting knife. The only bow to antiseptic standards was the alcohol which she used to swab the abdomen before the "operation," and the alcohol-drenched cotton bandages which were used later.

Finishing the incision, Pachita placed her knife on the table and instructed me to place my hand in the incision. She asked me to hold the intestinal wall out of the way. As I moved my hand forward, it seemed as if Pachita placed it in the abdominal cavity, and instructed me to push the intestines upward and out of the way.

As I followed her directions, I also paused a few seconds to check my breathing, heartbeat, and general relaxation. Over the years, I have trained myself to self-monitor my physiological state. Everything felt normal so I again directed my attention to the "healer." By this time, she had picked up the hunting knife and appeared to begin cutting out the cancerous tumor. Pachita seemed to be holding the knife in one hand and holding the outer edge of the skin to one side with the other hand. I, in turn, appeared to be holding the other edge of the skin, making a large area of the abdominal cavity accessible.

As I held up what Pachita referred to as the intestinal wall, my right middle finger jutted out slightly more than the others. Suddenly I felt the sharp edge of Pachita's hunting knife next to my hand; unexpectedly, she began to cut my finger. I prudently moved my hand further up the intestinal cavity.

Moments later, Pachita exclaimed that she had finished cutting out the tumor. She released her hold on the knife, moving her hand so as to hold apart the two edges of the incision. Meanwhile, the knife seemed to remain inside the abdominal cavity with the handle and half the blade jutting out. Pachita told me that I should grab the handle and gently remove the knife. To the best of my recollection, I took the bone handle and started to pull it. There was an initial resistance, but the knife was soon free and I placed it on the table.

Pachita, who was still holding the incision open, instructed me to pull out the loose cancerous tissue that she had just cut. I recall reaching into the cavity, finding a piece of tissue about one and one-half inches square, and throwing it on the floor.

Only five minutes had elapsed since the "operation" began. Pachita then asked one of her assistants to bring in the replacement organ. The assistant brought in a glass container with what appeared to be a human bladder in it. As he transferred the material from the glass jar to a basin, I had a chance to smell the unusual herbal mixture in which the bladder had been preserved since it was purportedly obtained that morning from a medical school.

Pachita picked up the bladder-like object by the urethra, brought it to her lips, and blew the bag-like organ full of air. I observed this process from less than twelve inches away. Pachita then handed the bladder-like organ to me, saying I should take it by the urethra so as not to let the air escape.

As I took the moist and slippery organ, most of the air did escape. Pachita calmly retrieved it and refilled the organ with air. This time I clamped the urethra tightly between my fingers and no air escaped. Pachita, in the rough voice of El Hermanito, said that we were running out of time and that I must put the organ in the abdominal cavity. Without hesitating, I seemed to place the bladder-like object in the lower part of the bodily opening. Pachita appeared to adjust the organ into place, connecting the urethra simply by massaging it.

Ten minutes after the intitiation of the "operation," Pachita appeared to bring the two sections of the healee's skin together, holding them closed with one hand. She then turned my right hand over, palm up, and stretched a strip of cotton over it. She placed my hand on the healee's abdomen, then removed her hand from underneath mine. The moment the palm of my hand touched the healee's body, an intense tingling sensation rushed up my arms and through my body. During this final part of the procedure, my right hand appeared to be the only thing holding the two halves of the cut skin together. Pachita then removed my hand and bandaged the healee. The "operation" was over.

Dr. Cousens, in a separate account, verified Villoldo's observations. In a statement prepared for the authors about this experience, Dr. Cousens wrote:

> My visit to Pachita on July 5, 1974, was a most unique experience. In looking back over my notes I recall that we

didn't expect to get in to see her as easily as we did. Usually there is a guard at the door and it is very difficult to be admitted. In this instance—and I remember that it was a rainy, full moon night—we had no difficulty at all. As Alberto, Luisa (Dr. Barbera's wife), and I approached, we found the door open and were invited in. Coming in, I saw people standing in the courtyard, lining up to go into a small one-room garage. I found it difficult to get directly to Pachita because of the many people she had around her.

From time to time, a healee comes to doña Pachita requesting a diagnosis. In this instance, the healee must bring an uncooked egg. Pachita rolls the egg over the visitor's body to clean the "aura." She then cracks it in two and discards it. Sometimes healees claim that the egg smells foul, or that they see a dark substance inside the egg. Pachita responds that the egg has absorbed the "poisons" from the healee's "aura." As we joined the line, we realized we needed to have several eggs for our psychic cleansing. Luisa went out, purchased the eggs at a market, and returned. Apparently while talking to some people we missed our turn in line, which put us back at the very end. At this time we were told there would be no "psychic surgery" that evening.

Luisa went in for her cleansing and I was the very last one. For a moment I was afraid they would not let me in, but they did, possibly because I was a visitor and had come a great distance. It was very rapid. As Alberto was translating, Pachita did the spiritual cleansing on me, passing the egg over my body. I was allowed to ask what I wanted. The guidance I wanted concerned my own spiritual development. I was asking for spiritual guidance, yet before I could get the words out of my mouth she said, "Love one another and go straight forward on the path you are on." She turned me around very quickly and walked away, which left me alone in one corner of the room. The next thing I found was that she was going to do "psychic surgery," which was quite a surprise.

Once inside the room, I observed that there were two beds on the room's left hand side. On the right side there were several Christian figurines on a table with a burning candle. The floor was slightly wet as it had been a damp day, and it was somewhat cold. The room smelled a bit dusty and musty. I stood to one side with Alberto, so as not to get in the way. Then they brought in the people to be "healed."

The first case was a vertebra replacement. At this point I was sitting at the foot of the bed and saw Pachita pull out a huge butcher knife and cut into the skin. I could smell the blood when Pachita cut into this woman's back. It was amazing, to say the least. She removed a vertebra and apparently put another vertebra in. She banged it into place with the handle of the knife. I don't know how she took it out or how she put it back in, but I did see her bang something into the woman's spine with the handle of the knife. Then she pulled the skin together, rolled the woman up in a sheet, and moved her to the side of the bed.

Then another person came in—a woman from Texas. This was the lady who had cancer of the bladder.

At this point Pachita asked Alberto to help her. During all this process I noticed a very strong "aura" over Pachita's head. It was bright white, going up maybe four feet, and then there was another "aura," extending maybe two or three inches and surrounding her head and neck. I was perhaps three feet from her, at the foot of the bed.

During this "operation," Pachita cut into the lady's abdomen with the large knife. I think she might have wiped it clean after the last "operation," but I'm not sure. She cut the skin while Alberto was assisting. All this time there was a kind of white glow around the area she was "operating" on. She removed the bladder, and took the replacement bladder one of her attendants had brought in. She brought it up to her mouth and blew it up with air, then gave it to Alberto, asking him to put it in, with her guidance. It's hard to say exactly what went on inside the woman's abdomen. Again I could smell the blood. During this time, I was also trying to comfort a friend of the Texas woman, another American who felt uneasy about the whole process.

The person being "operated" on demonstrated some degree of pain or anxiety. It wasn't the kind of process in which a person could actively participate; it seemed to be done upon you rather than as a process of conscious interaction. Among the things I felt strongly was that this was done to people who were not aware of what was happening by a woman who was in a profound trance state. Yet, the people appeared to have a deep trust in Pachita, although I also sensed fear in the room. And there was some pain present. Furthermore, I'm not really sure that anyone was particularly "enlightened" by the procedure.

During the process I was also involved in preparing some gauze for Pachita, handing her cotton to swab the lady's abdomen, and wiping blood from the wound.

At this point Alberto decided to examine some of the material removed during the "operation," and he handed me a piece of the tissue which somehow fell on the floor. One of the attendants noticed this and became very angry with Alberto and me. He began yelling at us and kicked us out. It was fine, because by this point I felt my need to see "psychic surgery" had been fulfilled. I had seen two "operations," one of a vertebra being replaced in which I saw the vertebra taken out and a new one pounded in, and the second a cancer of the bladder in which I saw the bladder tissue taken out and saw her put in what I perceived to be a bladder. I was very thankful for having been permitted to see that "psychic surgery" really happens.

There was no question in my mind that she was opening the skin; there was no question that I was smelling blood. I could see the wound on the person's back; my eyes were about three feet from where the "operation" was taking place. I could see the opening in the abdomen of the second lady and I could see Pachita's hands going into the bladder area, into the abdominal cavity. There is no question in my mind that things had been taken out from these incisions and things put back in. I had no doubts that I have seen authentic "psychic surgery."

I didn't understand the use of a knife, except that it was very gross and bloody. Yet the pain was minimal.

Approximately 90 minutes later, one of the attendants, a very gentle man, came and encouraged us to ask for strength, faith and love from Brother Cuahutémoc. Since we both still had blood on our hands, we were allowed to come back in and cleanse our hands in a ceremonial way. They poured a special liquid over our hands. We were then allowed to interview the four people that had been "operated" on. The best I could understand from the English-speaking woman was that she had experienced some pain. They were still wrapped in sheets and it appeared as if they were experiencing some kind of trauma—psychological or physical, or perhaps both. They were dazed; this brought back memories of being in post-operative anesthesia rooms in hospitals where people had not regained full consciousness. People were not given medication or drugs of any kind before or during the "operation." I examined the woman from Texas and found there was a scar, and it had apparently "healed" more rapidly than any scar I have ever seen immediately after "surgery." There were no stitches. It looked reddish but not particularly inflamed and as if it were perhaps a month old. I was told that the scar tended to disappear within a few weeks.

Many people have expressed their opinions about Pachita and there is little agreement. But if the question of "psychic surgery" is set aside, Pachita still has a number of procedures that are worthy of study. For example, the careful attention she has paid to her healees' belief systems may be an important component of any successes she might have obtained. And her sense of the dramatic, as exemplified by the pet falcon, is an additional factor in any "healing" she might facilitate.

The New Life Clinic

In 1965, one of the authors (S.K.) was introduced to Ambrose and Olga Worrall by Zelda Suplee, an editor living in New York City. Suplee stated that she had once fallen on the ice, injuring her right arm. When she went to Ambrose Worrall for treatment, she could not raise her arm. The "healer" made passes—moving his hand near the sore area

without touching it—and Suplee began to feel the sensation of heat. He then touched the middle of her back near
the right shoulder. The pain disappeared and her arm immediately began to function normally again.

Krippner had the opportunity to see the Worralls again
and to hear about their weekly healing services at the New
Life Clinic at Baltimore'ş Mt. Washington Methodist
Church. Krippner continued his contact with Olga Worrall
after her husband died in 1972, attending several confer-
ences on "paranormal healing" with her and discussing
"healing" processes.

In these conversations, Worrall referred to her gift as
"spiritual healing" rather than "psychic healing," because
such psychic abilities as telepathy and clairvoyance are not
necessarily involved with the phenomenon. She went on to
say,

> The "spiritual healing" I do is enhanced by my psychic gift,
> but "spiritual healing" can be, and usually is, accomplished
> by people who are neither clairvoyant, clairaudient, nor
> mediumistic in any way. The "healing" current flows
> through every clear channel available, whatever the
> "healer's" psychic abilities or, for that matter, religious be-
> liefs. People will frequently come to the New Life Clinic
> without realizing the root cause of their problems.

Worrall's clairvoyance has helped her understand hidden
elements underlying the illnesses of people attending her
"healing" services. She told Krippner how the services
originally were intitiated:

> It just sort of happened. Somebody at work had heard from
> somebody in the . . . office in Cleveland where Ambrose
> used to work, that Ambrose had done some "healing" out
> there. He asked Ambrose to help someone here. Well, one
> thing led to another and, before too long, we were handling
> people in our house here almost every night. It all just grew
> by word of mouth.

Bookjacket of *Olga Worrall: Mystic with the Healing Hands*, a biography by Edwina Cerutti. (Courtesy Harper & Row)

Olga Worrall was born in Ohio, but her parents were European, her father having been sent to the United States by the Czar to organize parishes of the Russian Orthodox Church. Her first unusual experience occurred at the age of three when she reported seeing "people" in her room at night. Eventually these reports were accepted as genuine by her parents after she had alleviated her mother's kidney ailment and other family illnesses with a "laying-on" of hands.

Worrall has claimed that about 90 per cent of the people who have been personally treated by her or her late husband, have improved. As for "complete cures," she has estimated a figure of about 50 per cent, on the basis of her files. On the other hand, she has insisted time and time again that there are no "guaranteed healings." Furthermore, Worrall has stated that she does not do the "healing"—"the spiritual power comes from God; I put my hands on someone and pray, but it is God who does the work."

From Worrall's point of view, this is the reason why the "healing" services do not exhaust her. She has asked, "Why should it tire me? The power comes from spiritual sources, not from me."

A first-hand report of a "healing" session at the New Life Clinic has been given by Edwina Cerutti, in her biography, *Olga Worrall: Mystic with the Healing Hands*:

> From 10:00 to 10:30, Olga speaks and answers any questions that are asked; from 10:30 to 11:00, there is time for meditation and prayer while the organ softly plays; from 11:00 to 12:00, a brief sermon is delivered by the minister of the church, or by a visiting minister, following which Olga, assisted by the minister and another worker . . . , administers the laying-on of hands for healing to those who come forward . . . .
> It was an impressive, silent procession, about three hundred people long. Nothing was said aloud. For each

person Olga had a smile so filled with encouragement and compassion that even I could sense its radiating warmth. Occasionally she would exchange a few whispered words with a newcomer. In all cases, she would close her eyes and put her hands on the person before her, standing in this position for at least two or three minutes. The places where she laid her hands varied . . . . but her parting [murmur "God bless you,"] was the same for all.

. . . Several years before, I had sustained a bad whiplash injury in an automobile accident and the recurrent pain in my neck, which extended along to my shoulders, was something I had learned to live with the way one does with the annoying but inescapable nagging of a husband or a wife. There was nothing to do but bear it—which I always did with the help of some aspirin, since each new attack lasted for many hours.

. . . Heaven knows I had never intended to join the line or take any part in the service. I was an investigator, not a participant . . . . Still, what better way to investigate than to participate? . . . Why not go up and see what, if anything, there was to see or feel?

Even as I moved forward, though, I was not as immune to the power that filled the sanctuary as I tried to pretend to myself . . . . Something was in this gathering, beyond any doubt—an intangible, invisible something that seemed to generate an emotional force of its own. I saw it on the faces of the hushed congregation; I felt it in the air around me, and I was most conscious of it as Olga placed her hands upon me.

When I resumed my seat, however, it was with almost a sense of disappointment. Except for an unusual degree of heat that seemed to generate from Olga's hands, nothing had happened, at least as far as I could see . . . .

As I turned my head to look about, I suddenly became aware that the pain in my neck was *gone*. . . . Incredulously, I craned my neck in all directions and gyrated my head in several ways to test for any twinges until it must have looked ridiculously like a telescope searching frantically for enemy craft from a submerged submarine. The fact remained: the pain was definitely gone.

Olga Worrall's "Healing Hands"

In recalling her early history, Worrall has said:

> I've done this all my life—one way or another. Somehow,
> even when I was a very little girl back in Cleveland, we all
> sort of knew that there was some kind of healing in my
> hands. My mother would ask me to put my hands on her
> when something hurt her and I would be asked by the
> neighbors, too, to help . . . .
>
> When I got older, and after I married Ambrose, I came to
> see that we were meant to do this. Not at first, of course.
> When we moved to Baltimore, I was determined to be an
> ordinary housewife and Ambrose was going to be just an
> engineer. No more clairvoyance or healing or anything odd!
> Why, even when our babies were sick, it never occurred to
> us to try to heal them. But afterward, we both came to
> realize that our gift of healing should be shared—freely and
> for free.

The phenomenon of Worrall's "healing hands" is illustrated in Edwina Cerutti's biography. Dr. Cerutti asked
Worrall:

> "What do you feel when you put your hands on someone?"
>
> . . . Olga didn't have to grope for her response. "When I
> put my hands on a person," she said, "a heat seems to be
> generated from my hands. People say it feels like hot pads.
> Sometimes I experience a sensation, sort of like an electri-
> cal discharge, with pins-and-needles pricking on my palms
> and fingertips. Here," she suddenly interrupted herself,
> "see how cool my hands are."
>
> She held out her hands for us to feel and they were very
> ordinary, average-sized hands, neat, ringed, and entirely
> cool.
>
> "Just watch," Olga continued, "I'm going to place my
> hands on Father Wellesly's back . . . and you tell them,
> Father Wellesly, how do my hands feel now?"
>
> "By jove!" he exclaimed in astonishment, "they're hot.
> They're really hot! Incredible."

Cerutti has written about an unusual experience she had while observing Worrall doing a "laying-on" of hands.

> I watched intently as Olga's hands rested on Keith's body, one hand in front and the other hand on his back. As she stood thus, in absolute silence and with her eyes gently closed, I suddenly became aware of an almost colorless, thin kind of vapory stuff that floated like smoke from the absolutely non-existent space between Olga's hand and Keith's body . . . .
> Olga was delighted, but not terribly surprised. "Did you really see it, Edwina?," she asked. "I've seen that many times . . . but of course, I've never watched myself. It's an ectoplasmic mist and it can be seen emanating from a healer's hands when healing—sometimes."

In 1974, during one of Worrall's experimental sessions at U.C.L.A.'s Radiation Field Photography Laboratory, she agreed to participate in a "psychic photography" experiment. Thelma Moss placed a piece of unexposed film in an opaque container and asked Worrall to hold it between her hands. When the film was developed, it was found to be covered with filament-like streamers. When asked what she thought the streamers were, Worrall answered, "I don't know what you modern scientists call it, but in my day we called it 'ectoplasm.' " After Worrall left the laboratory, Moss discovered that all the film in storage was unusable; it was covered with thin filament-like streamers.

Less spectacular, but still important, have been the evening "healing" hours held by Olga Worrall each night at 9:00 P.M. At that time, Worrall has stopped her other activities to pray for the thousands of people who have written her, seeking help for themselves or others. In addition, many friends, admirers, and healees also pause at 9 P.M. to send out "healing" thoughts. Helen Kruger, in *Other Healers, Other Cures*, tells of one man who joined a 9:00 P.M. "healing" group after writing the Worralls about his heart attack. He claimed that he felt "a sort of electricity" flow through his body at the meeting. Subsequently, his cardiologist called his condition "entirely relieved."

The reports of electricity-like sensations have been frequently cited by the Worralls' healees. Olga Worrall has reported receiving frequent messages from her late husband on the "spirit plane." In one of these messages, a comparison was made between "psychic healing" and electricity:

> It is a force in healing that stimulates the sick cells and acts as a tonic to the cells, strengthening and helping them get back into their proper orbit—as they are off orbit when disturbed. This power works through the mind of the healer and is projected into the mind of the patient, from which it reaches the lowest level of the cells in the body where the need for healing is. Our bodies actually produce this type of energy constantly unless they are overworked or interfered with by wrong medication. Then a spiritual healer is needed to throw off—by touch or thought—the emergency switch that each body possesses and flips on when things are not going well.

The message attributed to Ambrose Worrall went on to say that he worked through Olga Worrall each Thursday at the New Life Clinic Healing Service and that he was being instructed on the "spiritual plane" in ways to improve the forces used in "psychic healing."

In the meantime, Olga Worrall has described to one of the authors (S.K.) how she has used her psychic gifts during "healing." An example would be her reported ability to see "auras" surrounding the human body and to diagnose a healee's ailments from the color, shape, and size of the "aura." And Helen Kruger has reported one of Worrall's most dramatic cases—an eight-month old baby with a twisted right leg that was shorter than the left leg. The defect purportedly disappeared when Worrall placed her hands on the child's back.

When asked about the possibility of malevolent "spirits," Olga Worrall has admitted that they may be the cause of a person's illness on rare occasions. In an interview published in *Psychic* magazine, she stated:

> In a true case of possession, a discarnate spirit—one who is "unenlightened" and nonbenevolent and who desires the pleasures of earth—will occupy the body of a person who is easily influenced. Generally it is a type of person who wants to be directed by others and who wishes to avoid all responsibility. It could also be a person who is under the influence of drugs or alcohol, or on the verge of a mental breakdown.
>
> . . . In general, we deal with cases of possession by communicating mentally with the possessing spirit asking it to go away, and by seeking help from benevolent souls on the other side who are experts in dealing with such entities . . . .
>
> It is essential that all of us take special care of our minds and bodies to keep physically and mentally healthy . . . . Be master of your mind, master of yourself, thus no other mind can control you. And you can be controlled in a similar way by a person in the flesh; a possessing entity does not necessarily have to be from the other world.

Worrall has differentiated between "possession" and "obsession," the former being the intrusion of an "entity" and the latter being the centering of one's mind on a destructive thought to the exclusion of all other ideas.

Worrall has often been described as a "Christian mystic." And she has observed that popular interest in psychic phenomena has occurred because "religion no longer represents the mystical Christ." To Worrall, the person "is a spirit and needs to know the mysteries of the spirit. His soul cries out for this knowledge, this contact." Although she has found no evidence for reincarnation, Worrall has stated:

> I also believe that one important reason for developing one's psychic powers is to prove immortality, both to oneself and to others . . . .
>
> In the early days of the Christian religion, the gifts of the

spirit were practiced in the churches and healing was demonstrated and accepted. For instance, proof of immortality was demonstrated through clairvoyance. But today, can you imagine an orthodox church having a medium stand up during the service and say, "I have a message for brother so-and-so from his deceased mother or father?" Can you picture the pandemonium?

Yet these were the manifestations that took place in the early Church and gave substance to the religion. Christ himself . . . healed the sick, gave clairvoyant messages, demonstrated the immortality of the soul and its personal characteristics. And the Apostles were trained by him to do the same work.

Olga Worrall's world-view emphasizes the importance of the "spirit plane." In addition, Worrall has conceptualized the human being as consisting of both physical and "spiritual" elements:

On earth, he has a spiritual body encased in a body of flesh. He operates primarily through the spiritual body; the physical body merely responds to his orders, producing effects on the physical level, and carrying sensation back to the spiritual body from the physical world. We are therefore living in the spiritual world even while encased in flesh, but our attention is so strongly concentrated on what is happening on the physical level that we are virtually oblivious to the activities on the spiritual level.

During the time when the physical body is unconscious . . . , the spiritual body takes a temporary leave of absence. It can stay in the immediate vicinity of the physical body or it can travel vast distances . . . .

Olga Worrall's model of "paranormal healing" emerges from this world-view. According to Worrall, her "healing" involves the channeling of energy into a healee. This energy comes from a "universal field of energy" which is common to all creation. It stems from God—the universal source of all intelligence and power. "Emanations" surround each individual, purportedly caused by electrical currents flowing in the physical body. These can be observed as "auras" by some persons with psychic ability. There are also sound waves from the various physical organs and "thought waves" from the mind as well as "vibrations" from the "spiritual body." Energy from the "universal field" becomes available to the "healer," through the act of "tuning" his or her personal "energy field" so as to act as an "energy conductor" between this "field" and the healee. Worrall has stated:

> Of course, Ambrose, as a scientist, has always made sense of this explanation. He says that spiritual healing is a rearrangement of the microparticles of which all things are composed. The body is not what it seems to be with the naked eye. It is not a solid mass. It is actually a system of little particles or points of energy separated from each other by space and held in place through an electrically balanced field. When these particles are not in their proper place, then disease is manifested in that body. Spiritual healing is one way of bringing the particles back into a harmonious relationship—which means, into good health.

Olga Worrall in the Laboratory

Unlike some purported "healers" who object to a scientific inspection of their abilities, Olga Worrall has made herself available for any number of laboratory experiments. It is quite possible that Olga Worrall has been studied by more parapsychological researchers than any other "healer" in history. Unfortunately, many of the laboratory reports have never been published. However, Worrall has a collection of the reports and makes them available to persons who are interested in "healing" phenomena.

In her lectures, Worrall has sometimes referred to a report written by Dr. Robert Miller in 1967,* concerning

---

*This report appears in chapter nine of *Olga Worrall: Mystic with the Healing Hands* by Edwina Cerutti.

. . . an experiment to determine if prayer can have beneficial effect on remotely located plants. The growth rate of rye grass was measured to an accuracy of 1.0 mil per hour by means of a mechanical electrical transducer which was attached to a blade of grass through a lever arm.

On January fourth, 1967, in Atlanta, Georgia, the growth of a new blade of rye grass had been stabilized at six mils per hour. At eight P.M., a telephone call had been made to Ambrose and Olga Worrall in Baltimore, Maryland, asking them to pray for the plant, which was the subject of the experiment, during their nine P.M. silent time. The Worralls agreed to do so, and at nine P.M., as per this request, they employed the following method of prayer on behalf of the plant: they visualized it as growing vigorously under ideal conditions.

The next morning, observations were made from the trace on the strip-chart recorder. It was found that before the prayer was begun, the trace was a straight line with a slope showing a growth rate of 6.25 mils per hour. At nine P.M. sharp, the trace began to deviate upwards, and by eight A.M., the following morning, the growth rate was 52.5 mils per hour—an increase of 830 per cent. The plot was then continued for forty-eight hours more, during which time the growth rate decreased but never returned to the original rate.

During the entire period of the experiment, the door of the room in which the plant was housed and kept locked, the temperature was constantly maintained at seventy to seventy-two degrees Fahrenheit; the fluorescent lights were turned on continuously. There was clearly no known variable which could cause such a dramatic increase in growth rate of the rye grass. Therefore, these facts would indicate that Ambrose and Olga Worrall, six hundred miles away, had been able to cause an eightfold increase in a plant's growth rate simply by concentrating their thoughts on the plants and by doing so for less than five minutes in all.

Dr. Miller has conducted several other pilot studies with Olga Worrall. Although the results are preliminary rather than conclusive, they do point the way for important future research. In one experiment, Miller attached three silver chloride electrodes to the leaf of a philodendron plant. The wires from the electrodes were connected to a preamplifier which, in turn, was connected to an amplifier and a strip chart recorder. When Worrall placed her hands four inches away from the plant, the amplitude of the signal, which was registering on the strip chart recorder, increased greatly. When other members of the research team held their hands near the plant, only a slight effect was produced.

In another experiment, electrodes were attached to Worrall's head to measure her brainwaves before and during "healing." When she performed a "laying-on" of hands, the percentage of her alpha and theta brainwaves suddenly increased while the percentage of beta brainwaves decreased. Beta brainwaves are faster than alpha and theta brainwaves; the rapid shift from one brainwave pattern to another suggests Worrall's ability to alter her state of consciousness very quickly.

Miller also prepared a solution of copper salts, pouring five drops on each of two polyethylene discs. One specimen served as a "control"; Worrall held her hands around the other one for three minutes. After two days, the "control" specimen had crystallized and was jade green. The treated specimen had also crystallized but had a coarser grain and was turquoise blue in color. Both specimens had been stored under identical conditions of temperature and humidity.

Dr. Miller also co-authored a report with Dr. Philip B. Reinhart and Anita Kern for *Thought as Energy* edited by Willis Kinnear. It describes Worrall's work with a cloud chamber:

> Worrall visited Agnes Scott College in Atlanta, Georgia, during January of 1974. . . . One full day was devoted to paraphysical tests which were conducted in the physics laboratory. The key experiment had the objective of determining whether or not some type of measurable energy is given off by a healer's hands. A cloud chamber, an apparatus

originally developed by nuclear physicists for making visible the path of high energy nuclear particles, was used as the detector.

The Atomic Laboratories' Model 71850 cloud chamber was used in the experiment. It consists of a cylindrical glass chamber seven inches in diameter and five inches in height, which has a sheet aluminum bottom and a viewing glass across the top. The unit is operated by covering the floor of the chamber with a one-quarter inch layer of methyl alcohol and placing the entire unit upon a flat block of dry ice.

When the liquid surface of the alcohol is in contact with a closed volume of air, some of the molecules of the liquid evaporate into the air to form a vapor. Equilibrium conditions are reached when the rate of evaporation from the liquid surface is just balanced by the rate of re-entry of the alcohol molecules from the vapor state into the liquid.

When the bottom of the chamber is chilled by the dry ice, a supersaturated zone about one inch in height is created in the chamber. Condensation in the form of a mist then occurs. A charged particle, such as an alpha or beta particle, in passing through the chamber ionizes molecules of air and vapor and produces a trail of positive and negative ions along its path. The alcohol vapor preferentially condenses on these nuclei and a visible trail of droplets is formed. A spotlight mounted at the side of the chamber provides the lighting necessary for photographing the tracks.

During the experiment, Dr. Worrall placed her hands at the side of the cloud chamber without touching the glass. She then visualized energy flowing from her hands, much as she does when treating a patient. The observers saw a wave pattern develop in the mist of the sensitive zone, which, until she placed her hands in position, had been quite uniform in appearance. The waves were parallel to her hands and the apparent direction of motion was perpendicular to the palms.

After several minutes, Dr. Worrall shifted her position 90 degrees to see if the pattern in the cloud chamber would be affected. The waves began to change direction and were soon moving perpendicular to their original path. Unfortunately, no camera had been set up for the experiment and a photographic record was not obtained.

On March 12, 1974, a follow-up experiment was conducted. In this experiment a camera was mounted so as to enable photographs of the cloud chamber activity to be made. In addition, the experiment was designed to determine if Worrall could affect the cloud chamber at a distance. To achieve this result the cloud chamber was in the physics laboratory at Agnes Scott College in Atlanta, Georgia, but Worrall remained in Baltimore, Maryland, some 600 miles away.

After the cloud chamber had attained a steady state condition, a telephone call was made to Baltimore to let Worrall know that all was in order and to ask her if at 8:50 P.M. she would concentrate her thoughts and energies upon the cloud chamber. It was suggested that she mentally hold her hands at the sides of the chamber for several minutes and then change the orientation 90 degrees as she did when she was actually present in the physics laboratory.

Just before the telephone call was made, the sensitivity of the cloud chamber was checked by inserting a radium 226 alpha source into the chamber and observing the condensed vapor trails generated by the alpha particles. A photograph was taken at that time. Except for the alpha tracks only a fine mist, uniformly distributed, was visible. At 8:53 a definite change occurred in the cloud chamber. The mist began to pulsate and dark waves were visible in the chamber. The waves were parallel to the long direction of the table. The pulsation continued for about seven minutes but never changed direction. Then the motion in the chamber gradually subsided.

At 9:10 P.M. a second telephone call was made to get Dr. Worrall's report of her mental impressions. She said she had been able to transfer her consciousness to the laboratory and then she mentally placed her hands at the sides of the chamber and focused her attention on producing motion in the chamber. She felt a cool sensation as if a cool breeze was flowing over her hands. She also said that she did not shift the position of her hands during the experiment. It was decided to . . . ask if she would again concentrate on the cloud chamber.

The experiment was repeated and the sensitive zone of the chamber again became turbulent and undulations at the rate of about one per second were perceived. Photographs were taken of the interior of the cloud chamber before, during, and after the second experiment. A time interval of approximately eight minutes was required for the turbulence to subside after the second test . . . .

The experiment appears to be repeatable. However, because of the limited number of tests conducted, the possibility of coincidences and extraneous influences cannot be entirely ruled out . . . .

In summary, through the use of the cloud chamber, a recognized and accepted research tool, the theory that a tangible energy issues from the hands of healers is given support. A change in the cloud chamber pattern resulted when Dr. Worrall held her hands around the chamber. Other members of the investigating team placed their hands around the chamber with no results. The results of the second experiment, in which she was 600 miles away from the cloud chamber, indicate that . . . visible manifestations in the physical world can be produced mentally from a distance.

This study is provocative, but would be even more impressive had it been conducted on a "blind" basis, without the experimenters knowing when Worrall was going to attempt PK. As long as the experimenters knew what they were looking for, the possibility exists that their own PK was at work or that they misinterpreted a change that had nothing to do with Worrall's attempt.

Worrall has been awarded an honorary degree—Doctor of Humane Letters—from the Church of Religious Science Institute in California. In discussing the history of "paranormal healing," she has noted:

There are records of spiritual healings dating back over a period of five thousand years. Moses, Elisha, Elijah, Jesus, and many others demonstrated the gift of healing. Healings have taken place in shrines and temples without the benefit of any intermediary psychic or medium. This indicates that it is right to heal. Healing is an inborn capacity of the body.

It can be accelerated by proper treatment, by physicians, and spiritual healing.

Another laboratory report on Worrall has been filed by Dr. Hiroshi Motoyama, Director of the Institute of Religious Psychology in Tokyo.* Motoyama has constructed a special electroencephalographic device by which acupuncture "meridians" and Yogic *chakras* are purportedly measured. The report reads:

> One characteristic belonging to the psychic person is standard deviation of skin current of the 28 meridian (seiketsu) points which is very high compared with the ordinary person. For instance, in the average person the value is from 0.1 to 0.26, but Mrs. Worrall showed 1.0, a much higher value . . . . Then after comparison between readings before and during faith healing through her hands and fingers, meridians of the left hand fingers showed a highly significant difference . . . .
>
> Consequently, we can infer that her psi ability is more easily projected from the left as compared to the right hand. The meridians which showed significant difference are of the genitourinary system, the digestive system, and the heart circulatory system, which, according to the Yoga chakra system, means in her case that the analata, manipura and rishuda chakras are predominantly working.

Worrall has worked with Dr. M. Justa Smith at Rosary Hill College in Buffalo, New York. Worrall has recalled:

> She had me hold, in healing, enzymes, whole blood, serum, tap water, and distilled water to see if my touch on the different vials affected them. Kirlian photographs were taken of the specimen before testing—for control purposes—and after I had administered the healing touch, and the results showed that the specimens were affected.

---

*This report appears in chapter nine of *Olga Worrall: Mystic with the Healing Hands* by Edwina Cerutti.

Olga Worrall, then, has set an example for other "healers."
Her work with scientists has yielded valuable information
about "paranormal healing." At the same time, the laboratory data has reinforced Worrall's view of the world and her
model of the "healing" process. Rather than being an-
tagonists, scientists and "healers" should cooperate; each
has much to learn from the other.

Chapter Four

Hernani Andrade and the Spiritist "Healers" of Brazil

Anthropologists often use the term "shaman" to refer to certain primitive "healers." The best definition of this term is given by Mircea Eliade in his book *Shamanism: Archaic Techniques of Ecstasy*. Eliade calls the shaman the first "technician of the sacred," pointing out that shamanism in the strict sense is an historical phenomenon of Siberia and Central Asia where the term originated. Later, similar developments were observed in North and South America, Indonesia, Oceania, and elsewhere. Because shamanism coexists with non-shamanistic forms of magic and religion, it is necessary to employ the term in its strict and proper sense. Eliade has written:

> . . . Though the shaman is, among other things, a magician, not every magician can properly be termed a shaman. The same distinction must be applied in regard to shamanic healing; every medicine man is a healer, but the shaman employs a method that is his and his alone. As for the shamanic techniques of ecstasy, they do not exhaust all the varieties of ecstatic experience documented in the history of religions and religious ethnology. Hence any ecstatic cannot be considered a shaman; the shaman specializes in a trance

during which his soul is believed to leave his body and as-
cend to the sky or descend to the underworld.

Furthermore, a shaman differs from a medium who is possessed by "spirits." Eliade has observed that "the shaman
controls his 'spirits,' in the sense that he is able to communicate with the dead, 'demons,' and 'nature spirits,'
without thereby becoming their instrument." Eliade further
notes:

> . . . the specific element of shamanism is not the embodi-
> ment of "spirits" by the shaman, but the ecstasy induced by
> his ascent to the sky or descent to the underworld; incarnat-
> ing spirits and being "possessed" by spirits . . . do not
> necessarily belong to shamanism in the strict sense.

In comparing Rolling Thunder, doña Pachita, and Olga
Worrall, it is apparent that all three can be referred to as
"healers." All three are reputed to have psychic gifts;
therefore, it might be said that they all have engaged to
some extent in possible "paranormal healing." However,
the mode of "healing" is somewhat different for each of
them. Olga Worrall is a "mystic" who has spoken of making contact with a "universal field of energy" and of being a
"clear channel" for "healing" which she seems able to do
intuitively. Doña Pachita's claim to being taken over by the
"spirit" of El Hermanito places her in the tradition of
mediums who supposedly exhibit paranormal abilities when
they "incorporate" a benign and powerful "spirit entity."

Rolling Thunder, however, appears to fall most clearly
into the shamanistic tradition with its emphasis upon altered conscious states in which "out-of-body" experiences
occur and one travels to another world. These reports are
commonly heard by those who study with Rolling Thunder.
Furthermore, the Shoshone medicine man reportedly has
communicated with various types of "spirits" and has
demonstrated purported paranormal powers as well. Rolling Thunder's reputed occasional use of "psychic surgery"

resembles Eliade's notation that the North American shaman will sometimes appear to extract objects from a sick
person's body by suction.

Eliade has observed that the "spirit world" is part of the
traditional American Indian culture in which a person could

> . . . obtain a "tutelary spirit" or a "power" of some sort
> that makes him capable of "visions" and augments his re-
> serves of the sacred; but only the shaman . . . is able to
> enter deeply into the supernatural world . . . . He alone
> succeeds in acquiring a technique that enables him to under-
> take ecstatic journeys at will.

The "Spiritist" groups in various parts of the world also
emphasize special relationships with "spirit entities."
However, the "healers" produced by these groups belong
more to the mediumistic than to the shamanistic tradition.
The most highly publicized "Spiritist" groups operate in
Brazil.

"Spirits" in São Paulo

In the spring of 1973, the authors received a grant from the
Erickson Educational Foundation to visit various "psychic
healing" centers in São Paulo, Brazil. It is of historical
importance to realize that the first African slaves had been
brought to Brazil about 1550 to work on plantations in the
northeastern part of the Portuguese colony. The slaves had
been appropriated, often with the complicity of avaricious
people from their own tribes, on the West African coast,
home of the Yoruba culture.

Permeating the Yoruba culture was a religious tradition
steeped in myth and legend. The Yoruba "spirits" or
orishas were powerful and terrifying, yet so human that
they were talked to, pleaded with, and cajoled through special offerings and gifts. Olorun was the most powerful
orisha of them all. He created human beings but simply did
not have the time to deal with them. To speak to humans on

his behalf, Olorun created a son and a daughter, Obatalá, and Odudua, from a handful of clay. Obatalá, the god of purity, was put in charge of the heavens and Odudua was given charge of the earth. Their children, Aganjú and Yemanjá, gave birth to a son named Orungan. Unlike his father and grandfather, Orungan had no sister for mating purposes. So, upon reaching adolescence, he raped his mother, Yemanjá, who immediately gave birth to a number of *orishas:* the gods of thunder, the rivers, fertility, vegetables, mountains, wealth, war, the hunt, the sun, and the moon. Because water flowed copiously from her breasts during this period of multiple births, Yemanjá became known as "mother of the waters." A number of *orishas* were born later: Sakpata (who prevented disease), Ifá (the hearer of prayers), the Exús (or *orishas'* messengers), and the Ibeji twins (who symbolized the fact that human beings had both an earthly body and a "spiritual body").

When the slaves were transported to Brazil, they were squeezed into ship quarters so small that they could not stand erect. Many of the Yorubas died en route; the survivors thanked Yemanjá, "mother of the waters," for helping them to survive. But their problems were not over. Upon arriving in Brazil, they were spoken to in Portuguese and separated from their family and friends. The slaves had nothing but their religion to sustain them—and the missionaries attempted to take this away as well. The slaves were baptized as Christians and forced to attend the Roman Catholic mass. They were allowed to hold their own religious services but ran into trouble if the priests did not find pictures of Jesus, Mary, and the saints upon the slaves' altars.

So it was that the slaves cleverly adopted the Christian *orishas,* combining them with their own Yoruba *orishas*. Olorun, god of creation, became Jehova or God the Father. Obatalá, the god of purity and the heavens, was merged with Jesus, while Odudua—Obatalá's wife—was forgotten.

Their son, Aganjú, was also neglected, but their daughter Yemanjá—victim of the incestuous rape—became the Virgin Mary. Sakpata, god of health, merged with St. Lazarus, the man who Jesus was said to have raised from the dead. The Ibeji twins became St. Cosmos and St. Damian, Roman twins whose faith was so strong that when they were executed, they purportedly picked up their severed heads and sang hymns before expiring. Every now and then, Ifá and the Exús mixed up someone's prayers. These mischievous gods were as close as the slaves could come to finding an analogue to Satan.

Once the slaves had spent a number of years in Brazil, they added a few additional *orishas* to their panoply. The "Old Black Ones" (in Portuguese, *Os Prêtos Velhos*) were archetypal black father images, while the "Indians of the Seven Arrows" (or *caboclos*) embodied the best traits of the indigenous American Indians who were as badly treated by the European settlers as were the slaves.

The "Spirit" Religions

At the present time, there are four major spirit religions in Brazil which have grown out of the Yoruba tradition: Candomblé, Umbanda, Quimbanda, and Spiritism (or Kardecism). Candomblé is the oldest of the spirit religions. It uses the original Yoruba names for the orishas. Fortunes are told by cowrie shells, and religious services are led by women—the "Mothers of Saints."

Umbanda places somewhat more of an emphasis on the Christian names of the saints than does Candomblé. It is organized into seven "lines." Each practitioner is assigned to a "line" on the basis of one's birthdate, then adopts the foods, colors, numbers, symbols, charts, incense, and perfume of that "line." Umbanda allows both males and females to adopt priestly roles and lead drum-and-candle religious services. Held at locations referred to as *Casas do*

The priestesses, or "daughters of the saints," chant as the ceremony begins. (These photographs were not two ceremonies were similiar. All photos, pp. 112–115, courtesy S. Krippner.)

The high priest, dressed in white, drinks native wine and smokes strong cigars to alter his consciousness at the beginning of the session. (The use of wine and tobacco was not observed in the ceremony attended by the authors.)

The altar is unveiled, revealing various Christian saints as well as *Os Prêtos Velhos,* the "Old Black Ones" representing "spirits" of slaves who return to "heal" the sick, using priests and priestesses as their vehicles.

The high priestess, or "mother of the saints," smokes a pipe to help alter her consciousness. She will then ask for the aid of the high priest in "spirit incorporation."

113

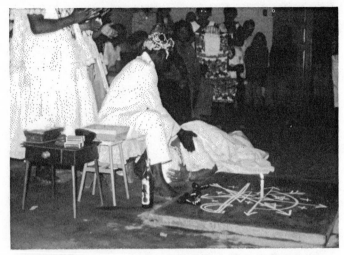

The high priestess enters an altered state of consciousness and falls on the floor, "incorporating" the "spirit" of a *Prêto Velho*. The drawing on the floor is said to invoke the aid of the "Old Black Ones."

The high priest begins the dancing. The priestesses join the dance except for the "mother of the saints" who is still in altered consciousness after "incorporating" a *Prêto Velho*.

The dance continues but the curtains have been drawn over the altar as it is now midnight—hour of the *Exús,* or mischievous "spirits."

The high priest emerges, now wearing the symbols of the *Exús.* They have taken over his body and must be placated by the others until the hour of the *Exûs* ends at 1:00 A. M.

Umbanda the services involve the "incorporation" by the priests and priestesses of minor "spirits" such as the Old Black Ones or the Indians of the Seven Arrows. The priests and priestesses then are felt to be capable of "healing" the sick.

When the authors were in São Paulo, they had the opportunity to attend an Umbanda session. One of them (A. V.) described the experience:

São Paulo, we were told, contains about 14 loosely affiliated Umbanda groups, each of which sponsors a number of weekly ceremonies. We found out the location of one of them but the hotel clerk warned us not to go to that section of town. Several taxicab drivers told us the same thing, warning us that we might not return alive. But eventually we did find a taxi which took us to our destination.

We arrived at the session and received a warm welcome. The congregation had already gathered, sitting along both sides of a hallway which led to the living room of the house. There, the white-robed priests and priestesses danced in a circle to the beat of a conga drum. There was an elaborate altar in one corner of the room covered with dozens of pictures and statues of Yoruba orishas and Christian saints. There were also photographs of elderly people—deceased relatives whose "spirits" were encouraged to join the proceedings.

After half an hour of dancing, the priests and priestesses appeared to have entered profoundly altered states of consciousness. They began to sweat profusely. Their colored bead necklaces—the colors representing their "line" and protecting orisha—swayed back and forth. One of the priests walked through the congregation with a smoking incense holder to purify us for the "healing" ceremony.

During the first session held each month, Umbanda priests and priestesses "incorporate" the Indians of the Seven Arrows. The same is done at the second session for the "spirits" of the Old Black Ones. Next come the "spirits" of the babies who have died early in their lives. During the final session, the "spirits" of the congregation's dead ancestors are "incorporated." Yoruba orishas such as Yemanjá and the Ibeji twins cannot enter a person's body or there would be an explosion from the unbearable concentration of power.

As we were there during the second session of the month, the priests and priestesses "incorporated" the "spirits" of the archetypal slaves–the Old Black Ones. They would writhe during this act, as if having a minor seizure; after a few minutes, the "spirit" would leave, and they would continue dancing.

All members of the congregation who required "healing" were then taken into the circle. After removing our shoes, both of us entered the living room and sat in front of a priestess. I had been experiencing a pain in the area of my right kidney. After the priestess' massage and ritualistic "passes," the pain disappeared and did not return.

The priests and priestesses left the room and the congregation entered the kitchen for refreshments. In a few minutes, the priests and priestesses returned, dressed in street clothes, and joined us in conversation. It was a pleasant way to end an especially dramatic evening.

Quimbanda also holds sessions in various *Casas* but the ceremonies center around the worship of the Exús and various harmful "spirits." The practice of the other spirit religions is protected by Brazilian law, but Quimbanda is illegal.

Understanding the "Perispirit"

Kardecism, the fourth spirit religion, has some of its roots in the Yoruba tradition but is principally based on the writings of the French Christian Spiritist, Allan Kardec.

Kardec was born in France in 1804 under the name Léon Hippolyte Denizarth Rivail. In 1848, two of the young daughters of John and Margaret Fox, in Hydesville, New York, reported hearing strange raps in their house. Soon the entire family reported hearing the raps and the sisters developed a code, claiming they were in touch with "spirit" entities. Soon an older sister joined them and they began lecturing on "Spiritualism" around the United States. Eventually two of the Fox sisters fell victims to alcoholism, were promised a great deal of money if they would write an article confessing fraud, and eagerly agreed—especially since it would embarrass the third sister with whom they had parted company. To this day, the controversy has not been resolved.

Kardec, however, was fascinated by the table rapping phenomena which had spread to Europe by 1850. Kardec observed that if "every effect has a cause, every intelligent effect must have an intelligent cause." The phenomenon of table rapping, and the associated phenomenon of tables which responded to certain individuals by tipping and spinning, were thought by Kardec to be due to an intelligence of some sort.

Kardec changed his name (from Rivail) at the advice of the "spirits" and adopted the term "Spiritism" to differentiate his belief system from that of the "Spiritualists." The word "Spiritualist" can be applied to anyone who believes in "spirits," but a "Spiritist" is said to be able to communicate with the "spirits." Kardec's best known volume, *The Spirits' Book*, was brought from Europe to South America by a member of the Brazilian aristocracy in 1858. It was immediately translated into Portuguese and created a sensation. Celebrated psychic sensitives and mediums were interviewed for their reactions to *The Spirits' Book* by newspapers which serialized it and ran frequent comments on Kardec's philosophy.

Many Brazilians who had covertly yearned for a religion somewhat more sophisticated than the primitive Yoruba tradition converted eagerly to Spiritism (or Kardecism, as it was also called). Here was a belief system that preserved what their black nurses had taught them about the "spiritual world," yet circumvented the drum beating and played down the *orishas*. Kardec proclaimed the immortality of the "spirit" which was said to enter the body at the moment of conception, choosing the family in which it wished to be born.

Kardec believed that the "spirit" is enveloped in a semi-material body of its own which he named the "perispirit." This "perispirit" is composed of a magnetic fluid (or "aura") which contains a certain amount of electricity. It serves as an intermediary between one's "spiritual body" and physical body. Thus Kardec stated that "healing" can be accomplished by "psychic healers" who send "magnetic rays" from their fingertips into the "auras" of ill persons. By using these "magnetic passes," a "healer" can also "magnetize" water which can be used for "healing" purposes. "Healers" may sometimes be mediums and communicate with various "spirits," but instead of *orishas,* these entities are usually relatives, or distinguished people such as doctors, writers, and teachers.

Kardec taught that when one's body is worn out, it is discarded and one's "spirit" is freed in much the way that a fruit sheds its peel. Death, according to Kardec, is like the setting aside of old clothing that is no longer of any use. The "spirit" leaves the body, still sheathed in the "perispirit" which constitutes for the "spirit" a "spiritual body" or "etheric body." It has a human shape because it once acted as a pattern or blueprint for the physical form. Ordinarily, the "perispirit" remains invisible, yet it can momentarily be seen if a "spirit" wills it. It is through the "perispirit" that a "spirit" acts upon matter, producing such phenomena as table-rapping.

Kardec thought that people who regard "spirits" as sources of absolute wisdom were making a grave mistake. Some "spirits," Kardec wrote, "send us communications that are very sublime in their depth" yet "there are others which are lowly and vulgar, trivial and deceiving."

To Kardec, God represented "supreme intelligence." God, since the beginning of creation, has instituted laws. Yet it is the choice and free will of the "spirit" whether to follow these laws. Kardec wrote, "We can say that good is all that which conforms with these laws, and evil is that which is contrary to these laws."

Kardec taught that it was through successive reincarnations that one's "spirit" develops. Incarnated "spirits" constitute humanity—both on earth and on other planets. In each incarnation, a "spirit" has a task to carry out which is in accord with its development; each incarnation provides the tests which can bring the "spirit" closer to its full potential. It is up to a "spirit's" will to diminish the number of these incarnations by working actively toward moral perfection in each lifetime.

Between its incarnations, the "spirit" travels through space. It is able to examine the incidents that aided or retarded its development in the former incarnation, and prepares for the forthcoming incarnation. Finally, a "spirit" reaches the last of its incarnations. It then becomes part of the order of "pure spirits" or "angels" and is liberated from the cycle of death and rebirth.

The Role of Mediums

Kardec took the position that some highly evolved "spirits" incarnate at certain times in history to illuminate humanity. Moses was one of these, yet the laws of Moses were meant to be appropriate for people living at that time. Jesus arrived to complete the law of Moses with a more elevated teaching about the "spiritual" life. Kardec gave special meaning to one statement attributed to Jesus, "Verily I say unto you, unless anyone is born from water and spirit, he cannot enter into the Kingdom of God."

Kardec rephrased Jesus' statement, writing that "Outside of charity there is no salvation." Charity, or love, was seen as the antidote to the harmful influences that greed, ambition, and pride bring upon the soul. Frequently, people are the cause of their own unhappiness and suffering. If they search for the cause of this condition, they often find it was a result of their own lack of charity, thus departing from the laws of God. Kardec wrote, in *The Spirits' Book:*

> The poor person who divides his bread with one poorer than he, is more charitable and has more merit in the eyes of God than he that gives his excess without depriving himself. When a person lives in selfishness, he is in constant struggle. With charity, he lives in peace. He will only assure his happiness in the world by making charity the basis of his institutions. This is why Spiritism has its maxim, "Outside of charity there is no salvation."

Kardec held that mediums could assist "spirits" to communicate with their relatives and friends. Certain "spirits" communicate through table rappings, sometimes making up a code in which each letter is represented by a certain number of taps. But this method is slow and does not allow for an extensive dialogue. A medium, however, can be guided by a "spirit," allowing one's hand to write what the "spirit" dictates. Other mediums "incorporate" the "spirit" and speak whatever the "spirit" wants to communicate. Kardec warned that a "spirit" will not come running at the call of any medium. There must be a clear purpose for the communication to take place; further, the medium must be an adequate and appropriate "instrument" for a particular "spirit."

Some mediums do not undergo discipline and training; in some instances, they are influenced by "spirits" of a lower order and become black magicians. Some other people with mediumistic capabilities do not realize their talents. It is easy for a "prankster" type of "spirit" to find affinity with them, and produce poltergeist phenomena. The poltergeist is often described as a "noisy ghost" because the phenomena include rappings, explosions, and household objects which appear to fly through the air and crash on the floor. For Kardec, poltergeist activity indicated that a mischievous "spirit" is at work, implementing its effects through the unconscious cooperation of a person with mediumistic tendencies. Kardec compared mischievous "spirits" to children who drive adults to distraction; if one can find humor in what they do and not take them seriously, they will go away.

Most "spirit" manifestations are not prankish but occur, according to Kardec, to convince the skeptics that life is eternal. When "spirits" operate through a medium, they do so through the "perispirit" of both. Because the "perispirit" purportedly contains a magnetic fluid, the fluids of the "spirit" and the medium must resonate. A medium may be a splendid "instrument" for some "spirits" but a poor "instrument" for others. In many cases, there is an "assimilation" which occurs over a period of time as the "spirit" and medium get used to each other.

In still other cases, the medium has a "spirit guide" who obtains information from another "spirit." In these cases, if the "spirit guide" is ignorant or deficient, the message from the other "spirit" will be garbled.

A "spirit" draws its "perispirit" from the magnetic fluid found in each planet or sphere. It is not the same everywhere, so a "spirit" changes its "perispirit" while going from one sphere to another. To human eyes, "spirits" do not have a specific shape. But to each other, according to Kardec, "spirits" appear as a brilliant flame which varies in color in accordance with their purity. The "perispirit" of the less highly evolved "spirits" resembles matter. For this reason, many of them act as if they were still on earth; they do not realize that they have died.

Kardec believed that some mediums are also "healers." In *The Mediums' Book*, he wrote:

> This type of mediumship consists mainly of the gift of curing through simply touching people, or by looking at them, or

through a gesture—without any medication. Surely some people will think that this is simply hypnosis. Yet, it is evident that magnetic fluid plays an important role in these cases.

Kardec claimed to be in contact with a highly evolved "spirit" which told him about "healing" through a medium. In *The Mediums' Book*, he recorded a dialogue on the topic.

Kardec (K): Can we consider those gifted with magnetic healing powers as mediums?

"Spirit" (S): Undoubtedly.

K: The medium is an intermediary between spirits and humans. Yet the magnetizer employs his own force and does not appear to be an intermediary.

S: This is an error. Magnetic force belongs to humans, yet its power is enhanced through the aid of spirits.

K: But there are healers around who do not credit spirits.

S: Do you think that spirits only assist those who believe in them? Anyone who magnetizes for a good purpose is calling the spirits without being aware of it.

K; Can this power be transmitted from one person to another?

S: The power itself cannot be transmitted, but the knowledge necessary to use it can be taught. However, there are those who do not suspect that they have this power; they need to believe it has been transmitted to them in order to use it.

K: Are there some formulas which are more effective than others in these cases?

S: Not really. Only superstition attributes virtue to certain words. It is the ignorant spirits who hold these ideas and prescribe formulas for people to follow.

K: How can we classify spirits correctly?

S: Classification is never absolute. The transition from one degree to the other is invisible, as the colors of the rainbow flow from one to the other, and as the night imperceptibly flows into the day. Spirits are always in a constant development from the inferior to the superior classes. This is a slow and gradual process, taking many lifetimes and the experience of many worlds to occur. All spirits were created simple and ignorant; it is through experience that growth occurs.

Kardec held that during sleep, the "spirit" is able to journey through space and interact more directly with other "spirits." Even during rest, the "spirit" is freer and able to escape the physical chains of the body. This is why the medium relaxes, entering an altered state of consciousness, before contacting a "spirit."

According to Kardec, the medium with "healing" ability can help people either through prayers or by a "laying-on" of hands. All devout Spiritists have this power to some extent and "spirits" can often heighten their ability when it is needed.

"Psychic Surgery" in Brazil

Another type of "healing" associated with Brazil's spirit religions is "psychic surgery." G. L. Playfair, * in *The Unknown Power*, discusses six such "healers" he has either seen personally or about whom he has interviewed witnesses:

1. José Pedro de Freitas, better known as Arigó. In 1956, a well-known political leader, Lucio Bittencourt, announced in public that he had been operated on by Arigó for a tumor of the lung; subsequent X-rays

---

*The authors know Playfair and consider him to be a reliable and honest observer. However, first person reports, including those of the authors themselves, do not constitute absolute proof of the existence of "psychic surgery." These reports represent a certain type of evidence which can be used to stimulate research which, in turn, can produce different types of evidence. Casual observation can lead to controlled observation which, in turn, can lead to experimentation.

showed no trace of the former tumor, and Arigó's fame began to grow. Apparently, the incident took place when Arigó was in an altered state of consciousness, as he did not remember what happened. Further, he was a devout Roman Catholic and such reports seemed to support Spiritism which had always filled him with apprehension. Shortly afterwards, however, Arigó was credited with having extracted a tumor from a woman in public, using nothing but a kitchen knife and being guided by the "spirit" of a certain "Dr. Fritz," a German physician he had seen in visions since his youth.

Once he accepted his mediumistic skills, Arigó moved away from Catholicism to Spiritism. In 1958, he was sentenced to jail for the first time for the illegal practice of medicine. However, he was rescued by President Juscelino Kubitschek because Arigó had correctly diagnosed a serious kidney condition of Kubitschek's daughter. In 1964, however, Kubitschek was out of office and Arigó went to prison after stating, "We all have a mission here on earth, and mine is to heal." After seven months, Arigó was released.

Arigó continued to "heal" until his death in 1971. Sometimes he would give prescriptions—often for obsolete medicines—but he was best known for his precise incisions into the body without using anaesthesia. Nobody died of blood poisoning and few complained of pain, despite the fact that Arigó often used a rusty knife or blunt scissors. After the "surgery," Arigó would close the incision. A radiologist named Madeiros is quoted by Playfair as stating, "The flesh simply comes together leaving a faint red line, which subsequently disappears altogether, where the incision was made." Arigó's "spirit guide," Dr. Fritz, supposedly explained the phenomenon (through Arigó) by stating, "We disconnect the biomagnetic organizing fields that link the 'perispirit' body to matter so that the tissues become an amorphous mass. Then we remove the foreign matter, which is not connected to the structure of the organism, and reconnect the fields." In other words, the predetermined structure established by the "perispirit" does not include diseased or damaged tissue. So if there is some way of making contact with the "perispirit," the unhealthy tissue can be removed and healthy tissue restored—in much the same way that a cook can bake a new cake, after the first has collapsed, by using the same mold.

2. Antonio Sales. Described by Playfair as a "barely literate" bricklayer, Sales began to develop his mediumistic abilities after working on the construction of a Spiritist center where he was told that he had the potentials of a medium. He began his career as a "psychic surgeon" in 1966 under the "guidance" of several "spirit physicians," including Arigó's Dr. Fritz. Using no anaesthesia, Sales has specialized in eye "operations," using surgical instruments. Playfair has reported that the only apparent difference between Sales and conventional physicians is Sales' speed, despite his lack of formal training.

3. Lourival de Freitas. Better known in Europe than in Brazil, Lourival has allowed many people to observe him during "psychic surgery" sessions. In 1934, he is supposed to have launched his career by "operating" on a plantation owner with a pocket knife. Lourival has claimed that the Roman emperor Nero has been his "spirit guide."

4. Zeca. A dealer in second-hand oil drums, Zeca was observed by Playfair to use ordinary surgical instruments. Playfair has written, "Several times I saw him take pincers and drop what looked like small pieces of meat into a plastic shipping bag an assistant held out for him . . . . Zeca had little chance to conceal these pieces of what looked very much like human tissue . . . . He wore tightly fitting sleeves that only reached a few inches below his elbow, and he never put a hand in a pocket throughout the evening." Playfair insists he never caught sight of anything concealed in them. Zeca "was always holding some implement in them, and he worked without a break, even for a glass of water, although the room was uncomfortably hot and stuffy."

5. Maria. Playfair also observed Maria at work, reporting,
    "The room was lit by the bright light . . . and there was
    no difficulty in seeing everything . . . . Maria . . . took
    a pair of scissors in her right hand . . . . She had made
    some brief cutting motions, then put down the scissors,
    took the cotton and pressed it into the neck, handing it
    back at once to the assistant. There was a bright red
    blob in the middle of it . . . . There . . . was . . . a
    completely unmistakable hole in the patient's
    neck . . . , and it was partly full of dark
    liquid . . . . The light was good enough for there to be
    no doubt whatsoever" Playfair continued, "Maria pro-
    ceeded to plunge the pincers slowly and carefully into
    the hole . . . . The pincers came out again, holding a
    black object that reminded me of a small burnt sardine
    just over an inch long . . . . Then the hole simply closed
    itself up." Maria's main "spirit guide" was identified as
    an Austrian physician; she began to "heal" at about the
    age of ten. Reportedly, her "operations" have been
    performed with her eyes closed; she has had no memory
    at all of what happened during an "operation" except a
    vague awareness of the "spirit doctors" guiding her.

6. Edivaldo. Playfair first met Edivaldo at a Spiritist
    center in Rio de Janeiro. He was given a prescription
    for a digestive problem that was the same as that given
    him earlier by a physician. But Edivaldo also advised an
    "operation" and five months later, Playfair returned.
    He recalled, "Edivaldo's . . . thumbs pressed hard,
    and I felt a very distinct plop as they penetrated the skin
    and went inside. My stomach immediately felt wet all
    over, as if I were bleeding to death. I could feel a sort of
    tickling inside, but no pain at all. The most unusual
    sensation was a sudden strong smell of ether, which
    seemed to come from my stomach area and drift up-
    wards past my nose. Then it was all over . . . . There
    was a bright red mark on the place where Edivaldo had
    pressed with his thumbs, and nearby there were two
    bright red dots. The red line was not a scar, just a jagged
    line only about three inches long . . . . Within two days
    it had disappeared. The red dots never faded, and I still

have them." Edivaldo later told Playfair that several
"spirit guides" had helped him over the years; their
number included Dr. Fritz as well as deceased physicians from France, England, Italy, Japan, and Brazil.

Playfair, a member of the Brazilian Institute for Psycho-
Biophysical Research, has noted Kardec's statement that
one's "spirit" chooses those illnesses that afflict the body
so as to learn patience and sympathy for other sufferers.
Incurable diseases—those which cannot be ameliorated by
conventional medicine, psychotherapy, or "paranormal
healing," are ailments which the "spirit" cannot give up
because a lesson is still to be learned.

The Spiritist Federation

The Brazilian adherents of Spiritism make little reference to
the Yoruba *orishas*, but have a special fondness for the Old
Black Ones and the Indians of the Seven Arrows who
sometimes speak through a Spiritist medium. The Spiritists
are also very active in providing social services for people;
the number of Spiritist clinics, orphanages, libraries, old
people's homes, and schools for handicapped children out-
number those run by the Brizilian government and the
Roman Catholic church combined.

One of the authors (A. V.) filed a description of a visit to
the Spiritist Federation of São Paulo:

*Shortly after arriving in Saõ Paulo, we were fortunate
enough to meet Jarbas Marinho, an engineer, and his wife
Carmen Marinho, a medium. One day, Carmen Marinho
took us to a large clinic run by the Spiritist Federation. We
were received by Carlos Jordão, the clinic's director. He
explained that "spiritual healing" is not in conflict with
medical healing; rather, it is a compliment to Western medical practice. Indeed, many of his healees were sent to*

*physicians when it was thought that the physical compo-
nent of their illness could be best treated medically.*

*Upon arriving in the clinic, the ailing person is received
by one of the mediums who makes an immediate psychic
evaluation of the healee. A colored ticket is given the
healee which directs him or her toward a certain type of
treatment. First, however, everyone attends a lecture in an
auditorium where the sick are told about Kardec and his
belief that physical sickness reflects "spiritual" sickness. If
one does not undergo "spiritual" growth, the physical
sickness might disappear temporarily but would return.
Many of the people giving these talks (and reading from
Kardec's works) are former healees whose service to others
has become part of their own continuous "healing" process.*

*One uses the colored ticket for the next phase of the
treatment. In each of several rooms, "healers" use
"spiritual passes" to work with one's "perispirit." Carmen
Marinho guided us to one such room in which there were
two dozen chairs and as many "healers."*

*We were invited to sit down and receive the "spiritual
passes." Stanley Krippner reported a "tingling" sensation
in various parts of his body during the session, and was
quite refreshed at the end. I went to sit before a large black
woman who stood directly in front of me. I felt very relaxed
and breathed deeply as she proceeded to make movements
in a criss-crossing fashion over my body. I felt a release of
tension on my stomach. When she finished, she tapped me
lightly on the shoulder. I walked out of the room feeling
very light and bouncy.*

*The last phase of the treatment involved individual coun-
seling with one of the Federation's mediums, many of
whom had been trained by Jarbas Marinho.*

The Marinhos have worked closely with Hernani
Guimaraēs Andrade, Brazil's leading parapsychological in-

Stanley Krippner with H.G. Andrade at the Psycho-biophysical Laboratory in São Paulo, Brazil. (Courtesy A. Villoldo)

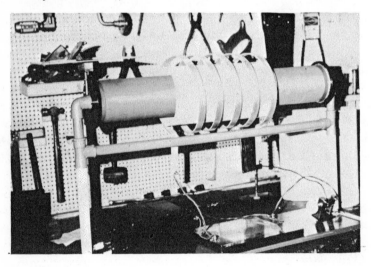

H.G. Andrade's electrophotography device, the first constructed outside the U.S.S.R. after Semyon and Valentina Kirlian published their original findings. (Courtesy S. Krippner)

vestigator. Andrade was born in 1913 in the State of Minas Gerais and graduated in civil engineering from the University of São Paulo in 1941. In 1952 he came to São Paulo to work for the state's Water and Electricity Department. In 1968, he became technical director of the Department's Electricity and Telephone Division.

At the age of seventeen, Andrade read one of Kardec's books. Although raised as a Roman Catholic, he concluded, "I had been a Spiritist all along without knowing it." In 1963, he established the *Instituto Brasileiro de Pesquisas Psicobiofísicas* (IBPP)—the Brazilian Institute for Psycho-Biophysical Research.

The investigations conducted at the IBPP include inspections of poltergeist phenomena, reincarnation-type cases, and bioelectrical fields. The latter area is studied with Kirlian photography apparatus and the *tensionador espacial electromagnético* (TEEM)—the electromagnetic space "tensioner." The TEEM consists of six electromagnets set perpendicular to each other. It also contains two stoves heated by continuously circulating water, the temperature of which can be carefully controlled. Bacteria were placed inside the TEEM to see if they would reproduce at a faster rate than control bacteria kept outside of the device. A series of eighteen tests was conducted; the overall results showed that bacteria placed inside the TEEM increased eleven per cent more quickly than the control batch. Three separate control cultures gave identical results, showing that the system was capable of giving consistent figures. Furthermore, the percentages of increase appeared to rise in accord with the strength of the electromagnetic field generated. To Andrade, these results indicated that biological effects could be elicited electromagnetically.

Andrade suspected that the mechanism at work in the TEEM experiments was a biomagnetic field. Andrade's world view posits the existence of a psychic or psi dimension which interacts with the ordinary dimensions of the

universe. It is the biomagnetic field which connects the psi
dimension with the more obvious aspects of reality.
Biomagnetic fields can be produced and enhanced through
"tensioning space" electromagnetically. The TEEM,
therefore, is seen as a device which can "tension" space,
enhance the bacteria's biomagnetic fields, and thus increase
their rate of growth. Biomagnetic fields can also be enhanced by "psychic healers," thus assisting a healee's recovery from an illness or an accident.

   In addition to his stature as a parapsychological investigator, Andrade has also gained a reputation as a remarkable facilitator of "healing." It is to people like Andrade
that Brazilian Spiritists go if they are suffering from a health
problem so serious that it cannot be handled effectively in
one of the Spiritist clinics. Two examples of these serious
conditions would be "obsession" and "possession."

   In "obsession," it is felt that the magnetic field of the
healee is in disequilibrium due to poor mental control and
disharmonious thoughts. As a result, they assimilate
magnetic forces from the environment of the same poor
quality, exaggerating the condition and producing a mental
pattern that is diagnosed as mental illness. The environ-
mental forces which are attracted include those of discarnate "spirits" of a lower order. These entities attach themselves to the person and, although they do not usually
"possess" that individual, they do "obsess" or influence
the person, creating various mental "imbalances" and
illnesses. The ailments that characterized an entity in its
previous incarnation have a certain "vibration" which
often matches the "vibrations" of the healee who frequently manifests physically the ailment of the "spirit."

   A "healing" service arranged to assist an "obsessed"
person begins with a series of inspirational readings which
encourage the mediums to direct their thoughts to God. A
"spirit guide" is then called upon to serve as "mentor" for
the group. The "obsessing spirit" is then asked to express
itself through a medium in all of its anguish, pain, and igno-

rance. One of the mediums holds a dialogue with the "obsessing spirit." Gradually, the entity is encouraged to leave the ailing person. If no dialogue with the "spirit" is possible, the medium purportedly hypnotizes the "spirit" and coaxes it to leave.

In order for "psychic healing" to be effective, the healees must change their behavior so as to develop an affinity for higher "vibrations." "Magnetic passes" can temporarily remove the lower "energies" that have accumulated in the "perispirit" due to the entities' attachment. But if the healees are to be free from future "obsession" both from lower entities as well as from their own psychological complexes, they must direct their will toward a "reinvestment" of their personalities. This can be done by "investing" their efforts in higher thoughts rather than in overindulgence in tobacco and liquor and in other bad habits. As a result of the "reinvestment" process, the healees will develop affinities for the more highly evolved "spirits" who can serve as guides and as sources of inspiration.

Once the ties are broken to the lower entities, the physical manifestations of the illness should begin to disappear. It not, a healee would be taken to a medium who can "see" the "obsessing" entities and persuade them to leave the healee. The entities are told that they, too, are on an evolutionary path and they will do better to break their attachments to the earthly plane.

"Possession" is a more serious matter. In this case, the "spirit" entities have taken over a person's body and will. Andrade has taken part in many "exorcisms" in which the healee would be placed in a circle of mediums, one of which could "incorporate" the offending entity. Another medium, the "indoctrinator," would stand outside the circle and would speak to the "spirit." The entity would be lured out of the healee's body and told to enter the body of the "incorporator." The healee would then be sent to a different room. At this point, the "incorporator" would expunge the "spirit" from his or her own body, firmly telling the entity not to return.

Mediums at Work

A variety of skills are needed for "psychic healing" procedures such as those carried out by Andrade and his group. Jarbas Marinho has developed three-year training programs at the Spiritist Federation of São Paulo for several categories of mediums:

1. The intuitive mediums, who receive information and inspiration through intuitive means.
2. The clairaudient mediums, who "hear" information as if it were being whispered to them.
3. The "healing" mediums, who are able to act as receptors for both earthly and cosmic "energy fluids," using them in "healing" through "magnetic passes," "cleansing the aura," and other "spiritual" procedures to "heal" and strengthen the body.
4. The clairvoyant mediums, who are able to "see" into the world of "spirits" (this is often said to be the highest type of mediumship, as these mediums can "see" into other worlds and other dimensions).
5. The transportation mediums, who have the capacity for out-of-body experience which transports them into the "spirit" world.
6. The incorporation mediums, through whom the discarnate "spirits" can communicate during a séance.
7. The psychographic mediums, through whom the "spirits" can write.
8. The precognitive mediums, who have the ability to perceive beyond the usual range of the senses, as well as the capacity to look into the future.

Marinho has taught the mediums during their first year in the instructional programs. The classes, which typically would meet weekly, consist of several dozen people. First, Kardec's theory of Spiritism would be outlined, including the importance of the "perispirit." Then Marinho would tell about the yogic concept of *chakras* or "energy centers" of the body. The class would practice projecting their "psychic energies" into each of their *chakras,* cleansing and purifying them.

Marinho would then teach his students to feel the proximity of "spirits" thus identifying their nearby presence. The students would then be taught to establish contact with their own personal "spirit guides" and "spirit instructors."

The "spirit guide" eventually "touches" the student; following this contact, the "spirit guide" begins to teach the student mediumistic practices. The "spirit instructor," on the other hand, gives the student lessons on theoretical aspects of Spiritism—typically by "speaking" through a medium.

Ken Kimell, while doing graduate work in psychology at California State College, Sonoma, embarked on a field study during which he spent several weeks with Andrade and the Marinhos. Upon his return to the United States, he reported his impressions of the mediumistic training process:

> A weak medium permits the "spirit" to send telepathic messages. The "spirit" supplies the ideas but the mediums use their own voices to report the information. The strong mediums, on the other hand, allow the "spirits" to speak directly through them. If the "spirit" is describing an object, such as a flower, the medium can visualize that object. This phenomenon is called a "manifestation"; Marinho teaches the mediums to discriminate between "manifestations"—which are associated with the "spirits"—and telepathic impressions which can be picked up from other people in the room.

As the students progress in their mediumistic training, more time would be spent practicing the various skills taught by Marinho. Some individuals would terminate their training if it is decided that they are not ready for the "opening" demanded by mediumship. Others have the potential to become mediums, but are not accepted into the program because they lack readiness for this experience. As the training advances, the students must learn how to differentiate between "spirit" messages as those projected by their own personal needs—or those projected by other people through telepathy. Ken Kimell observed:

> Jarbas Marinho claims to know how to differentiate the messages from the "spirit plane" from wishes, hopes, aspirations, and desires. The mediums are taught how to make these differentiations. They are also taught how to differentiate "spirit obsession" from psychosis, although the factors that went into their judgment were never made clear to me.

Andrade and the Marinhos have organized weekly "healing" services in coordination with dona* Regina Moura—a medium of the "incorporation" type. The authors attended one of these sessions; one of them (S. K.) reported:

Dona Regina was a gentle but vivacious woman with sparkling, dancing eyes. Although no longer young, she gave one a feeling of youthful strength by her vivacity. We began the session with several prayers requesting "healing power." We then joined hands, forming a "healing circle." Soon, our hands began to shake and vibrate; dona Regina assured us that the "healing power" was present.

Alberto Villoldo asked dona Regina to attempt a "healing" of a close friend in New York City. After receiving her name from Villoldo, Regina asked us to send "pink healing vibrations" to the distressed party. The medium then became very still.

---

*"Dona" is a Portuguese term of respect, similar to the Spanish word "doña."

A few minutes later, dona Regina revived, telling us she had taken an "out-of-body" trip to New York, had located Villoldo's friend, brought the friend's "perispirit" to São Paulo for "healing," then transported it back to New York City. Regina gave Villoldo a description of his friend which he confirmed as being accurate, and said that the young woman in question had a serious "spiritual" problem which was the cause of her physical ailment.

Dona Regina's voice became somewhat strained; she asked us to direct "positive energies" toward her. She stated that these "energies" could be generated by visualizing a pleasant scene, a happy memory, or someone we loved. Then she shook violently for a few seconds, as if a wave had broken over her body. She clenched the table lightly, then slowly opened her eyes.

Dona Regina's eyes remained open, rarely blinking. She spoke, and her quiet, gentle voice was now the strong, deep, throaty vocalization of an old man. It was announced that Regina had "incorporated" the "spirit" of O Prêto Velho, *the Old Black One. Words of greeting were given to the Andrades and the Marinhos whom he recognized from previous séances. Villoldo and I were introduced to the Old Black One and we received messages.

Then dona Regina "incorporated" the "spirit" of a man with a cultured voice who had been a Spiritist leader in the nineteenth century. The voice told us of the need to relate Spiritism to the findings of science. The next voice coming from Regina was less cultured and more brusque; it was purported to be the same "spirit" who had appeared previously, but in a different incarnation. The "spirit" had personal messages from friends and relatives "on the other side."

The last voice was that of a young girl from Vienna. Then dona Regina regained her composure. She remembered few details of the experience but remarked how pleased she was that the Old Black One had made an appearance while we were there.

Andrade as an "Indoctrinator"

Ken Kimell was present at another session held in dona
Regina's home in which Andrade served as an "indoctrinator," one who speaks with the "spirits" after the
medium has incorporated them. It was noted that a young
woman under treatment was "obsessed" by a "spirit."
This "spirit" spoke through another incorporation medium
while dona Regina directed the procedure:

> "Spirit" (S): I'm confused. So confused.
>
> Dona Regina (R): You are going to stay right where you are
>> for awhile. The only thing you will be able to do is
>> speak. I order you to tie your hands together.
>
> S: But I want to move.
> R: Tied the way you are, the only thing you will be able to
>> move is your mouth.
> S: That's the trouble. People don't want me to enjoy my-
>> self.
> R: That's not true. When a pastime is healthy, everyone
>> enjoys it. But when the pastime is mischievous, it must
>> be stopped.
> S: Ha!
> R: You will not laugh. Think about who you are.
> S: I am a bad, old, ugly woman.
> R: The spirit world has no age.
> S: There are only ugly people in the spirit world. That's
>> why I prefer to stay on earth.
> R: With the help of Jesus, I'm going to show you your
>> face in a mirror. Then you will see for yourself that
>> you are really young and beautiful with long, black hair
>> and dark eyes. And you are not bad. You are a mis-
>> chievous little one, but we all love you.
> S: Put the mirror away!
> R: Look! Do you recognize yourself?

S: No, that's not me! Get away!

R: Not you?

S: No.

R: Did you forget that death only exists for the physical body, not the spiritual body? To help you remember, I'm going to show you how your physical body died. Come with me. We are going to return to your home.

S: You mean that I am going to see my house?

R: Yes. You are sick. Very sick. You are in bed with tuberculosis. You are in an iron bed.

S: How did you know it was an iron bed? Why are you doing this to my head? I'm confused.

R: Look. You have two doctors and a nurse beside you. You have a terrible pain in your chest. Observe it. A painful ache in your lungs.

S: You are really confusing me.

R: And now you are passing into the spiritual plane. You have gone through what is called death. You have left your material body and are now in space. The spirit really exists. And divine mercy is so great and bountiful that it has allowed you to enter the body of a healthy medium. Observe how many years you have suffered, bothering people, until God's mercy came to you.

S: What can I do?

R: We are going to ask God to help you. As I told you, you are in a medium's body to clear your mind and clarify your doubts. All of us have to die. At this moment I am asking Jesus to help you.

S: To do what?

R: I'm going to have to take you to your grave.

S: No!

R: Let's go to your grave. I must do this. You will now leave the medium's body and will travel with me to your grave. I will leave my body and will take you there. You will see your body and your skeleton.

S: No! No!

R: Come along now. Open the door. Flesh of the human body, take unto you this spiritual entity and give it form! Can you now see your skeleton?

S: Yes. But how do I profit from this?

Andrade (A): You now understand reality better. Don't you feel the difference?

S: There is a great change from what I felt before. But I don't know if I can believe you.

A: Why not?

S: You could be betraying me.

R: Order her to look at the medallion on her skeleton. Behind the medallion there is a photograph.

S: How did you know about the medallion?

A: Do you remember the medallion? Do you remember the photograph?

S: Of course.

A: This is to convince you that we are telling you the truth. The photograph is of your beloved; he has been waiting for you in the spirit world for several years.

S: Things are changing. I was thinking in one way, and now I am thinking differently.

A: Are you afraid to enter the spirit world?

S: Not anymore. At least I will see if I have better results there.

A: Yes. I think you will find it a better place.

S: I sincerely think so. I will try to do better. Let's see if I can. Do you think I am better than I was?

A: I am sure you are. Very soon you will be very calm. Then you will leave us.

S: I feel calm. Thank you. Goodbye.

This episode demonstrates how some "spirits" supposedly are shocked by physical death, and are unable to leave earth for the "spiritual plane." The mediums allegedly take these "spirits" back to their traumatic death experience and make them relive it. A type of catharsis is experienced; indeed, in the example reported by Kimell, the incorporating medium was said to have vomited a black substance during this episode. After working through the death experience, these "spirits" are purportedly able to enter the "spiritual world" and cease their mischievous activities on earth.

Biological Organizing Models

Andrade's work as a Spiritist has been combined with his career as an engineer and his avocation as a parapsychological researcher. He noted Kardec's insistence that Spiritism must be scientific as well as philosophical and religious, if it is to survive and grow.

In his book, *A Corpuscular Theory of the Spirit*, Andrade put forward the point of view that absolute space has no dimensional limitations. Within absolute space, energy can organize itself, forming corpuscles of any number of dimensions. The physical world is a case in which individuals are aware of three dimensional (3D) particles having width, length, and height. However, there might be other particles with more than three dimensions. Another world might be superimposed upon the physical world forming a more complex 4D world.

Interaction may be possible between 3D corpuscles and 4D corpuscles; after all, interaction between 2D and 3D items is quite common. A person's shadow, for example, has two dimensions while a person has three dimensions.

Andrade has hypothesized the existence of a biological organizing model (BOM) for each living organism. The BOMs determine the growth and development of that organism; however, they are part of the 4D world rather than the 3D world. The BOMs, and the biomagnetic fields that assist their interaction with matter, appear to be scientific reconceptualizations of the "perispirit" which Kardec described as the "spiritual" counterpart of one's physical body. In the Yoruba tradition, the Ibeji twins symbolized the notion that people had "spiritual bodies" as well as physical bodies. Therefore, Andrade's hypothesis reformulated this poetic notion in such a way that it could be discussed scientifically.

According to Andrade, the interaction between BOMs and organic matter has been taking place ever since life originated on the earth. While living matter is formed and destroyed, the BOM connected to it remains intact, and every time there exists the necessary biological substances and conditions, the BOM contributes to the formation of a new being. No form of life, whether it be a tree, a toad, or a person, can be formed without one.

If it interacts with a seed or an egg, the BOM will guide that seed or egg to develop along the proper lines. The BOM creates living things by the process of holography, the technique of reproducing images by reconstructing their wave fronts. G. L. Playfair expands upon this comparison in *The Unknown Power*:

> . . . Nowadays a laser can record a diffraction pattern, from which a 3D image can be projected, on a 2D photographic plate. Just as the laser reduces a 3D object to two dimensions, so the BOM reduces a 4D object to our familiar three.
>
> Now, how can these 3D and 4D worlds interact? First of all, we must assume that what we call paranormal phenomena really do exist . . . . The most important feature of such paranormal phenomena as have been proved to exist, for our present purposes, is that they exist at least in part in our familiar physical world. They do not, and cannot, originate in our world, but they can and do interact with it on certain occasions.
>
> . . . Andrade asks us to assume that one of the most likely ways the 3D and 4D worlds interact is through the human

brain. This already serves as intermediary between mind and body. Now since the human brain is known to be made of matter, whereas there is no physical matter as we know it in the psi world, or 4D world, there must be something specific in the structure of matter itself that makes this interaction of the two worlds possible.

This, he suggests, might be termed a *Biomagnetic Field* . . ., behind which we have the already mentioned BOM, a pre-existent structure connected to the normal biological process but located outside our familiar physical space.

Andrade put his theories into practice with the electromagnetic space tensioner which produced a field where bacteria multiplied more rapidly than would have been expected. Similar work had been done by other scientists; some of them found that eggs could be incubated more quickly by using radio frequency waves and that tumors implanted in rats grew less quickly when the animals were placed in a strong magnetic field. R. O. Becker and J. A. Spadaro found that electrical stimulation increased the speed by which severed animal tails and limbs would regenerate.

Another researcher whose ideas resemble those of Andrade is Harold Saxton Burr, a Yale University professor who attempted to investigate electrodynamic fields by measuring the difference in voltage between two points on the surface of the body. He used a vacuum-tube voltmeter for these experiments because it required a minimum of current for its operation. When measuring the electrodynamic fields of living subjects, Burr usually placed one electrode on the forehead and another on the chest. Alternately, the index finger of each hand was dipped into bowls of saline solution and connected to the voltmeter.

Among female subjects, these voltage measurements helped to measure the exact moment of ovulation because this event is preceded by a steady rise in voltage—one which falls rapidly after the egg has been released. Abnormalities in the voltage measurements were found to give advance warnings of cancer in one study. In another study, high voltages were found to correlate with the subjects' psychological feelings of well-being, while low voltages were associated with negative statements and moods. It was discovered that wounds would change the voltage measurements and could serve as a useful measure of healing rate. The electrodynamic fields identified by Burr could measure the depth of hypnosis and assess drug effects. In his book, *The Fields of Life*, Burr noted that "as the force field extends beyond the surface of the skin, it is sometimes possible to measure field-voltages with the electrodes a short distance from the surface of the skin— *not* in contact with it."

Burr maintained that these electrodynamic fields help determine the growth of an organism just as Andrade hypothesized that there was a BOM or biological organizing model around each organism. Examining frogs' eggs, Burr noted different voltage gradients across different axes of the eggs. He marked the axis, or line, of the largest voltage gradient and later found, as the eggs developed, that a frog's nervous system always grew along that axis.

Burr found that he could segregate, with his technique, those seeds with superior growth characteristics from the others. And when he placed electrodes in the cambium layer of trees, he found correlations with such astrophysical events as sunspot activity. Investigating protoplasm, Burr discovered that a polar reversal of the voltage usually occured just before there was a directional change in protoplasmic flow.

The "Phantom Leaf"

In 1970, Andrade built the first electrophotographic device outside the U.S.S.R. based on the Kirlians' procedures. He knew of the Soviet reports that on occasion, when a small part of a leaf is cut off and the leaf is photographed, a "phantom" of the missing part appears. He thought that this "phantom effect" might be evidence of the BOM.

One day, Andrade took a leaf from the chayote plant and accidentally nipped off a small part of it while fitting it into position to be photographed. An associate took the color film sheet away for processing; when he brought it back, Andrade found that he had reproduced the "phantom effect" in color for the first time anywhere. The outline of the chayote leaf was well-defined and there was a faint but unmistakable line corresponding exactly to where the leaf had been torn. Like the Soviet researchers, Andrade apparently had photographed something which had no right to be there.

Or had he? The American physicist and electrophotographic researcher, William A. Tiller, issued a cautionary statement suggesting the possibility that ionized gas emission from the solid leaf could have flowed into the adjacent space which then allowed some streamer discharges to occur there. "Perhaps," Tiller continued, "a type of mechanical resonance develops in the remaining leaf setting up constraining waves in the adjacent air to confine the vapor emissions largely within the original leaf envelope." Tiller also noted that some "phantom leaves" have been produced by placing the leaf on film, then cutting off a small portion. This procedure is clearly unacceptable because it can result in either chemical sensitization or electrostatic sensitization of the film.

The Soviet investigator, V. M. Inyushin, has written several papers describing "biological plasma" or "bioplasma," a hypothetical state of matter which differs from solids, liquids, and gases. "Bioplasma" purportedly consists of subatomic particles which form a "bioplasmic body" that surrounds and interpenetrates all living organisms. Inyushin and his colleagues at Kazakh State University have conducted many experiments to determine

whether "bioplasma" exists and, if so, what its properties
are. One of the authors (S. K.) attended a conference in
Moscow at which Inyushin presented a paper stating:

> . . . We have been attempting to . . . estimate the stability
> of the bioplasmic emission . . . . Our aim is to control the
> bioplasmic processes and to ascertain how these are related
> to psychic phenomena . . . . Bioplasma is emitted from the
> body and does not come from the atmosphere. A structure
> in the bioplasmic field is produced which acquires tempor-
> ary stability, conveying . . . information from the living or-
> ganism. This structure endures for up to five minutes, long
> enough to make an impression upon the film emulsion.

Later, another electrophotographic researcher, Thelma
Moss, produced films and videotapes of several "phantom
leaves," but noted that the effect disappeared in a few minutes. This finding corroborated Inyushin's statement.
Further, Inyushin has never suggested that the Kirlian process photographs "bioplasma." However, he suspects that
the "bioplasmic body" around each organism might organize the pattern of gaseous emissions, electron discharges, and streamers which are produced by the Kirlian
apparatus. If so, Kirlian photography might be a technique
which could be used to indirectly study "bioplasma." In
the meantime, it is of interest to note the similarities among
Inyushin's "bioplasma," Andrade's biological organizing
models, Burr's electrodynamic fields, and Kardec's
"perispirit."

Some scientists might balk at the suggestion that scientific methods could be used to explore Spiritist concepts.
But A. H. Maslow, in his book *The Psychology of Science*,
stated:

> If there is any primary rule of science, it is, in my opinion,
> acceptance of the obligation to acknowledge and describe all
> of reality, all that exists, everything that is the case. Before
> all else science must be comprehensive and all-inclusive. It

must accept within its jurisdiction even that which it cannot understand or explain, that . . . which cannot be measured, predicted, controlled, or ordered.

Gardner Murphy has commented on this issue in his book, *Outgrowing Self-Deception*:

> . . . Humankind has very curiously and subtly, very ingeniously and systematically, prevented itself from reaching out to new types of reality. This is partly because we defend ourselves against a bolder type of extension of knowledge . . . . Man is forever at work keeping vast areas of unwelcome reality out of his view, trying especially to suppress knowledge of his own nature.

Science can help individuals prevent self-deception in several ways. It can bring data to people's attention that they would otherwise ignore; psi phenomena would be an example of the data which indicate there are types of reality which may be unwelcome but which, nevertheless, must be faced. On the other hand, science can also help people to study and scrutinize their assumptions of reality to see if their world-view is valid. Do "spirits" really exist or are they explainable as part of people's unconscious wishes, needs, and drives? Is the "spiritual body" a fact or is it imaginary? These are some of the issues that need to be explored scientifically and that can be resolved by scientists who approach the task with dedication and intelligence.

Andrade's interest in Spiritism has led him to accept a world-view which holds that there are realms of the "spirit" as well as of the body. This world-view has led to a model of disease which emphasizes the role of "spirits" in health and illness. From this model, Andrade has generated theories which he thinks are testable. If his theories, such as that of the biological organizing model or BOM, are ever verified, they will be important factors in bringing about a paradigm shift. A future science that incorporated BOMs, biomagnetic fields, and the like, would alter the world-views of significant numbers of people. These revised world-views interestingly enough, might have a great deal in common with Kardec's notion of the "perispirit" and the Yoruba myths about the Ibeji twins—those *orishas* who were created to remind human beings that they had both physical and "spiritual" components in their makeup.

Chapter Five

The Esoteric and the Intuitive Paths: Peru's Fausto Valle and Czechoslovakia's Josef Zezulka

Hernani Andrade, in his "healing" practice, utilizes what he has learned from the Spiritist tradition. However, he also uses techniques obtained from yoga, the Kabbalah, and the Tarot. These represent another path to knowledge, often referred to as the "esoteric" traditions because special discipline is typically required before one can gain an understanding of these teachings.

The esoteric schools trace their roots to the earliest eras of recorded history. They claim among their number Hermes Trismegistus (the mythical founder of alchemy), Imhotep (the legendary Egyptian physician), Moses, Solomon, Aristotle, Pythagoras, Jesus, and Paracelsus. Purportedly, it has been the task of these teachers to transmit secret doctrines; in fact, the word "esoteric" is supposed to have originated about 335 B.C. with a group of Aristotle's students who differentiated between their master's "outer" teachings which were available to the general public, and his "inner" (or esoteric) lessons which were more difficult to understand, therefore being limited to his select students. Contemporary esoteric writers claim that agriculture, architecture, astronomy, medicine, and philosophy have their roots in the secret traditions. Various Egyptian doctrines passed into the hands of Hebrew writers and may have influenced the writing of the Kabbalah—an esoteric interpretation of the sacred books of Judaism. King Solomon himself is reputed to be the author of one of the Kabbalistic texts. This material is said to have influenced the Essenes—the sect with which Jesus reputedly had some contact during the early period of his life. Jesus is regarded by the esoteric writers as a "high initiate" in the secret traditions; one school of thought even claims that he taught in the inner cloisters of the initiate school for 40 years after his resurrection.

Esoteric Symbolism

The Freemasons are a contemporary society dedicated to preserve sacred teachings which they date back to Moses. The Grand Master Serge Reynaud de la Ferriere once wrote that the word "Mason" is related to "Moses" and symbolizes the gathering of God's people during the time of great crisis. It was also held by this Grand Master of Freemasonry that the Egyptian Great Pyramid and a sacred serpent were once on the emblem of the Masons; over the years, they were transformed into a carpenter's square and plumb line.

Most of the esoteric teachings are highly speculative and one of the tradition's most controversial themes is that of astrological periods. It is held that the sun takes 25,920 years to journey through the 12 signs of the zodiac. This period is divided into 12 cycles, each of which lasts 2,160 years—the time it takes the sun to "travel" through one sign. While the sun was in Taurus, the world's religions emphasized such symbols as the winged bull and the minotaur. Some 2,160 years later, the sun entered Aries, the sign of the ram. This supposedly coincided with Moses' descent from Mount Sinai, denouncing the golden calf the

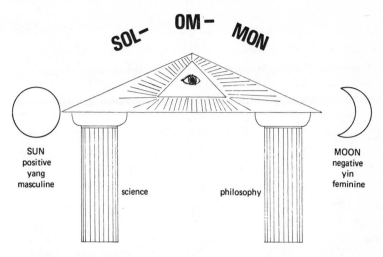

SOL- OM- MON

SUN
positive
yang
masculine

science

philosophy

MOON
negative
yin
feminine

The spiritual rebuilding of Solomon's Temple and its
esoteric message of the union of opposites.

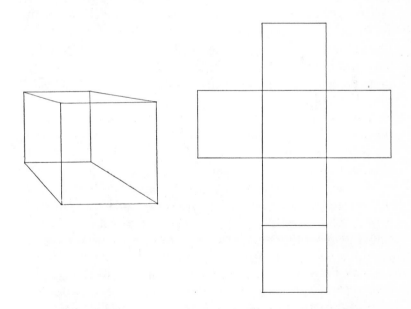

The philosophers' stone, a sculpted six-sided cube,
opens to become the cross, representing the material
and "spiritual" dimensions of the person.

Israelites had been worshipping, and proclaiming that the time had come to begin sacrificing lambs during worship services. Some two thousand years later, Jesus called himself "the lamb of God." His coming marked the arrival of the Age of Pisces—and the early Christians used a fish as the symbol of their belief. The twentieth century marked the beginning of the Age of Aquarius the water-bearer (different writers attribute somewhat different dates to its exact advent). Many esoteric teachers call for the "spiritual" rebuilding of Solomon's temple and approvingly quote, as did Kardec and the Spiritists, Jesus' statement, "Verily I say unto you, unless anyone is born from water and spirit he cannot enter into the Kingdom of God."

The "philosopher's stone" is yet another esoteric tradition. It is said that neophytes would carve and polish replicas of this stone to participate in its meaning. One's will, symbolized by a mallet, must strike the chisel of reason sculpting the crude rock which slowly is shaped into the prized stone, a six-sided cube. When opened, the cube becomes a cross, the horizontal arm symbolizing the material dimensions, while the vertical arm stands for its "spiritual" dimensions.

The esoteric oath, "To will, to know, to dare, and to be silent," is said to date back to the disciples of Hermes Trismegistus. It implies that the divine design is sound; however, neophytes can choose whether or not to follow these laws. Therefore, one vows to know the secret teachings (and to remain silent about them), to desire nourishment of the "spirit," and to risk taking the arduous journey which will eventually lead to initiation. This initiation process involves a total transformation of one's character; alchemical transformation of base metal to gold was said to symbolize this "rebirth" of personality.

Some traditions stress a preparation period which involves such yogic practices as bodily postures, breathing exercises, dietary practices, and other forms of "purification." Yoga was mentioned in such Hindu texts as the

Upanishads and the *Bhagavad-Gita*. But the great system-
ization of yoga as a discipline was accomplished by a writer
(or writers) referred to as Patanjali. The psychologists
Gardner and Lois Murphy regard this effort as "one of the
great psychological achievements of all time." In their
book *Asian Psychology,* they add:

> Aristotle said, "The mind is the thing known," and we sus-
> pect he meant what Patanjali means. . . . There is a con-
> tinued insistence upon the purity—we would say the
> homogeneity—of the self, free of all fuzziness around the
> edges due to any sort of contacts with other things. This
> involves a true and absolute stability, unchangeability. This
> content is not a process, because a process would involve
> temporal change. The self is immune to all effects of change
> or time: there is a thinker over and above the temporal flow
> of thought process. . . .

Yoga has the effect of "purifying" one's body, preparing
one's *chakras*—or "energy centers"—for the rising of
"kundalini energy." Some traditions hold that "kundalini
energy," or "serpent power," resides at the base of the
spine, like a coiled serpent waiting to rise. After one's
"kundalini energy" rises through all seven *chakras*, one
becomes an initiate. (In the Kabbalistic tradition, this is
comparable to reaching the *Kether Sefiroth*.) The initiate is
regarded as having gained masterful control of his or her
body and mind, and as being firmly on the path to more
fully acquiring knowledge of divine laws and the workings
of nature.

Alchemy and the Kabbalah

In the alchemical tradition, the purported production of the
philosopher's stone would begin by combining a neutral
substance (salt) with sulphur and mercury. From a symbolic point of view, sulphur would represent the burning,
solar, "male" principle (what the ancient Chinese referred

to as *yang*) while mercury stood for the cool, lunar, "female" principle (the Chinese *yin*). The chemicals would interact in the flask in the same way that a neophyte would evolve into an initiate. Stanislas Klossowski de Rola, in his book *Alchemy: The Secret Art,* wrote:

> There are . . . three degrees of perfection within The Work. The first work ends when the subject has been perfectly purified . . . and reduced into a pure mercurial substance. The second degree of perfection is attained when our same subject has been cooked, digested, and fixed into an incombustible sulphur. The third stone appears when the subject has been fermented, multiplied and brought to the Ultimate Perfection, a fixed, permanent . . . fixture: The Philosopher's Stone.

Aristotle's description of the "basic elements" is used as proof by some esoteric writers that the Greek philosopher was also an alchemist. Aristotle wrote that the relations among the elements was mediated by their dryness or humidity, heat or cold:

> Earth: cold and dry
> Water: cold and humid
> Fire: hot and dry
> Air: hot and humid

Aristotle wrote that there was a fifth element, ether—one which was eternal and unchangeable.

Alchemy apparently was practiced in India and China as well. Some writers have observed correlates between alchemy and Tibetan tantric Buddhism. Lama Govinda, in *Foundations of Tibetan Mysticism,* has written:

> To the alchemist who was convinced of the profound parallelism between the material and the immaterial world, and of the uniformity of natural and spiritual laws, this faculty of transformation had a universal meaning. It could be applied to inorganic forms of matter as well as to organic forms of life, and equally to the psychic forces that penetrate both.

Thus, this miraculous power of transformation went far beyond what the crowd imagined to be the Philosopher's Stone, which was supposed to fulfill all wishes (even stupid ones!), or the Elixir of Life, which guaranteed an unlimited prolongation of earthly life. He who experiences this transformation has no more desires, and the prolongation of earthly life has no more importance for him who already lives in the deathless.

In the same book, Govinda relates the tale of a robber who approached a tantric master, asking him how he could acquire a magical sword which would make him the invincible ruler of the world. The tantric master prescribed a large number of complicated physical and mental exercises that the robber had to practice for several years. At the end of the appointed time, and after fervently practicing the exercises, the robber went to a location designated by the master. He recited an incantation and the sword appeared. As the robber reached for the sword and touched the handle, he attained enlightenment. He lost all interest in the sword, invincibility, and ruling the world. Govinda comments:

> This is emphasized over and over again in the stories . . . . Whatever is gained by way of miraculous powers loses in the moment of attainment all interest for the adept, because he has grown beyond the worldly aims which made the attainment of powers desirable. In this case, as in most others, it is not the end which sanctifies the means, but the means which sanctify the end by transforming it into a higher aim.

A related tradition is that of the Kabbalah, a term which means "received wisdom" in Hebrew. Although Kabbalism did not gain prominence until the twelfth century, its ancestry can be traced back to the earliest Hebrew scholars, some of whom constructed a system of knowledge that was inaccessible to the majority of Jewish people. Kabbalism has two branches—the speculative, dealing mainly

The tree of life of the Kabbalah showing the ten
Sefiroth. (From a 16th century drawing by Paulus
Ricius)

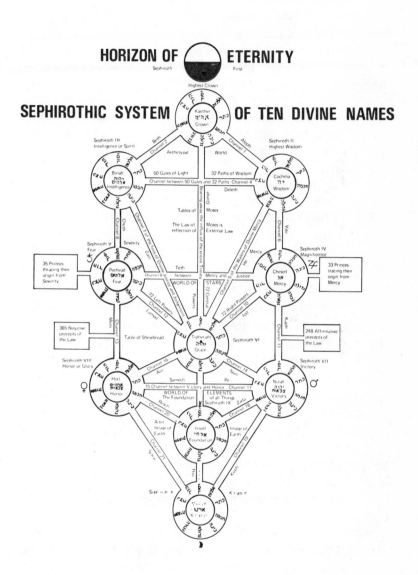

The ten *Sefiroth* of the tree of the Kabbalah, with the 22 interconnecting paths said to correspond with the Tarot divinatory deck.

with philosophical deliberations, and the practical, dealing with applied "magic" and the innovation of heavenly powers.

Charles Poncé, in his book *Kabbalah,* has discussed the differences between the secret doctrines and traditional rabbinical Judaism:

1. Kabbalism holds that the God in the scriptures is a limited God, one subordinate to a higher, limitless, and unknowable God—the "En-Sof."

2. The universe, according to Kabbalism, is not the result of creating something out of nothing, but the result of a complex operation performed by the "Sefiroth" ("crowns of knowledge")—emanations of the En-Sof.

3. The Sefiroth are a bridge connecting En-Sof with the finite universe.

The major Kabbalistic text, *The Book of Splendor,* contains 19 volumes. One of them, *The Book of Concealed Mystery,* describes the "Macroprosopus," En-Sof's greatest manifestation, known only by the exclamation "Yah" or "I am." This manifestation is represented by the first of the ten Sefiroth in the "Tree of Life" and is regarded as the first movement of the En-Sof toward manifestation.

There are 22 paths connecting the ten Sefiroth; these are spoken of as the various roads a neophyte can journey in the process of "spiritual development." They also show up in the symbolism of the 22 Tarot cards, a technique of divination which some writers believe emerged from the Kabbalah.

Again, "kundalini energy" is referred to; neophytes must strengthen their bodies to prepare for the rising of the "kundalini." When the neophyte reaches the sixth Sefiroth of the Tree of Life, there is an integration of one's personality which prepares the way to initiation. The neophyte eventually attains initiation as the gate between the second and third Sefiroth is crossed. This "conjunction" resembles the Chinese blending of *yin* and *yang,* as well as the alchemical mixing of sulphur and mercury.

After "Macroprosopus," the "I am that I am," the first Sefiroth is attained, the Tree of Life which has been journeyed through fades away but a new Tree of Life appears. The path, the adept discovers, is never ending.

Occult Medicine

Various types of "healing" are part of each esoteric tradition. Sometimes, these practices are referred to as "occult medicine" because the word "occult" derives from a Latin word meaning "to conceal." A study of this field was undertaken by C. Norman Shealy, a neurosurgeon, and published under the title *Occult Medicine Can Save Your Life.* Shealy observed:

> To some, the occult is not only hidden but also rejected knowledge: information that has been discarded or refused or disbelieved. Initiates feel that the occult is rejected either because it represents a threat to the establishment and to society and its lifestyle, or because society is too blinded by its own prejudices and ignorance to see the truth.
>
> But the establishment itself feels that it rejects the occult only because it was long ago disproved. . . . The occult . . . covers acupuncture, astrology, alchemy, herbology, the Cabala,* ritual magic and Witchcraft. . . .

Shealy has pointed out that amulets, sacred charms, tattoos, and talismans were in use at medicine's beginnings. Also, medicinal practices have typically been known to only a few initiates—whether they call themselves witch doctors or physicians.

---

*Cabala is one of several spellings for Kabbalah.

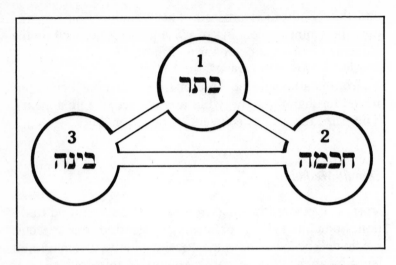

In crossing the "gates" between the second and third *Sefiroth*, initiation is attained as well as the rising of the Kundalini or "serpent power."

The seven *chakras* and the paths of the Kundalini energy.

When the Code of Hammurabi was set down by the Babylonians about 2,000 B.C., they used the word "healer" to denote a physician. For them, demons were considered the source of disease and incantations were among the tools used by physicians.

The two oldest medical papyri are even more ancient, describing three types of Egyptian practitioners: physicians, surgeons, and sorcerers. They also contain information about the pulse and the role the heart plays in blood circulation. A later record, the Ebers papyrus of 1550 B.C., states "Lay the hands on him . . . and the pain will leave him."

Egyptian, Greek, and Roman physicians all utilized "sleep temples" where patients could not only obtain sleep and rest, but, perhaps, dreams in which the nature of their diseases would be revealed. The holes near the patient's bed in some of these temples suggest that a priest could have whispered to the sufferer during sleep, providing information which could have been recalled on the following morning and thought to have been of divine origin.

Hippocrates, the founder of Greek medicine, often referred to the constellations of the stars in his writings. Galen, the famous Roman physician, often used occult practices to select drugs for his patients. And the Greek philosopher Democritus held that everything, "spiritual" as well as material, was made from atoms; he wrote that psychic phenomena consisted of "the finer atoms of the soul."

The greatest medical figure of the Middle Ages, the Arabian physician Rhazes, was a student of alchemy. European physicians of the era typically used astrology while various kings and emperors believed their "royal touch" could cure disease. In the 1500s, when the Spanish invaders of Mexico conquered the Aztecs, they found two classes of "healers"—physicians and sorcerers—as well as astrologers and seers, all of whom were consulted in matters of sickness and health.

A Journey to Cuzco

"Healers" of different types still abound in Latin America. One of the authors (A.V.) had the opportunity, in 1974, to visit Fausto Valle—a Peruvian "healer" whose work reflects the esoteric traditions. Villoldo reported from Cuzco:

This ancient city of the Incan empire lies nested in a valley 10,000 feet high in the Peruvian Andes. For hundreds of years, it was the governing seat of the great empire that stretched from present-day Chile to Colombia.

Robert Menzies, a California herbalist, and I arrived in Cuzco after days of grueling overland travel through the Andean mountains. Ten hours after leaving the warm coastal city of Lima, we found ourselves 15,000 feet above sea level in snow-covered tundras; it felt like the top of the world. Life on these plateaus consisted mostly of llamas— the furry American version of the camel—and hardy Indian people living in much the same manner that their ancestors had lived. Agriculture for these descendants of the Incas consisted in the cultivation of potatoes, corn, and other basic staple crops on terraced mountainside gardens. At these altitudes, the Indians relied on chewing coca leaves for stamina. They would wrap several of the leaves around a piece of chocolate and place the small bundle between their teeth, moving the gums slowly until the mixture dissolved. This plant (from which cocaine is derived) increases circulation, allowing one to work for long periods of time under the stress of high altitudes.

Upon arriving in Cuzco, we heard that Fausto Valle had been residing nearby for several months, performing various forms of "healings." He was well known not only for his "healing" practices, but because the local medical association was pressing a lawsuit against him for practicing medicine without a license.

Villoldo and his companion arrived at Valle's Spanish-styled apartment house early one evening and were welcomed by his wife who said, "Brother Fausto is treating someone but he will be with you soon."

She brought out a pot of strong Peruvian coffee and invited us to join the group of Valle's friends who were sitting around a table. A few minutes later, an old Indian woman walked out of the bedroom, followed by Valle. He was short statured, of strong build, with deep, penetrating eyes. He turned toward us, smiled, and remarked, "Ah, welcome my brothers, I was expecting you." Turning to me, he said, "But I did not expect you to be so tall!" At this point, Señora Valle and the others at the table broke into a laugh; we learned that Valle had predicted the arrival of the North Americans earlier that week and that they had been expecting us.

The next morning, Valle took the North American visitors to the local cathedral where Señor Paliza, an accomplished Peruvian artist, was exhibiting his paintings. They were told that Paliza had been confined until recently to his bed with total paralysis of his extremities as a result of an accident. His brother, a physician, had advised him that his case was medically hopeless and that he must accept his paralysis. Paliza then met Valle who, within a month, had helped him recover the use of his arms. Four months, and many treatments later, he was walking normally and painting again. Villoldo reported:

Valle commented that it is precisely with those cases where medical science has given up that he has achieved his greatest success. Paliza's fiancée, who had cared for him during his confinement in bed, confirmed the surprising changes in Paliza's health. Although one could still detect a slight lack of coordination in his walking, and an occa-

*sional tremor in his hands, it was inspiring to observe with
what dedication this young painter was committed to re-
gaining full movement and furthering his art.*

*Valle had treated him through the "laying-on" of hands
technique, massage, water treatments, and herbal remedies. In addition, he employed the help of one of his two
"spirit guides," one whom he addresses as "The First
Brother Superior." These "spirits," Valle claims, aid him
in his diagnoses as well as during "healing" itself, many
times carrying out "healings" at a distance. According to
Valle, in Paliza's case the "spirit guides" performed an
elaborate series of treatments which involved "re-
energizing" the nervous system from the "spiritual plane."
However, Valle does not "incorporate" these "guides" as
do many of the Spiritists; this demonstrates a critical difference between the esoteric and the Spiritist traditions.*

Fausto Valle told Villoldo that he had been initiated into an
esoteric tradition similar to Freemasonry. His training included work in "cosmobiology" (applied astrology), the
Kabbalah, the Tarot, yoga, nutrition, and herbology. Of
special importance to Valle were the regional herbs he used
in his "healing" work. He went on to say:

> Each of the herbs has valuable individual properties which
> may be different when two or more herbs are combined. For
> one thing, each of the plants has its own astrological sign,
> just like we do, and in blending herbs you must make sure
> the combination is favorable astrologically. If not, the prep-
> aration will not work, or it will cause negative results. There
> also has to be a correspondence between the plant you
> utilize and the position of the planets of the sick person.
> That is why this science is called "cosmobiology" and why
> it is such an invaluable tool to us. On the other hand, it is of
> even greater importance who prepares the herbs. The plants
> have a subtle "spirit" that must be awakened by the initiate.
> Then the power of the herb is multiplied many times. It is

for this reason that you can employ an herb for other than its primary uses.

For example, you might use a plant whose primary function is as a diuretic, stimulating urination, to treat a headache. You could make it into a tea and bless the preparation before the ill person drinks it, and it would cure the headache. Although your science cannot reasonably account for this, it has to do with which virtues of the plant the "healer" activates. The "healer" infuses the tea with his power; this complements the awakened "spirit" of the plant. This preparation, in the hands of an initiate, takes on powerful "healing" qualities. Actually, you could even use water, as long as you infuse it with the "psychic power" which comes through you and awakens its dormant virtues.

Villoldo asked Valle how a person could "tap" into this source of power. Valle answered:

We are all connected to the source of this "psychic power." How clearly it comes through is another matter; this depends on your own degree of "personal power." This "personal power" is awakened through the gentle disciplining of your body and your mind through yoga and healthful eating, and strengthening your nervous system to be able to transmit this "energy" without burning up your *chakras*. So when you treat a person suffering from an illness, you cannot treat only the physical body. The "energy body" represented by the *chakras* must also be balanced and brought to health, as well as the psychological and "spiritual" aspects of the person. Otherwise, the "healing" is not complete, and there will be a relapse at one of these other levels.

Several days later, Villoldo and his companion attended Paliza's wedding. After an engagement of several years, he was finally marrying his fiancée. When the moment for the nuptial waltz arrived, Paliza and his wife rose, took two wavering steps, then waltzed across the room to a cheering audience.

Children of the Sun

Cuzco is not far from the citadel of Machu Picchu, the
sacred mountain of the early Incan and late Incan culture;
its ruins are thought by many to have been an observatory.
The region is dotted with ancient ruins of fortresses, cities,
and ceremonial sites, many of which have become tourist
attractions. Two weeks after arriving in Cuzco, Villoldo
and Menzies left to seek out Mariano Guatara, a well-
known sorcerer from a nearby village. Villoldo reported:

*There were seven of us, including Valle and his wife, and
Antonio Paredes Baca, a professor of philosophy at the
University of the Andes. Paredes, who is also a fine herb-
alist, took us to the village where Marinano lives.*

*The sorcerer's specialty is "healing" children who are
suffering from* susto—*the "evil eye," a psychological
shock from which small children reportedly suffer. We were
told that Mariano also frees people from the effects of
"black magic" through massage and rituals. The rituals
might involve making offerings to the Virgin Mary or to a
particular saint, leaving tobacco or coins in front of someone's house, or lighting a candle at a crossroad—next to
which they might place certain magical beads or offerings.*

*Mariano and his family live in a small one-room adobe
house similar to others in the village. In another adobe
structure in front of the house is the family's cooking area,
consisting of a closed fire pit, pots and pans, and grain
storage bins. The streets are of stone, and there is no electricity in the town. As the sorcerer spoke only Quechua, a
native language, Paredes acted as our translator. He explained the technique of diagnosing with the coca leaves,
called the* rastreo de coca. *In this method, the sorcerer
picks three coca leaves from a bundle kept in a special
cloth, blows on them, and tosses them back on the cloth.
Depending on the positions in which they fall, they indicate*

the answer to particular questions. The sorcerer diagnosed Fausto, accurately identifying several of the "healer's" ailments.

Leaving Mariano's house, the seven of us drove to the ruins of Tipon. These ruins are tucked away at the end of a dirt road three miles up a mountain. We reached the top of the hill just before sunset. That was the evening of the full moon, and Paredes and Fausto explained they were taking us to the Inca initiation caves, still several miles away, but for which we had to prepare with a water cleansing ritual.

As darkness descended, the colors and shadows of the sunset began playing on the ruins of the old city, softening and transforming the countryside. As we examined a now-darkened temple, Señora Valle called, motioning for us to follow. A few yards away was a stream of water bursting out of the side of the rock wall, forming a powerful spout. By now the evening had become quite chilly, the cool wind reminding us that we were in the Andes, 10,000 feet high. We descended the stone steps that led to the spout, and found it was located in a niche between two walls, protected from the wind. Señora Valle felt the water and called back to us that it was warm. She explained that this was a "magnetic stream," the water of which had cleansing and "healing" properties.

We proceeded to take our clothing off and bathe, carefully following the "healer's" instructions to wash the skin over each of our chakras. *At no time did we feel chilled; to our surprise, we felt instead a warm tingling sensation that spread throughout our bodies.*

As we walked back towards the road, the "healer" explained that this was the beginning of our preparations for the evening and our encounter with the initiation caves. We drove back down the steep mountain road and headed towards Cucillichayo, which in Quechua means the "Palace of the Monkeys." It was close to midnight when we arrived at our destination, which was nevertheless brightly lit by the full moon.

In Cucillichayo, we were interested in the two caves located on the slope of a rock formation. The sides of the 150-foot high slope had been carved into an intricate array of steps and stone seats. The first cave, the one closest to the ground, had a triangular entrance large enough for only one person to go through at a time. Next to it rested a heavy triangular stone which may once have served to seal the cave door. Inside the spacious antechamber we found a small window, with its edges well-worn and polished from much use. The window, not quite large enough for a person to fit through, opened to a small cave which led to the outside. Toward the rear of the antechamber was a smaller chamber with an altar and a thronelike seat carved out of the stone.

This was the cloister where final initiation was attained and was, the "healer" explained, used by the Inca rulers and priests when they sensed their physical death approaching. With healthy bodies and clear minds they would enter the cave, closing the stone door behind them, and await their death in meditation and prayer. Aspirants to the priesthood would act as attendants, bringing food for the departing Inca noble or priest through the window of the antechamber. When the old priest or ruler had not taken any food for a few days, the cave purportedly was opened and generally found empty, as traditions say that the priests and rulers, at the time of their death, would transmute not only their "spirits" but also their material bodies and vanish.

I felt there could be a strong resemblance between this cave and descriptions I had read in Buddhist literature of similar "Samadhi" caves. I was also reminded of a Tibetan Samadhi story of a small igloo that was built around the departing monk. A narrow entrance was available in the front, large enough for a food tray to be pushed through. When the monks attained Samadhi, their physical forms would not be there when the igloo was dismantled.

Valle described the next cave, which was further up the

hill than the first one, as a site of ancient Incan initiations. He said these caves were used by the early Inca people, the Children of the Sun (in Quechua, "Inca" means "The Child of the Sun"). These were the original builders of the Holy Citadel of Machu Picchu, who with their technology were able to cut stones flawlessly, making perfect angles and edges. He explained that these people inhabited the region long before the late Inca empire flourished. I thought of the fortress we had seen several days before at Sacsayhuaman, with its meticulously cut stones, some weighing tons, which fit so finely it was impossible to insert the edge of a knife between them. In our Western culture such perfect masonry on that large a scale had been difficult until the development of super-fine cutting instruments.

Carved on the outside of the initiation cave was what seemed to be the face of a large elephant with two distinct tusks and a long trunk. On the right hand wall of the opening passage a glowing serpent was carved in the rock, with its head pointing inside the cave. To enter the main chamber, one needs to descend three stone steps, the last of which is a carved feline animal resembling a jaguar, on whose back one must step to enter the chamber.

It is very curious that the face of an elephant should be carved on the entrance to the cave, as there had never been any elephants in South America. How did these ancient people know of the existence of elephants, and what they looked like? We know the elephant was an important religious symbol in many of the Eastern traditions. Could it also have held important religious symbolism for the early Incas?

We entered the spacious main chamber, and then stepped into a smaller rear room where we found a low altar about six feet in diameter carved in the stone. To the right of the altar was a smooth hollow area which might have served for the placing of ceremonial objects; to the left of the altar was a seat carved out of the stone. Inside this small chamber we felt the reverence and profundity usually associated with solemn moments in ancient cathedrals. Yet the "heaviness" I had always associated with those places of worship was not there. It was truly a magnificent spot.

A most curious thing then happened; up to this point all of us had kept perfectly silent, examining the initiation chamber by the light of our small candles. Valle then extinguished the candle and the chamber became pitch black. As our eyes became accustomed to the dark, we noticed that there were small flashing lights on the domed ceiling above the stone altar. At this point, I felt an intense warmth in my belly, radiating into my chest, followed by a trembling in my arms.

The cupola-like ceiling above the altar which previously had seemed to be eight or nine feet high, now appeared to be 30 or 40 feet high, and outlined on it were flickering dots which looked like the entire evening sky, perfectly clear, without a cloud. My arms continued to tremble and I felt as if my stomach had dropped into a chasm and there was a great big open space in my belly. I looked at my companions in front of me, and then closely at the "sky" and I seemed to recognize Ursa major, Orion, and the outline of the Milky Way, even though I knew some of these constellations could not be seen in the southern hemisphere.

I lowered my vision to the altar and felt faint and nauseous. Standing on the altar, a form about eight or nine feet tall seemed to appear. It was a majestic figure radiating light; in fact, its tall shape appeared to be made of "streams" of light. As I examined this apparition of light, my uneasiness left me and a sense of warmth and well-being permeated my body. The figure appeared to be a man with a long white beard that fell over his crossed arms which he held against his chest. This figure emanated a solemn majesty; its face appeared like a radiant mass of light, sometimes resolving into the features of a man, yet most of the time remaining a glowing "ball" of light. A great sense of peace filled me.

The being then appeared to speak and seemed to say, "Welcome my sons; welcome to the land of your ancestry. We are the Children of the Sun. We are your ancestors. The time has come for the ancient initiations of the Children of the Sun to be renewed on the Earth. The energy of the planet is changing. We will be with you wherever you are. Welcome my sons."

The image then vanished. We remained in the darkness keeping absolutely still. A few moments later, Valle struck a match and lit the candle again. I felt welcome and warm though a bit awed. The sense of being in the sacred place and presence of the Children of the Sun evoked a deep sense of reverence in me. We held each other's hands and prayed. We participated in a ceremony where Valle blessed each of us in the tradition of the Incas. Of the seven of us, four reported seeing and hearing this luminous being. The other three had not seen or heard anything, yet had experienced a deep sense of reverence and awe. This was the first contact some of us had had with this type of phenomenon.

The experience in the dark cave reported by Villoldo and the others is reminiscent of experiments in sensory deprivation reported by A. H. Riesen, J. P. Zubek, and other investigators. When one's visual perception is completely blocked off, there is a tendency for internal stimuli to be projected and perceived externally. Whether or not this is what occurred in the cave is an open question. But whatever happened is an unusual and provocative phenomenon worthy of careful attention.

Esoteric "Healing"

A few days later, back in Cuzco, Villoldo had the opportunity to observe some of the interesting techniques Fausto Valle had been employing in his work. One of the healees was a woman with severe sexual problems. She felt she was frigid and unable to relate with her husband in a fulfilling way. Villoldo reported:

As I observed her posture and her pattern of breathing, I could surmise that she held considerable tension in her lower abdomen. Valle sat facing the woman and her husband, listening to a long and involved description of her condition. A few minutes of listening to her convinced me that a good part of her problem was of a psychological nature, and that both she and her husband could benefit from psychotherapy. The "healer" rose from his chair and announced that he would give her an acupuncture treatment, which would return her proper hormonal balance, and then recommend some exercises for the two of them to do. We stepped into the adjoining room where the woman lay down with her back exposed. Valle first massaged her upper back, applying a fragrant lotion, then took a long pointed metal probe and began to stimulate various points at either side of her spine.

Though the pressure on the metal probe was light and at no time did it pierce the skin, the woman would wince in pain, sometimes screaming loudly. After stimulating each of 12 points several times, the "healer" laid the instrument down and began to put his index finger one by one on each of the same points. With only the light touch of the "healer's" finger, the woman would again wince in pain. Slowly her moans became interspersed with laughs, and in a few minutes she was simultaneously laughing and crying loudly. The "healer" finished by massaging her back, indicating to her husband that as part of her treatment he must massage his wife's back three times a week. As she rose, I could observe that her breathing had become deeper and her posture more relaxed, with much of the tension around her lower abdomen gone. They left, promising to return the following week.

In the case of this couple, I observed a variety of different processes occurring. The employment of psychothera-

peutic techniques was evident when the "healer" gave the husband "permission" to touch his wife in a way that would not be threatening to her, and which would allow her to learn to receive pleasure without having to return it. He then appeared to use a form of acupuncutre; when asked if he was stimulating acupuncture points, Valle replied that they were "energetic points." Perhaps this procedure may have served to release some tension and allow her to express some pain. If so, it could have assisted in the relaxation I observed after the session had ended.

In other words, whatever Valle's paranormal talents may have been, there are a variety of psychological and physiological explanations to account for this woman's reactions.

Fausto Valle had moved to Cuzco from Lima, the capital of Peru, four months before Villoldo's visit. He had been a participant in the Kumba Mela, a festival held in Machu Picchu during November, 1974, in celebration of the purported shift of the "equatorial magnetic stream" from Tibet to the Peruvian Andes. According to some esoteric writers, there is a "magnetic stream" continuously flowing into the planet, the focal center of which was previously in Tibet. Now this center had shifted to the Peruvian Andes, as it was in the time of the Incan ruler, Manco Capac, who is typically pictured holding a golden rod in his hand. This golden staff, Valle said, allowed the ruler to tap and direct the power of the "magnetic stream."

That was the reason given by Valle why Cuzco and Machu Picchu "are now becoming a new center of 'spiritual energy' for the planet." He continued, "It is again becoming like the olden days of the late Incas and the Children of the Sun before the late Incas, where the initiated world would gather in Machu Picchu to communicate with the universe."

At the top of a building at Machu Picchu, which may have been an observatory, there is an oddly carved stone

Alberto Villoldo in the fortress of Sacsahuaman near Cuzco. The massive stones are so carefully fit together it is impossible to insert the edge of a knife between them, even when they curve to make a 90 degree turn. (Courtesy A. Villoldo)

The Citadel of Machu Picchu.
(Courtesy S. J. Lynn)

named *Inti Huatana* meaning, in Quechua, "the hitching post of the sun." Some esoteric writers claim that it held a large crystal by which the Incas could receive communications from the children of the sun living on other planets or in other dimensions of reality.

The esoteric world view held by Valle, stresses the existence of various levels of reality. To the esoterics, there are "spirit" worlds which embrace not only human beings but plants and the other animals as well. Individuals who have worked their way through various initiation ceremonies are in touch with these forces—conceived to be just as "natural" as are the more readily observed laws of the physical world. The models of "healing" emerging from these traditions are based on "God's laws." An initiate can restore an ill person to health by performing rituals, prescribing herbs, and utilizing techniques that place the healee within the natural scheme of things—techniques that restore an internal balance reflecting the balance of the universe.

The "Intuitive Healer" and Mystical Experience

Shamans, such as Rolling Thunder, undergo training and initiation as part of a tradition maintaining that they are members of an "elect" that has access to an area of the sacred which is inaccessible to other members of the community. Esoteric "healers," such as Fausto Valle, study a body of occult knowledge, undergo rituals of purification, and eventually are initiated into a select priesthood. Spiritist "healers" such as doña Pachita and the Brazilian mediums "incorporate" various "entities" for "healing" purposes. Some "healers" represent more than one tradition; Hernani Andrade is a Spiritist who uses many techniques gleaned from the esoteric traditions.

Olga Worrall underwent no special training or initiation, nor has she "incorporated" an "entity" when attempting "healing." Although she has claimed to be guided by her late husband during "healing" sessions, she has retained her own personality and identity. Instead, Worrall has spoken of the "spiritual power that comes from God" during her "healing" sessions. It is this conceptualization of herself as a "channel" or "conductor" between the "universal field of energy" and the healee that places Worrall in the tradition of the intuitive "mystics."

Worrall can be referred to as an "intuitive healer" because her practice as a "healer" has been based more on her own experience than on esoteric literature, teachings from a revered teacher, or messages from a "spirit guide." These experiences often appear to have been "mystical" in nature and have been reported by individuals who lived throughout history in a number of geographical locations. In Europe one can cite Plotinus, Meister Eckhart, St. John of the Cross, St. Teresa of Avila, and Emanuel Swedenborg. In Asia, there were Sankara, Kabir, Vivekananda, Ramakrishna, and many others. Whatever their specific differences, they all spoke of conceptualizing reality in ways different than those used by their culture. These concepts emphasize the fundamental unity of all things, the illusionary nature of such constructs as time, space, etc., and the importance of gaining information by means other than the commonly accepted senses.

In addition, the mystics all reported similar experiences. These experiences, according to W. T. Stace in *Mysticism and Philosophy,* involved perceiving that the whole multiplicity of things which comprise the universe are identical with one another and therefore constitute only one thing, a pure unity. According to Stace, this sense of unity "is the central experience and the central concept of all mysticism, of whichever type." Another scholar of mysticism, Alan Watts, noted that in these experiences, one discovers oneself as "inseparable from the cosmos as a whole in both its positive and negative aspects, its appearances and disappearances."

When intuitive "healers" conduct "healing" sessions, they usually enter an altered conscious state in which various types of unitive experiences occur. Lawrence LeShan, in *The Medium, the Mystic, and the Physicist,* has described what typically happens:

> The healer goes into an altered state of consciousness in which he views himself and the healee as one entity. There is no attempt to "do anything" to the healee (in Harry Edwards' words, all sense of 'performance' should be abandoned) but simply to meet him, to be one with him, to unite with him. Ambrose Worrall put this simply and clearly: "I followed a technique I have of 'tuning in,' to become, in a metaphysical sense, one with the patient." . . . Edwards wrote that in psychic healing the healer "then . . . draws 'close' to the patient so that his being is merged, as it were, into that of the patient, so that 'both' are 'one.'" . . . Ambrose and Olga Worrall have said, "We must care. We must care for others deeply and urgently, wholly and immediately; our minds, our spirits must reach out to them."

Zezulka's World-View

Many mystics are literate, well-educated persons such as Kabir, the fifteenth century Indian poet. Others, however, are found in primitive societies, or—if living in a technologically developed part of the world—ignore or avoid studying the ancient and medieval traditions so important to the esoterics. This is the point of view taken by Josef Zezulka, the Czech "intuitive healer," who has stated:

> I perceive truth as simple and plain. I am not interested in the earlier teachings, I do not read, I do not listen. What I present, I received as simple knowledge, and I express it in simple words.

Zezulka has referred to the human senses as "weak." If a person depends on the senses alone to attain knowledge,

. . . he is like a blind man, staggering in the darkness among the truths of life. In the past there were great teachings, presented by people who had the ability to study their unconscious until they discovered the very basis of existence. With the passing of time, the teachings of the ancients fell into forgetfulness, becoming clouded as a result of human compromise with the truth.

Falling back on his own contemplative experience to attain knowledge, Zezulka has written about a moment in which he was struck by the intuition that,

. . . everything exists in the now. There is nothing that was or will be. There is only one great present that exists in timelessness. This is the great process that contains the individual destinies of everything. It can be compared to a body which consists of individual cells. Our individual destiny is such a cell.

According to Zezulka, each human being retains memories of past levels of evolutionary development—fish, amphibia, reptiles, lower mammals. When *homo sapiens* evolves to another species, a new quality of memory will develop, one which is tuned toward the future.

At first it will be feeble, limited to only a few events, but later as it becomes stronger it will have greater range in the process of destiny. The appearance of these abilities is slow and inconspicuous but already we may note it in the case of some events in our own lives that we have anticipated for no logical reason.

Zezulka has stated that all living beings go through life as if it were a "destiny." There are events in each destiny that are related to events in one's previous destiny, that is, in another lifetime:

A complete destiny lasts from one birth to the next birth. In the course of one's material life there is an event called death in which the being discards one's physical body. Just before entering into a new life does the sense of personality vanish as does the identification with past experiences. Only the higher, innermost consciousness remains.

One does not consider oneself a personality anymore, but rather a being which has gone through many different forms. All the lives one has lived through form an impression. As one chooses one of the many potential destinies for the future, this impression displays itself in its totality. One sees this for an instant as one prepares for the next incarnation—and then one knows what to prepare for in the coming life.

As soon as a being leaves the timeless and enters one's new destiny, one is trapped by time. What was previously stable and unified now appears to be divided. The story then develops and the destiny is perceived as one's life.

The being looks at everything as one's own, as a life which one will someday finish. And when the being dies, it finds itself standing above the destiny one has just passed through. Each entity is a pilgrim in a great chain of destinies.

Zezulka has expressed the point of view that one's actions in a past life bear seeds, the fruit of which manifest themselves in a present existence. The fruits of irresponsible deeds manifest themselves as hardship and one's successful journeying through these tests result in "spiritual" evolution. If one is more "spiritually" evolved, there is no rebound from the past and only the events of destiny remain.

Human organisms are composed of three basic spheres, according to Zezulka. Illness can occur on any one of these spheres:

1. *The Somatic Sphere*. Diseases in this sphere are caused by infections as well as by deficiencies of essential vitamins and minerals. Abnormal formations and growths also occur at the somatic level.
2. *The Psychological Sphere*. Malfunctionings in this sphere are characterized by psychological imbalances such as those that produce psychosomatic ailments and mental illness.

3. *The Sphere of "Vital Powers."* Disease at this
    level are caused by weakness or chaos in one's
    "vital powers"; for example, by deformation of
    the "lines of power" through which organs influ-
    ence each other or through destruction of the bodi-
    ly "power centers."

To Zezulka, every individual is characterized by a balance
of "vital powers" that are essential to survival, health, and
growth. Ordinarily, these "vital powers" are in a steady
state with only slight fluctuations. A disease is fundamen-
tally a disturbance of the physical balance in our bodies.
When our balance or homeostasis is disrupted, the "vital
powers" are weakened and are no longer able to resist inner
and outer influences that are harmful to the system. As a
result, the inner organs become affected and their activity
becomes feeble or chaotic.

These "vital powers" are essentially the pulsations and
rhythms of the life force itself. The physical and psychological spheres of our organism are vitalized and given life by
this third sphere—the "vital powers." Reciprocally, these
are the regions in which the rhythms and pulsations of the
"vital force" are manifested.

The discipline whose realm is the vital sphere is called
"biotronics," or "bio-energy therapy." According to
Zezulka, this is an independent branch of "healing" which
will supplement traditional medicine in the battle to con-
quer disease.

The "Biotronic Healer"

Zezulka, in an article appearing in *Psychoenergetic Systems,* wrote that a "biotronic healer" is concerned with the
malfunctioning of the "vital powers." Malfunctioning is
characterized by feebleness or by chaotic activity of the
"vital sphere." Disease is caused by a destruction of the
bodily centers of the "vital powers," and by deformations

of the "lines of power" through which organs influence each other.

It seems that simpler species are able to regulate their own "vital power" states. For example, Zezulka has noted that a diseased mouse in a terrarium will press itself against the healthy mice. This can be interpreted as an attempt to strengthen its own afflicted body with the powers emanating from the healthier organisms. Similarly, Zezulka refers to the folk tradition that if children sleep with old people in one bed, the old ones are strengthened while the children are weakened. His experience and observations have convinced him that "vital powers" tend to flow spontaneously from areas of high concentration to areas of deficiency.

The "biotronic healer" is a person whose special talent is, according to Zezulka, the ability to transfer "vital powers" from the environment to diseased individuals without losing any of his or her own "vital powers" in the process. This second or "excess stream" of powers has importance only for the healee, and is always separate from and in addition to the "healer's" own reserve of "vital powers." There are very few people who can do this, and still fewer who are able to develop and control their innate "healing" abilities.

Zezulka's model of "healing," then, is based on the notion of "vital powers." "Healers" can develop and control their reservoir of these "powers," transferring them to healees.

Zezulka has conceptualized two types of "healers," the "magnetizers" and the "sanitors":

> A "magnetizer" is a biotronic healer who has the innate ability to transfer vital powers, but who does not know exactly what the powers are or how to regulate them. The magnetizer usually discovers this ability accidentally or through someone who is familiar with healing processes and draws attention to it. The magnetizer works by drawing the hands over the body or by pressing them against the area that is supposed to be the cause of the disease.

The abilities of magnetizers vary according to the kind and amount of powers that they can direct to the ill person. Thus, their effects on individuals will vary. Some individuals will be easier to heal than others, and some magnetizers may be more suited than others for healing certain diseases. I would presume that the magnetizer's healing is accomplished by strengthening the centers of power in the sick person's body with the translated powers, so that the lines of force regain their balance.

The "sanitor" is a biotronic healer who works actively, regulating and controlling the vital powers. On the other hand, the magnetizer works passively. In the presence of a deficiency of vital powers, the magnetizer becomes a passive vehicle for the transfer of powers from the environment to the individual who needs them. The sanitor on the other hand, understands these powers. The sanitor learns to develop and apply them, controlling, transferring and combining them. The sanitor can also alter these powers during a treatment.

The vital powers flow in through the breath, solid food, liquid food, and sleep. In these ways one's basic supply is replenished. When an individual's supply is not sufficiently replenished, the sanitor is able to supply the needed powers through a special process in which the vital powers are brought under voluntary control. For these reasons, the sanitor is more likely than the magnetizer to experience fatigue. This is generally a bodily weariness, caused by the activity of healing, and not an exhaustion of the healing powers. Thus, a sanitor must be in touch with one's bodily powers and know one's limits. A magnetizer, who acts only as a passive vehicle, is more able to heal a greater number of healees at one time than is a sanitor. However, it is only the sanitor who can effectively heal complex diseases, and who can consciously apply one's powers to the real causes of the disturbances.

According to Zezulka, there are some individuals who have the ability to relieve pain, such as headaches, by using a "tranquilizing power." However, he has insisted that this is not a "healing power" by itself; it can be harmful in that only the warning signal—that is, the pain—can be subdued while the underlying ailment remains active.

Zezulka has conjectured that occasionally people may transfer some of their own "vital powers" unconsciously, and may suffer from "undernourishment" which will first manifest itself as fatigue, and later as disease or reduced functioning of an organ. However, this is exceptional. As a rule, the "vital powers" do not leave the body in great amounts or for long, so that the body is easily able to recover its proper level. Some people, though, try to consciously transfer their powers for the purpose of "healing" without the ability to do so. Such attempts create an unnatural outflow for which there is no easy compensation. The body may mobilize all its reserve and fight a physical breakdown for some time, but ultimately it must give way to a serious illness.

Zezulka has described a bodily "sheath" made of "plasma" that resembles Kardec's description of the "perispirit."

> Over the course of my experience, I have observed a number of methods by which a sanitor may exercise an influence. The sanitor is responsive to a "plasmatic" sheath that surrounds the body. The sheath displays the vitality and quality that the body is afflicted with, the sheath reveals a disturbance in that area, as if it were infected. Sanitors start their work by "taking off" the infected plasma from the body. This may be done by concentration, or by movements of the hands.
>
> After this procedure, it is essential that the hands be cleansed. Most sanitors wash their hands with running water, although some use earth or open fire. There is another method, cleaning by the air, but this is inefficient since the infected plasma is not negated, but remains in the air, where it can be attracted by other people, and may disturb their health. If a sanitor did not clean one's hands, the infected plasma would have harmful effects on any other person the sanitor were to touch. Infected plasma disrupts the unafflicted plasma of a healthy person and may lead to the contacting of a disease.

Joseph Zezulka's symbol of healing. The cross symbolizes the physical and psychic components of the organism. The three-pronged design represents the unifying quality of the "life force." The circle represents unity and timelessness. (Courtesy J. Zezulka.)

Joseph Zezulka holding his hand around a flame at the end of a "healing" session. (Courtesy M. Rojek.)

In 1974, one of the authors (S.K.) observed Zezulka during a "healing" session in Prague. Afterwards, Zezulka held his hands around a flame, purportedly to negate the infected "plasma." At this moment, Mark Rojek, a student from Michigan, took a photograph of the process.

When the picture was developed, a striking color photograph was obtained. But upon inspecting the picture, Rojek observed that Zezulka's hands appeared to be transparent; the flame could be seen clearly—just as if it were shining through the "healer's" hands. There is probably a reasonable explanation for this phenomenon from a photographic point of view; nevertheless, the picture is provocative and dramatic.

Four Basic Forces

According to Zezulka, a "sanitor" works with the four basic forces which form the healee's "vital powers." These forces can be referred to as "centripetal" (proceeding inward), "centrifugal" (proceeding outward), "excitative" (stimulating), and "tranquilizing" (calming) in nature. Zezulka has given an example of the regimen a "sanitor" might advise in treating a disease through the manipulation of these four forces:

1. Strict diet. Greatest possible concentration of raw and fresh food.
2. Strengthening activity of the liver by quick change of the "centripetal" and "centrifugal" forces. Increase of complex "vital power."
3. Balancing the bodily center.
4. Specifically influencing the disease through a "tranquilizing" force.

Zezulka added, "After the malignant process is stopped, I would use the tranquilizing and centripetal forces to restore complete health."

Zezulka has stressed diet in the "sanitor's" development as a "healer." The "sanitor" reportedly has to be careful of what he or she takes in as food as this will affect the effectiveness with which "vital powers" can be transferred to the healee. Zezulka has claimed that,

> . . . as a sanitor develops as a healer . . . he stops eating meat. There are many diseases in which meat plays a smaller or greater role. We must realize that we have too many harmful ingredients in our food nowadays, such as artificial colorings, flavorings, and preservatives.
>
> Eating meat stimulates the development of the intellect to the detriment of intuition. The role of balancing and regulating the intellect, which is achieved by intuition, is left unfulfilled. So we end up with people who are clever but not wise; neglect of intuition gives us barbarians with very little refinement.

Zezulka's stress on intuition—knowledge obtained without the use of reason—characterizes his approach to "paranormal healing."

While there are individuals who appear to be able to "magnetize" with very little training, it takes a certain amount of self-development to become a "sanitor." According to Zezulka, the "sanitor" must first acquire a knowledge of human anatomy and the interrelated functioning of the different organs, as well as the variety of diseases that exist. He or she then closes the eyes to visualize these organs; as the "healer" visualizes the disease, he or she also obtains a mental image of the disease disappearing.

> But knowing medicine is not enough. He must also develop positive values and attitudes toward life. This is important because the sanitor's character cannot help but influence and calm the powers that are transferred. His inner qualities must evolve so that he respects life and all living beings.
>
> One must develop the understanding that the lives of all creatures have the same value. The individual creatures differ from each other by their degree of development, but the

value of their life is the same. One must understand that all the lower creatures are his brothers. The value of their life is the same as the value of his life.

The sanitors become a positive element in the overall process of the universe through a deep understanding of the laws of life. Their sense of ethics have to become perfected and firmly established in a deep knowledge of truth.

The next step is to develop an understanding of one's own power. A sanitor's ability is not limited to the complex of magnetic powers. Though he uses them, he is much more concerned with employing subtle combinations of the different powers. We see this subtle combination of powers in nature, for example, the wind and rain in one combination can be very nourishing to plant life, while in another they can be devastating, washing away the young seedlings. The sanitors learn to know these powers, to control, and to transfer them. They also learn how, when, and which powers to use and which combination is applicable in specific healing treatments.

Zezulka has warned, "This path is neither simple nor easy. It consumes the person as a whole. One is expected to devote himself to it wholeheartedly. This is the reason that only a few magnitizers are willing and able to devote themselves to the discipline required to become sanitors." Zezulka reportedly took this path himself, evolving to the role of a "sanitor."

According to Zezulka, he began to practice "biotronic healing" in 1946. In 1955, he developed a program for treating cancer. This program has several elements, one of which involves diet. In Zezulka's opinion, one cause of cancer is the presence of carcinogenic (or cancer-producing) elements consumed in food and tobacco. Thus, he has advised his healees to abstain from smoking and to eat fresh foods containing "vital power."

Another factor involved in cancer is a lack of "vital power" or "energy" on the part of the ill person. Various psychological and physical conditions lead to this lack of "vital power."

Zezulka has found lung and throat cancer the most difficult types of the disease to cure, possibly because the healee often finds it difficult to stop using tobacco. Other prohibitions imposed by Zezulka include smoked cheese, smoked meat, roasted food, fried food, baked food, coffee, and chocolate. Cooking tins containing benzoic acid should not be used. Ointments containing tar should be avoided.

Instead, the healee should eat boiled foods, stewed foods, and fresh foods, especially fruits, vegetables, nuts, roots, milk, and butter. Every cooking utensil placed on a flame should contain water, according to Zezulka. He has observed:

> No other animal uses fire to prepare food. It is an incorrect presumption that the human body is organically built to use such food. If fire is applied without water or air, tar appears in food very quickly. In frying, roasting, baking, and smoking, unnatural food is produced which is not appropriate for the body. It may not be incorrect to suggest that cancer was initiated at the time when fire was first used to prepare food.

In regard to "vital powers" and food, Zezulka has indicated that leaves lose this "energy" very quickly, fruits and vegetables hold it somewhat longer, and it is relatively stable in roots, seeds, and nuts. According to Zezulka:

> We know that on this planet life is derived from life. Only green plants are able to accept inorganic nutrients. All higher organic bodies accept only organic nutrients; in addition, they often consume other living organisms. This means that besides the organic substance, they contain the vital powers or vital energy.
>
> Besides the solid, liquid, and gaseous elements which the body must use, the vital energy in food is equally essential. Lack of these vital powers weakens the body, making it susceptible to the toxic effects of the environment.

In Zezulka's sessions with cancer cases, he has attempted to remove the diseased "plasma" around the body and fill

the healee with "vital power." He has said that he directs
extra amounts of "energy" to the liver and the breastbone,
important connective areas for the body. The next phase
emphasizes the brain and Zezulka has noted:

> There is a morphological center I presume exists in the
> cerebrum which commands the form of the body as a whole,
> as well as the individual organ and cells. I suspect a correla-
> tion with the cerebellum, so I influence the cerebellum as
> well. The stream of energy is modulated toward tranquility
> and balance.

Only in the last phase of treatment would Zezulka attempt
to exercise local influence on the cancer. Between 10 and 15
sessions ordinarily would be required. He has told of his
process of visualizing the cells—seeing them in the mind's
eye. In addition,

> I try to pervade the organism and disturb the activity level
> of the cancerous cells. This is why I often use warm water
> and work with wet hands. In this way, one's tranquility is
> increased. The same manner is used if there is a tumor to be
> dissolved. If the process of dissolving it is too difficult, a
> surgeon should be asked to remove the tumor. It is then
> wise to repeat the healing process after the operation has
> been completed.

During the postoperational phase, Zezulka would use
"centripetal healing," with water as a complement. "Protective healings" would be advised twice a year for at least
five years. Again, ten to fifteen sessions would be recommended with a continuation of the prescribed diet.

Bioenergotherapy

Zezulka delivered a paper at the First International Congress on Psychotronic Research in Prague during June,

1973. He commented on the "sanitor's" use of "vital powers":

> The sanitor cannot administer an overdose of the vital
> power. No matter how much is given, the body will only
> take in what it needs. The excess will flow away. The
> sanitor's operation can restore health, but it cannot do any
> harm. It either helps or has no effect. This is an advantage
> over drug therapy where overdosing and habitual consump-
> tion are great dangers. Should a sanitor use a part of the vital
> power which is not necessary, the body will not accept it for
> the same reason. This phenomenon serves as a warning to
> the sanitor that the amount of power being transferred
> should be reduced. Often, the origin of a disease is not
> necessarily in the place of pain or symptoms. Thus, the
> body gives the sanitor indications that help one to discover
> and heal the cause of the disease rather than merely remov-
> ing the symptoms.
>
> The sanitor also works by rectifying the bodily center.
> This is a center in the brain which I know about through my
> experience, although I am unable to localize it. It controls
> every cell and forms a plan of the body and its organs. It is
> through this center that growth is directed. Defects in this
> center create defects in development or modification of
> bodily form. The center is also influential in the activity of
> the organism in healing wounds, and seems to control the
> growth of benign tumors. Diseases that stem from defects in
> the bodily center must be healed by directed attention to
> that area.

Finally, according to Zezulka, a "sanitor" affects the
healee through his or her personality. The quality of
thought and behavior, of values and motivations are also
transferred to the sick person, varying with the degree of
that person's sensitivity. This effect may be very direct as
when the "sanitor" wishes to "open up" the diseased person so that he or she is more receptive to treatment. In this
instance, the ill person would be given specific directions
on how to "open up" to the "sanitor's" effect.

In his concluding statement, Zezulka reiterated his use of

personal experience and intuition to formulate his ideas about "paranormal healing."

> I offer only my own views as they have been formulated during my practice. We are only beginning to understand this ancient form of healing. I presume that it faces a great future and that those who study it will have the opportunities and the capabilities for improving it. My only hope is that biotronic healing will be the work of honest, unselfish, and competent people so that it will be effective in alleviating suffering and curing disease. I also hope that, by its unique understanding of the life processes, it may lead people to more healthy and more appropriate ways of life.

Following Zezulka's presentation, one of the authors (S.K.) asked him if he would like to demonstrate his "healing" technique. Zezulka agreed, and Shelby Parker volunteered to be the healee. Parker, an educational consultant, suffered intermittent pain in her right leg, where she had an artificial hip. At the time she volunteered, she reported that her leg was in severe pain.

Zezulka performed a "laying-on" of hands on various parts of Parker's body. From time to time during the session, Zezulka also held his hands several inches away from her. Following this session, Parker reported the sensation of heat apparently coming from Zezulka's hands, even when they were being held several inches from her body.

One year later, Parker was again having difficulty. This time, there was so much pain and stiffness in her leg, hip area, and lower back that her movement was seriously restricted. Parker took Darvon, a pain reliever, daily and could only walk short distances; even then, she needed a cane. Much of her time was spent in bed due to the discomfort.

By mail, she arranged a series of fifteen minute sessions with Zezulka. They synchronized the time so that they would both be thinking of each other during the same part of the day. For eleven days, beginning on July 3, 1974, Zezulka attempted to "heal" Parker who, at that time, was residing in California. On July 3, Parker made the following entry in her journal:

> Today I rested in the sun, read, and took a walk, moving easily. Feeling quite well, I did not take Darvon. I had been in the habit of taking one Darvon capsule each morning along with my vitamin supplement. This would control the pain for most of the day. But today I am delighted that I have not needed it!
>
> It is now 6:00 P.M. and there is no back, hip, or leg pain. This has been a beautiful, peaceful, deepdown restful day.

On July 18, Parker reported experiencing sensations of warmth during the fifteen minute "healing session" which she spent in what she called a "a receptive meditative attitude." She wrote:

> After I relaxed, there was a tingling in my fingers. It was especially strong in my right hand. It seemed as if the healing energy was coming through my fingers and into my hands.
>
> Suddenly my open hands began to rise. I let them do as they wished. They made a circle as if they were holding a ball. It felt as if this imaginary ball or sphere actually had substance. My hands carried the sphere to my forehead. It seemed to enter my head as my hands pressed against it. My hands then moved outward and down to my lap, feeling empty as if the ball had dissolved. I wanted to lie very quietly and let this experience permeate my entire body.

Later that day, Parker walked on the California beach, something she had not been able to do for six months. On July 19, she wrote:

> Today I again walked to the beach and back, a distance of about one and one half miles. I used my cane, but it barely touched the ground. This is real progress!

In August, 1975, the authors interviewed Shelby Parker in Colorado. At that time, she no longer used a cane. She spoke warmly of her continued contact with Zezulka, and also of a visit to a "healer" in the Philippines—a visit which was associated with still further relief from her difficulties.

In the meantime, the Committee of Applied Cybernetics of the Czechoslovakian Scientific Technical Association organized, in September, 1975, a seminar on "biotronic healing," "bioenergotherapy," and "bio-energotherapeutics." Zdeněk Rejdák, the organizer of the conference, sent one of the authors (S.K.) a summary statement concerning the meetings:

> It was agreed that bioenergotherapy is the capacity of one organism to transmit the proper energy to some other organism in order to improve its psychosomatic state. On the basis of the latest Soviet research, the mechanism is probably biological plasma. It can be presumed, therefore, that an interaction is taking place between the two biological plasmas—that of the bioenergotherapist and that of the patient.
>
> The bioenergotherapist proceeds from the knowledge that the patient has the capacity for automatic regeneration and self recovery, just as long as the limits imposed by the patient's state are not exceeded. When the patient's own reserves are quite limited, the bioenergotherapist provides an additional reserve, designed to restore equilibrium to the patient, bringing him back to health—both at an objective and subjective level.

Dr. Rejdák went on to state that

> Every disturbance in an organism's equilibrium reflects a change in biological plasma—its color, form, and radiation. Biological plasma also participates in the creation of the pathology of a body organ or bodily tissue; there is feedback between the diseased part of the body and the surrounding

biological plasma. As the bioenergotherapist works with biological plasma rather than with the diseased tissue directly, bioenergotherapy can be seen as an auxiliary to traditional medicine and complementary to it.

Therefore, the bioenergotherapist can be conceived as an individual with the capacity to transfer energy that has healing characteristics to individuals capable of using this energy. As early as 1956, there was a verification of these procedures in the U.S.S.R. Particularly striking results were found in the treatment of arthritis, asthma, poliomyelitis, tuberculosis, and, of course, various psychosomatic ailments.

Zezulka's long career in Prague may have had some positive effect in the calling together of the scientists for this significant conference. Furthermore, Zezulka submitted a paper to the Second International Congress on Psychotronic Research which was held in Monte Carlo in 1975. Although he could not attend the meeting, his paper was accepted and was printed in the conference proceedings. Zezulka wrote:

> Slowly, the discipline of "healership" is beginning to occupy a place in medicine. By "healership," I mean a direct and conscious transfer of human vital powers—or energy—from a healer to a patient with the aim of ending the patient's disease. I think that this is an ancient branch of medicine which fell into oblivion when human beings lost interest in it.
>
> . . . The healer works by removing body plasma which has been spoiled by the disease and filling the healee with vital power. . . . Through these practices, "healership" can be revived and scientific methods can be used to study its effectiveness.

Zezulka's mention of science is typical of many contemporary "psychic healers" who recognize the value of scientific inquiry. Science itself is expanding its perspectives, taking positions which are favorable to the study of "paranormal healing." In *The Politics of History*, Howard Zinn has written:

> Science no longer confronts nature as an objective observer, but sees itself as an actor in this interplay between man and nature.

He suggests that intuition and emotion should be used as valuable tools to supplement reason. Furthermore, Zinn recommends that field studies should be made with no preconceived answers, only preconceived questions. This type of research is certainly appropriate for studying "psychic healers," especially those representing the shamanic and Spiritist traditions.

Zinn concludes that there must be discipline and a high level of accuracy maintained, but not in the context of complete objectivity which would result in "losing a vital understanding of the totality of the effect being studied."

It is interesting that Olga Worrall and Josef Zezulka, both "intuitive healers" who purportedly obtained their knowledge in non-rational ways, have been in the vanguard of those "healers" who have cooperated with scientists and who have appreciated the value of scientific inquiry in understanding the "healing" process.

Chapter Six

Josephina Sison and
the Filipino Spiritists

In 1975, Shelby Parker arrived in the Philippines. She had accompanied Don H. Parker to an important conference on education in India where he had been commended by Prime Minister Indira Ghandi for his contributions to educational development. As President of the Institute for Multilevel Learning, International, Dr. Parker's next stop was in Manila to see Luis Abiva who was publishing Parker's materials for use in Filipino schools.

Abiva took the Parkers to Alex Orbito's "healing clinic" where Orbito stated that Shelby Parker would need three "healing" treatments to be helped. During the first session the Parkers witnessed several "operations," many of which involved Orbito massaging a section of the body and appearing to remove various objects while red fluid seeped from the area the "healer" touched.

The second session was held the following day. When the Parkers arrived for the third session, they were told that there were 71 healees ahead of them. This gave Don Parker an opportunity to film several "operations" and to observe dozens of "healing" treatments closely. He later told the authors that he checked carefully for sleight of hand but could see no way that fraud could have been perpetrated. Parker said that he had been standing only a few feet from Orbito during the treatments, all of which were done during the day in a well-lit room. Parker added:

> Orbito appeared to be in a trance-like state. Often, he would not even look at the part of the body he was touching. Once, he worked on two people at once, appearing to pull a four-inch-long substance from one person's nose and something else from another person's arm.

Shelby Parker reported that a number of clot-like substances seemed to emerge from her leg during the three times that Orbito worked with her. She also told the authors that she felt "ripples of energy" in her leg during the session. Shortly after returning from Manila, she found that she no longer had to use a cane.

The "Wonder Healers"

When one of the authors (S.K.) visited the Philippines, he discussed the "healers" with Robert Fox, an American anthropologist teaching at Brent Junior College in Baguio City. Dr. Fox spoke of the "healers" as "astute social psychologists" who, in the more remote areas of the country, held the community's social fabric together by "curing" people of such antisocial tendencies as selfishness, jealousy, and petty theft.

Fox suggested that the "healing" ceremonies date back at least 2,000 years, possibly originating in the "cult of the dead," a series of practices by which one's ancestors were consulted. With the arrival of the Spaniards, the ceremonies—to survive—had to take on the facade of Roman Catholicism. More recently, Allan Kardec's writings, such as *The Spirits' Book,* influenced the "healers" as they echoed the notion of the aboriginal cult that "spirits" guide the practitioners during "healing" sessions. In other words, the historical developments in the Philippines mirror those in Brazil and both countries now have a number of active Spiritist "healers."

In both countries, attention is paid to Kardec's statement that physicians make a mistake if they "heal" only the ailments of the physical body while neglecting the "spiritual" ailments which are often the basis of an illness. Fox noted that most "healers" engage in more of a "healing séance" than was true of the original religious rituals; Fox had observed many séances, noting that everyone from Christian saints and primitive gods to one's ancestors and dead Japanese soldiers from World War II had been evoked. Fox lamented the lack of interest in the topic by social scientists. Fox suspected that the Filipino "healers" would manifest similar patterns which have persisted over the years. "Like the Hopi," he concluded, "the Filipino 'healing' tradition is not to resist cultural change but to adapt to social change." Therefore, the phenomena continue to manifest themselves as they have for centuries even though the cultural trappings have altered considerably.

In 1967, Harold Sherman published a book, *"Wonder" Healers of the Philippines,* in which he described his observations of two alleged Filipino "psychic healers." In one case, Sherman suspected sleight of hand; in the other case he reported "operations" in which the healee's body seemed to open up while a Filipino named Antonio Agpaoa appeared to remove a diseased piece of tissue, after which the body opening seemed to close.

In his book, Sherman presented opposing points of view as well. One of the dissenters was Sherman's associate, S. S. Wanderman, a cancer and arthritis specialist, who spent three days observing Agpaoa:

> He pulls a lamb's membrane over the abdomen . . . and saturates it with a liquid that looks like blood. . . . The times he does open the body, he uses a concealed razor blade.

When offered the tumor allegedly taken from the body of a healee, Wanderman said he did not need to examine it. He could tell "at a glance" the specimen was several days old and that the liquid was not actually blood.

Sherman noted that the Philippines Medical Association, in 1962, had denounced Agpaoa as a "conjurer," stating that tissue removed by Agpaoa during an "appendectomy" turned out to be a piece of chicken intestine when scrutinized in a laboratory. Sherman concluded that he could not personally recommend the "psychic surgery operation" until further studies had been made.

Sherman, and one of his companions on the trip to the Philippines, Henry Belk, attempted the first of these studies. They flew Dr. Hiroshe Motoyama and a portable electroencephalograph from Tokyo. After he attached the electrodes to Agpaoa's body, Motoyama asked him to relax his body and mind. A series of recordings was made, and Motoyama turned off the machine. He then asked Agpaoa to enter the state of consciousness that characterized his "operations." Shortly after he turned on the machine, there was a short circuit. Motoyama commented, "Ah, so! Very sad! Too bad! All the way from Japan—and this!" Sherman simply concluded that Agpaoa had blown out the machine. And Agpaoa himself held up his hands, proclaiming, "Sorry, Dr. Motoyama, your instrumentation will not work—but *mine* works all the time."

Agpaoa had another opportunity to demonstrate psychic phenomena several months later when Henry Belk took him to Motoyama's laboratory in Tokyo. In his book, Sherman describes how Agpaoa served as the transmitter in a telepathy experiment while Motoyama's mother served as receiver. Upon receiving a stimulus, Agpaoa concentrated upon Motoyama's mother until given the signal to stop. Motoyama reported that Agpaoa was able to induce changes in the receiver's electroencephalogram as well as three other psychophysiological measurements. Unfortunately, the two of them were in the same room, separated only by a wooden screen. The use of a sound-proof cubicle for the receiver would have ruled out sensory clues such as bodily movements and breathing irregularities.

In the meantime, Sherman's book had received considerable attention in the parapsychological community, including a somewhat favorable review in the *Journal of the Society for Psychical Research*. In response to this review, D. S. Rogo and Raymond Bayless wrote a letter which was published in the December, 1968, issue of the journal. It read, in part:

> While Mr. Fletcher states, "I am sure students of the occult would welcome further investigations with scientific proof before either accepting or dispassionately rejecting the alleged phenomena," in fact, three investigations have been made in the United States, two of which received wide coverage.
>
> The first exposé was the project of a Los Angeles television commentator, Mr. Joe Pyne, who flew to the Philippines in order to (1) photograph the operations and (2) get expert medical opinion on the phenomenon. Shortly after this investigation (in mid-1967), Mr. Pyne devoted a portion of his television program to his findings which were as follows:
>
> (1) The physician (who "posed" as a cameraman) accompanying Mr. Pyne, was invited to place his hand inside the patient's incisions. The physician stated that no incision had been made. The effect was created by "Dr. Tony's" pressing his fingers into the patient's stomach (Tony tends to choose obese persons for these operations) and then, with the aid of a hidden sponge soaked with blood, filling the crevice with blood, thus giving the illusion of an open cut in the skin. (You will notice on all photographs, Tony keeps a sheet close to the "incision," under which he keeps the sponge.) With the aid of a magician, a similar operation was performed on Mr. Pyne's program; however, instead of any organic tissue being removed from the incision, out popped a . . chicken!
>
> (2) A prominent Filipino physician stated on a filmed interview that having analyzed a piece of tissue removed by

Tony, he could safely say that the tissue was not human, but animal matter.

Better motion pictures of Tony's psychic operations were taken by Dr. Robert Constas . . . , a prominent psychiatrist. He presented his findings at a meeting . . . in May, 1967. Dr. Constas' motion pictures clearly show the modus operandi of the phenomenon: they readily show that Tony has a piece of tissue wrapped around his finger, being unravelled as he massages the "incision." He then jerks it up as though he had withdrawn it from the "incision." . . . . Another interesting feature of the Constas films is that the blood issuing from the "wound" is already coagulated.

While it has been claimed that few medical authorities have examined tissue extracted by "Dr. Tony," both the present writers were enabled to give at least amateur testimony as to its nature. At a small meeting (of the Southern California Chapter of the American Society for Psychical Research in April, 1967), a local investigator and self-styled champion of "Dr. Tony" appeared . . . and after a rousing condemnation of Joe Pyne's exposure, proceeded to bear witness to "Dr. Tony's" operations, claiming that his wife's hip had been operated upon. In corroboration of his claims he volunteered a small vial which bore a small piece of tissue allegedly withdrawn from his wife. One of us . . . recognized the material as nothing but an insect pupa (of the order *Diptera*). We did not challenge the speaker at that time. Later, when the discussion became more heated, we did challenge him with the information. The speaker angrily stalked from the room.

During the entire period that "psychic surgery" had been a popular fad in the U.S., many American citizens were interviewed on television and radio who claimed to have gone to the Philippines in order to have an operation by "Dr. Tony." These persons may be classed into three categories: (1) Cases in which there was little evidence that the person was in need of an operation at all. (2) Persons who were onlookers and who were told that they were in need of an operation by Tony himself! (3) And cases in which no subsequent medical examination was made to prove that any operations had taken place. On the contrary, many persons stated that after their "surgery," they were still afflicted by the growth allegedly removed by "Dr. Tony."

The increasing publicity surrounding the Filipino "healers" resulted in a charter flight of 111 desperately ill persons from the Detroit area.* The flight was so highly publicized that the Filipino authorities threatened any "healer" with arrest who worked with the Detroit group. James Osberg, a newspaper reporter, offered to submit his body to a "healer" if the police and medical examiners would sign immunity from arrest if the "healer" was able to perform an "operation" to everyone's satisfaction. The authorities refused, stating that even if such an "operation" were performed, the "healer" would have to be arrested for practicing medicine without a license.

Osberg modified his proposal so that the practitioner could be arrested if any surgical instrument or sharp object were used, or if the "opening" left a scar. However, the "healer" would not be arrested if the body were "opened" and "closed" without instruments and without leaving a scar. The medical examiners refused to agree to this contingency, even though they stated that the situation Osberg described could not possibly occur. Finally, the medical examiners walked out, the "healers" saw the healees, and—according to a reporter who interviewed them—about half the group felt that they had been helped.

More Reports, More Opinions

In 1973, two important reports were published bearing on the Filipino "healers." The *Parapsychology Review* revealed that an Italian neurologist had traveled to the Philip-

---

*This incident is described in *Psychic Surgery* by Tom Valentine.

pines to film Agpaoa's "operations."* On his return, the neurologist and his team reported:

1. One of the tricks we detected was that the "blood" produced on the patient's body was smuggled into the operation room in little vials that were deftly broken open at an opportune moment. The red liquid, which appeared during the "operations" was examined in a laboratory at Turin University and found to be neither human nor animal blood.

2. Two renal stones emerged during an "operation" on an Italian journalist. On examination in a laboratory at Rome University, they were found to be a lump of kitchen salt and a piece of pumice.

3. Pieces of bone which seemed to emerge from patients' bodies during the "operations" were later examined and found to be bones in an advanced state of decomposition. Tissue which was produced during the "operations" was also found to be decomposed. The Italians doubted that organic matter in this state could have come from the human body.

4. The neurologist complained that he never succeeded in seeing with his own eyes an "opening" in the skin; the operation field invariably remained covered by Agpaoa's hands.

The cameras brought over by the Italian group remained focused upon the "operation" but failed to produce satisfactory evidence that an "opening" was ever made.

Also in 1973, a journalist, Tom Valentine, published *Psychic Surgery*, an account of his own impressions of the Philippine phenomena. Valentine had read the negative accounts of Agpaoa, one stating that he held a small bag of animal blood in his hand, squeezing it out as he kneaded the skin, and another claiming that the "blood" was actually a chemical compound produced by a mixture of one sub-

---

*This expedition is described by G. Zorab in *Parapsychology Review*, May–June, 1973.

stance mixed with the alcohol and other hidden material in the cotton swabs he used. He also heard the explanation that a pig's membrane is spread over the healee's skin to simulate an exposure of the internal organs.

Valentine writes of his interview with W. J. Monaghan, an investigator for the American Medical Association. Monaghan showed Valentine a file of clippings which were critical of Agpaoa. In addition, Monaghan branded Agpaoa a "fugitive from justice," telling Valentine about the 1968 tour of the United States in which Agpaoa undertook several "operations" and fled the country before a warrant for his arrest could reach him. Shortly after this conversation, Valentine left for Manila to take a first-hand look at the phenomena.

Valentine did find at least one instance when Agpaoa resorted to trickery. And, in a discussion with Henry Belk, Valentine was told that when Agpaoa's powers "go on vacation, he can't do anything, so he's dishonest about it and perpetrates a hoax." Valentine reported that Agpaoa, whose letterhead referred to him as "Pontifex Maximus," rarely charged fees but that the "donations" from foreigners sometimes exceeded one thousand dollars. Agpaoa's father had even gotten into the act, charging fifteen dollars for massage treatments with special attention given to female customers.

However, Valentine saw Agpaoa work on many healees who reported that they were "healed." Valentine also visited some of the less publicized "healers," such as José Mercado about whom he wrote:

> The most astonishing operations . . . I witnessed were performed . . . in the Pangasinan lowlands. The healer there was José Mercado . . . . It was in his crowded chapel that we encountered the curious phenomenon of "spiritual injection" . . . . Those who wanted injections lined up along a wall, and Mercado went to work . . . .
>
> My turn arrived, and my left shoulder was the target. Mercado, grinning from ear to ear, pointed his right

forefinger at my upper arm. There was nothing in his hand and nothing protruding from the tip of his finger, yet when he made a slight jerking motion with his hand, I felt a distinct needle jab. A tiny welt and a droplet of blood appeared on the spot.

The "injections" were part of the diagnostic procedure and preceded the "operations."

One of the authors (S. K.) has met a physicist from West Germany who claims to have lined up for the "injection," having placed four sheets of polyethylene foil under his shirt. After Mercado gave the physicist an "injection," a tiny amount of blood is said to have spurted from the sheets which then were reportedly found to have holes in the center. This would be an impressive experience as there had been witnesses to it, and because the polyethylene sheets had been examined microscopically. The physicist wrote that he was convinced that no needle had been injected and that there was no trickery. Unfortunately the physicist has refused to publish this account, but it does provide a worthwhile procedure for future experimenters.

One parapsychologist who has shared his experiences with a Filipino "healer" is Ian Stevenson. Writing in a 1976 issue of the *Journal of the American Society for Psychical Research*, Stevenson tells how the "kidney stones" removed by a "healer" from two healees proved to be pebbles once analyzed.

The Spiritists' Union

In 1974, one of the authors (S. K.) received an invitation to be the final speaker in the Caliraya Conference on Higher Consciousness and the Environment, sponsored by the Caliraya Management and Development Foundation in Manila. He was met at the airport by the director of the Foundation and Dr. Hiram Ramos whose experiences in a Japanese prison during World War II had given him such a keen appreciation of life that he could not rule out any "healing" modality that would alleviate human suffering. Krippner reported:

Our first stop was at 56 Dr. Pilapil Street in Pasig, the capital of Rizal province. This was the site of "Savior of the World," the local chapter of the Christian Spiritists' Union of the Philippines, an organization which for over fifty years has represented most of the nation's "psychic healers." Antonio Agpaoa represented a notable exception, having never joined the union.

We were greeted by Juan Blance and his assistant, Felipe Biton. Blance told us how he used to detest the Spiritists as did many members of the Roman Catholic church in his neighborhood who were told by the priests that Spiritists were involved in "the work of the devil." Indeed, Blance remembered throwing rocks at the Spiritists when he was a boy.

In 1957, Blance witnessed a serious crime and was afraid that he would be unjustly arrested for complicity. Terrified, he went to several people for help but they could offer him little in the way of advice or solace. Finally, he talked to a Spiritist who correctly predicted that he would be approached by the police to act as a witness to the crime, but would not be accused of complicity. In gratitude, Blance became a convert to Spiritism and about two months later, he successfully attempted "psychic healing." He told us that for four years he would enter an altered state of consciousness when he began "healing" and would not remember the experience at its conclusion. As the years went by, he still went into an altered state during "healing," but was now able to remember the events once the session was over.

Blance's assistant, Felipe Biton, discussed his own serious interest in "psychic healing" which went back four years to an incident in which a blind man recovered his sight after Biton prayed over him. He then began to

specialize in "magnetic healing," a procedure which resembled that used by many of the Spiritists I had visited in
Brazil.

As we entered Blance's center, I noticed a group of ailing
people sitting patiently in the waiting room. I learned that
the room doubles as a sanctuary for the Spiritist services
that are held there once a month. At these services, I was
told, an abundance of spontaneous cases of automatic writing, mediumship, and speaking-in-tongues had been observed.

Blance was somewhat upset that morning because of a
group of American tourists he reported seeing earlier in the
week. Upon arrival in the Philippines for the sole purpose
of seeing several "psychic healers" in reference to their
ailments, the tourists reportedly had checked in at a hotel.
After a few days of sightseeing and shopping, the "healers" arrived. As the "healing" ceremony progressed, it
became obvious that a great deal of legerdemain was involved. For example, a stack of damp towels was said to
have been placed on the stomach of a tourist. Soon, bloodlike fluid began to flow and intestinal-like tissue began to be
extracted. However, the "tissue" and "blood" appeared
to be coming from between the towels rather than from the
tourist's abdomen. Nevertheless, the tourists proceeded
with the "treatments" and a few felt somewhat better.
Those who felt no improvement talked to the local populace
and found out that the men who had "treated" them were
well known for fleecing ailing visitors from abroad. The
name of Juan Blance came up; reportedly, he was referred
to as an honest person and some of the Americans ended up
in his center.

The Americans were said to have left Manila by the time
I arrived, but I did have a chance to observe several "healing" sessions in the small treatment room which was separated from the sanctuary by a curtain.

The first healee was a middle-aged woman who complained of an indigestion problem. Blance asked her to lie

*down on a high, narrow table, baring her abdominal re-
gion. He rubbed some coconut oil on his right thumb. He
closed his eyes, as if in prayer, and pressed firmly on the
skin. Slowly, a pool of milky fluid appeared around the
woman's navel. While continuing the pressure with one
hand, Blance reached for a tablespoon with the other. As
he ladled the fluid into a bucket, we observed some thick,
foamy, light-colored material. Dr. Ramos told me that this
material had been analyzed by a Manila laboratory and
found to be pus in some cases and a sugary substance in
others.*

*Blance wiped the remaining fluid from the woman's ab-
domen with a towel. She then pointed to a mole which
protruded slightly from her neck, asking that it be removed.
Blance applied some coconut oil to it, then picked it off with
his hand. A tiny portion still remained, but this too was
removed with his second attempt. There were a few drops
of blood which Blance wiped off with a swab of cotton; a bit
of cotton was left on her neck to absorb any other blood
that might appear.*

*What was I to make of this? The removal of the mole did
not seem unusual, although it did seem a highly dangerous
procedure medically, in that it could have led to considerable pain, bleeding, and possible infection. As for the appearance of the milky pus-like fluid, this could have been
stored in a capsule or vial which Blance had hidden in his
palm and then broken. However, I looked in vain for the
remains of the container. Also, I had been watching
Blance's hands carefully, once he folded them in prayer.
From the prayer, the hands went to the woman's abdomen.
So if there had been a hidden capsule, Blance would have
needed to hold it during several different manual operations. Could a capsule have been hidden under the spoon?
Perhaps. However, the fluid had already appeared by the
time Blance reached for the spoon. Nevertheless, some of
the fluid could conceivably have been hidden in a capsule
taped to the spoon. This procedure would have necessi-*

tated the existence of two capsules large enough to contain
the three tablespoons of liquid which Blance eventually ladled into the bucket.

Blance's second healee was a young woman suffering
from asthma. Instead of spending much time on her nose,
Blance had the healee remove her blouse and lie down on
her stomach. After folding his hands and uttering a silent
prayer, Blance indicated, by gesture, that I should extend
the forefinger of my right hand. He then took my right
hand and aimed my forefinger at the woman's back. He
brought my finger to a point about six inches from the skin
just underneath the shoulder blade. Suddenly, he made an
abrupt motion with my forefinger, then released it.

I had not taken my eyes off the woman's skin as this
procedure was transpiring. I maintained my attention because I knew that Blance was reputedly able to cut skin at a
distance as part of a "purification" ritual. And I noticed a
slit on the woman's skin in the exact area beneath my finger
position. Within a few seconds, a thin ribbon of blood filled
this slit.

How was this phenomenon to be explained? Blance
could not have used his left hand physically to cut the skin
as it was clasping my right hand. Blance's right hand was
resting by his side. Just possibly, he could have concealed a
knife, razor blade, or piece of mica in his right hand, making the slit while I was distracted and looking elsewhere.
However, I knew only too well the distraction techniques of
magicians, and resolved not to let my eyes wander from the
woman's skin from the moment I approached the table and
gave Blance my hand.

Could the slit have been produced before this? Perhaps.
Blance could have slit the woman's skin before I approached the table. But if that had happened, why did I not
notice the scratch earlier? The slit was clearly visible just
as soon as the cutting motion had been made by my finger.
If the incision had been made earlier, why did the bleeding
not start until after my hand had completed making its

abrupt movement? The possibility does exist that Blance scratched the skin before I observed the process; if so, the timing would have had to be extremely precise so as to precede the flowing of blood.

Blance then proceeded to place a Filipino copper coin on the slit, tore a small piece of cotton from a roll, dipped it in alcohol, and lit the cotton with a match. He then placed a glass cup over everything. The skin quickly rose to fill half the cup because of the partial vacuum which had been created. There was profuse bleeding and the cup and cotton were removed.

Blance, at this point, dipped his thumb into coconut oil and proceeded to squeeze and press the skin around the incision. An irregular disclike piece of matter could be observed in the middle of the blood. It resembled melted wax, and I noticed there were specks of foreign material in the disc. Ramos told me that he had examined several of these discs, finding such material as blood, small pieces of bone, and sugar deposits.

Blance showed the disc to the healee, then dropped it in a basin of water. He told me that the process "purified" the body in some way. I had not known about the disc and did not expect it to appear; conceivably, Blance could have secretly placed it under the coin as he put the coin on the slit in the skin. This procedure was not repeated, so I had no chance to examine another disc more closely as to its appearance.

The third healee was a young girl, the palm of whose right hand was disfigured by a mole which was about the size of a quarter. Blance closed his eyes in prayer and asked the girl to pray as well. He then soaked a wad of cotton in alcohol. He lit the end of the cotton and, while it was still burning, pressed the cotton firmly onto the girl's palm. After Blance removed the cotton, it was apparent that the mole had puffed up slightly. Then Blance, with a pair of scissors, cut out the portion of the mole which had risen above the skin. He repeated the process so that the remainder of the mole could be cut away.

I asked the girl if the process had hurt her and she replied, "Not very much." Blance stated that, "When there is little pain, the 'healing power' is greater than if there is much pain." This incident, of course, could be adequately explained on the basis of what has been discovered in hypnosis research. If a patient is hypnotized, or spoken to reassuringly, the experience of pain is lessened considerably.

The remainder of Blance's cases, which I observed later that morning, involved procedures which could have been painful but which elicited very minor reactions from the healees. In no other case did Blance return to the procedure in which he appeared to cut the skin. Was this avoided to prevent me from observing more carefully and perhaps detecting trickery? Or was it that this procedure was needed for very few of Blance's healees?

From Blance's center, Krippner and his hosts drove to 63 St. Mary's Street. There they visited "Merciful Endeavors, Inc.," a conglomerate of "psychic healers" and Spiritist mediums affiliated with the Association of Psychic Healers, a small group operating outside of the Spiritists' Union due to policy disagreements. The leader of the group was Nemesio Taylo; Ben Bustamante was the other "healer" they observed, while Rosario Gerard, Cornelio Miranda, and Perla Ocampo worked as mediums and "magnetic healers." The healees in the room appeared to represent a wide spectrum of social and economic classes.

The treatment room contained three "operating tables" above which hung illuminated pictures of Christ and Mary. Another painting showed a dove above which had been written the words "Christ the Healer" and below which were printed the words, "The Spirit of Man Is the Candle of the Lord." Krippner reported:

As we came into the room, an elderly lady was brought forward by her relatives, none of whom she recognized. Taylo had her lie down on a table, and proceeded to bring his large diamond-chip ring to the tips of her toes and fingers. Every time Taylo did this, the woman would wince with pain. When he brought the ring close to her forehead, she grimaced horribly. "Possession," Taylo muttered, and went to work.

For about five minutes, Taylo massaged various parts of the old woman's body, moving her limbs upward and downward as he proceeded. He then uttered a silent prayer and brought his ring near to the woman's body parts again. This time she demonstrated no reaction. Instead, she smiled at her relatives and, as Taylo pointed to each one, she called out the correct name.

In the meantime, Miranda was praying over a woman on the table at the far left and Bustamante was rubbing a young man's stomach on the middle table. Suddenly, a thick strip of white fabric emerged, apparently from his navel. Bustamante kept massaging the abdominal region with one hand, while pulling out three additional strips of fabric with the other hand. When Bustamante finished, the young man's stomach pains had ceased; the stomach as well as Bustamante's hands were cleaned with alcohol and the next healee came up to the table.

This was a young woman who complained of backaches; again, Bustamante had her lie on her back as he poured a small amount of water on her stomach. Within seconds, his hands were rubbing the water around the woman's navel; a polyethylene strip appeared; it was about an inch wide and six inches long. This was followed by a second strip of approximately the same dimensions.

The phenomenon could have been the result of the fabric strips being "palmed," the way a clever magician "palms" an object later "produced" from thin air. However, I watched Bustamante's hands very closely between operations. When he washed his hands with alcohol, the fingers were spread widely apart. At no time did he touch his hands to the table or his pockets (where he might have had the polyethylene strips hidden). Instead, he moved directly to the next healee.

With people on every table in the center, I faced the same problem I had encountered at a three-ring circus in my youth: Which area should I concentrate upon? I directed my attention back to Taylo. He was now working with an adolescent suffering from a case of swollen testicles. After pouring some water over the abdominal area, Taylo motioned for some cotton. As his assistant was not immediately available, I reached for the box, handed him the cotton, and remained standing directly in front of the healee during the entire session.

As Taylo pressed firmly into the abdominal area, he again motioned for cotton and as I gave it to him, I leaned so far over the healee that I was only a few inches from the site. As Taylo took the cotton, I could see nothing in his hands. After he wiped some of the water from the boy's body, I could see nothing in either hand. Then, Taylo appeared to grasp a strip of material and began to pull it. The material was about five inches long; upon examination it seemed to be a band of elastic. The sides of the elastic were coated with clay. Indeed, small lumps of clay floated to the surface of the pool of water surrounding the healee's navel and dissolved into the water which dripped down the side of his body.

Taylo's hands never left the boy's body. Taylo did not reach under the table or into his pockets. Unexpectedly, another piece of elastic appeared and Taylo seemed to pull it from the small pool of water on the healee's abdomen. All this occurred while I was handing cotton to Taylo. I had a large enough piece of cotton in my hand so I could keep a constant watch on Taylo's fingers. He would take a small piece of cotton as it was needed and wipe the clay from the boy's side.

Taylo deposited the two strips of elastic in a wastebasket as well as the clay-encrusted pieces of cotton. He poured alcohol on the boy's abdomen, wiped it off with cotton, and massaged the entire area with his hands. He told the boy's mother that her son had been "hexed" but that the "hex" was now removed. Nevertheless, if the swelling of the testicles did not go down, then she should return with her son for an additional treatment. After the two of them left, he told me, "Of course, this was not necessarily a 'hex'; the ailment could have been the result of the boy's anger or of resentment that he was unable to express."

Taylo's next healee was a young woman whose neck was swollen from goiter. Again, I stood ready with the cotton, this time placing myself in a different position so I could see Taylo's hands from the side rather than from the front. Taylo asked for some cotton, placed it on the woman's throat, and it soon began to become discolored with a red fluid. Taylo poked a hole in the center of the cotton and I could see several small, dark red, solid objects which resembled blood clots. This piece of cotton was discarded, a fresh piece was substituted, and the same phenomenon occurred.

Finally, Taylo wiped the area with alcohol, placed a fresh piece of cotton on the woman's neck, bandaged it with a piece of cloth, prescribed a special type of herbal tea and compresses of coconut oil, and suggested she return in a week. I noticed there had been no change in the size of the swelling on the woman's neck.

The next healee was having domestic problems of a personal nature (centering around impotence). Taylo asked for a handwriting sample, looked at the man's palm, and began to discuss his problem, turning occasionally to the Bible to quote an appropriate passage. As this procedure appeared to be quite time-consuming, I walked over to the table where Ben Bustamante had begun to work with a young boy.

The healee was losing his hair and his mother mentioned that she had taken him for a medical examination including skull X-rays which were "inconclusive." Bustamante melted a small piece of wax with a flame, allowing the drops to fall into a bowl of water. Bustamante told the boy and his mother that the shape of the solidified wax would resemble the shape of the "spirits" who were causing the trouble. Within a few seconds, he retrieved three pieces of wax from the bowl, all of which had unique shapes—one vaguely resembling a bird, one a spider, and one a person. He gave these to the boy's mother, telling her to place them under the boy's pillow at night, and to burn incense in the room daily. Through Ramos, who spoke the Tagalog dialect and acted as my interpreter, Bustamante told me, "The shapes represent things the boy is afraid of and these procedures will help him to overcome the fears."

Bustamante then pulled up the boy's shirt, lowered his pants, and began to massage the abdominal area. A strip of bark from a palm tree appeared to emerge. It was nearly an inch thick and approximately eight inches long. It was also quite rough—not the type of item that could be easily folded and "palmed." Bustamante threw the bark into the garbage pail which already contained the white fabric and the polyethylene strips taken from the other healees.

It was time for us to leave the center, but our departure was delayed by our driver who looked as if he were about to faint. Although he had lived in the Philippines all his life, he had never seen the "healers," having been told that they were fraudulent. Dr. Ramos had the driver sit down and revived him through a brief session of deep breathing and guided relaxation.

Later that day, I reflected on my experiences and the several unusual phenomena I had witnessed. In one instance, I had seen a slit appear in the epidermis of a person's skin for no apparent reason, save the "healer's" moving of my finger at a distance of several inches above the healee's body. In other instances, I had seen various fluids, waxlike and puslike substances, fabrics, polyethylene strips, elastic, and palm tree bark appear when a "healer" rubbed a healee's abdominal area. The diagnostic aspects of the process were, no doubt, important for "healing" to take place but did not hold the possibility of being paranormal in nature. However, many of the "healing" phenomena themselves were either psychokinetic in nature or incredibly sophisticated sleight of hand effects.

"Palming" and Palm Leaves

When an investigator studies purported psychic phenomena in the field, more than one observation is advisable. Between observations, the researcher needs to check out the ways that he or she could have been deceived, could have misperceived events, or could have misinterpreted what was going on. In the case of the Filipino "healing clinics," Krippner returned to "Savior of the World" and "Merciful Endeavors" the following day, without notifying the "healers" in advance. He reported:

Blance appeared pleased to see us and allowed me to observe the work he did. There were very few healees who came to the center that morning. None of them received the treatment involving a slit in the skin and so I did not have an opportunity to observe that procedure again.

When we arrived at "Merciful Endeavors," we discovered that Ben Bustamante was present that morning but he was not working because he could not get in touch with the "spirits" and so their "powers" were not available. Bustamante told us that he simply relaxes on those occasions; he expressed disdain for the "healers" who use legerdemain when the "powers" are not present.

Taylo was seeing healees, however, and asked me to come up to his table. This time I checked the bottom and the sides of the table to be sure there were no objects secreted there which could be "palmed" and produced during the *"healing" ritual. I also inspected Taylo's Bible and the ever-present box of cotton, basin of water, and bottle of rubbing alcohol.*

Following a short religious service consisting mostly of hymn singing, Taylo was ready to begin his work. I stood directly in back of Taylo when his first healee, a middle-aged gardener complaining of chest pains, climbed to the table. After Taylo administered the test for "possession" with his ring and noticed the gardener wincing in pain, Taylo poured water over the man's abdomen and began to massage the area with his hands. Within a few minutes, I could see red rivulets seeping down the side of the man's body. Taylo then pulled some dark clot-like formations from the area around the man's navel.

Taylo wiped this material away with cotton, then applied the rubbing alcohol. As Taylo kneaded the skin, clay began to appear in the pool of alcohol surrounding the healee's navel. Suddenly Taylo pulled out a pebble encrusted with clay. This was followed by two more, then another one, until six pebbles had been placed in an empty basin. Taylo told the man that, in his gardening, he had disturbed the resting place of some "elemental spirits" who had given him the pain in revenge. Again, Taylo placed his ring near the tips of several fingers and toes as well as the man's forehead. This time no reaction was observed and Taylo concluded that the "possession" had ended.

Taylo's second healee was a young girl who I took to be mentally handicapped by her awkward movements and the lethargic look in her eyes. The girl's mother told Taylo that her daughter had never talked, whereupon Taylo touched her head, then held her throat. He asked the girl her name; she whispered, "Maria." Taylo asked, "Again?" And the girl proclaimed her name in a louder voice. The delighted mother took away her daughter while I recalled that in my days as a speech therapist in Virginia, I had heard of similar reactions when parents took their mute or stuttering

children to Oral Roberts or other evangelists. Unfortu-
nately, with these evangelists the positive effects rarely
lasted more than a few days.

The third healee was a man suffering from rheumatism
who gave his age as 83. He winced horribly as the
diamond-chip ring was placed near his extremities. As I
stood directly in front of the man, I could see Taylo pour
rubbing alcohol on the man's abdomen and place the bottle
back on an adjoining table. At no time did Taylo touch the
side or bottom of either table. I was able to see both sides
of his hands quite well. The light was excellent and there
were no shadows concealing what went on. As Taylo wore
a short-sleeved shirt, there was no chance of hidden objects
resting under his sleeves.

As Taylo massaged the man's abdomen, he lifted up the
brown tip of a palm leaf. He gave it to me and asked me to
pull. I could very clearly see that although Taylo's left hand
was also holding the leaf, it did not curve under his hand
but appeared to be coming from the healee's abdomen. I
stopped pulling for a second; the leaf kept emerging and
began to buckle. I pulled again and it was obvious to me
that the rate at which I was pulling the leaf had nothing to
do with the rate at which the leaf emerged. Once the base
of the leaf was in my hand, I held it from top to bottom,
estimating its length at 18 inches. The man passed the
"possession test," got up from the table, put a peso in the
donation box and went on his way. (I noticed that one peso,
less than 20 cents, was the average donation.)

Upon leaving "Merciful Endeavors," I picked a long
green palm leaf from a tree outside. I tried to roll it into a
small ball that would fit into my hand and the fiber showed
several creases. I did the same thing with a withered,
brown leaf resembling the one I had seen inside. Not only
did it crease, but it also began to tear. I took a palm leaf to
my hotel room and covered it with hand lotion. The leaf
rolled more easily but it still creased. However, there had

been no creases or tears in the leaf I had seen on Taylo's table.

Krippner's next stop was 2012 Retin Street in Manila, the home of Guillerno Tolentino, a noted sculptor often hailed as the "Michelangelo of the Philippines." Tolentino was sculpting a statue of a Filipino legislator when the group entered his home. Krippner reported:

He and his wife were delighted to hear of my contact with the "healers"; Tolentino told me of his several years of work as an officer in the Spiritists' Union and of his visits to dozens of "healing" centers.

The couple also showed me their collection of inspirational "messages," written in Tagalog on thin paper, and found embedded in pebbles and unopened nuts which purportedly "dropped out of the air" during sessions with a medium. My immediate reaction was one of disappointment that a scientist had not been present to collect several of these objects and take them to a laboratory for a complete inspection before they were opened.

Tolentino described Spiritism as a way of life, not a religion; thus, many Filipinos who are nominally Roman Catholic have experienced no conflict when visiting "psychic healers" despite the fact that the Archbishop of Manila, in 1964, stated that the "healers" "follow a doctrine . . . contrary to the teaching of the Holy Roman Catholic Church."

Tolentino had written his credo in a pamphlet titled, "Why I am a Spiritist." It read, in part: "God is my father. Nature is my mother. The universe is my way. . . . The mind is my house. Truth is my worship. Love is my law. . . . Conscience is my guide. Peace is my shelter. Experience is my school. . . . Joy is my hymn. . . ."

As Ramos and I left the Tolentinos' home, I was deeply impressed by their sincerity and the description of their efforts over the years to keep the Spiritists' Union free from charges of fraud. I knew that Tolentino and the union had been accused of forming a conspiracy to defraud sick foreigners. Yet these accusations remained unproved; in my own experience, I had observed no request for money made at either center I had visited. Indeed, I was told of cases where a "healer" had been dismissed from the Spiritists' Union for becoming excessively oriented toward collecting money.

Later that afternoon, Ramos and I drove to Caliraya where I began my seminar. For three days I spoke of our work in the Maimonides Medical Center dream laboratory, where we had conducted experiments involving psi processes and altered states of consciousness, and of the parapsychological research I had observed in Czechoslovakia, the Soviet Union, and Brazil. Inevitably, someone asked me for an explanation of the phenomena manifested by the Filipino "healers." I had been giving the matter considerable thought since my observations of Blance, Taylo, and Bustamante, so I offered a few ideas.

In the first place, I observed, there is not one phenomenon, there are several phenomena. On the various films I had seen in the United States, I often observed outright trickery. At "Merciful Endeavors," I had witnessed prayer and supportive counseling. At both centers, "magnetic passes" were utilized. All of these procedures, including legerdemain, could result in "healing" but were not necessarily paranormal in nature. Possibly paranormal, however, was the scratch made by Blance on human skin. I conjectured that if it was not due to trickery, this may have been the result of focusing bodily fields, "psychic energies," or a combination of the two, in the way that a magnifying glass focuses sunlight to produce a burned hole on paper.

What of the sudden appearance of material such as the red liquid, the waxlike substance, and the brown palm leaf?

Did not this suggest some sort of "materialization" that would violate the laws in physics of conservation of matter? Not necessarily. Each of the items I saw was a common one. If their appearance was not due to sleight of hand, why could they not have been "teleported" from a nearby butcher shop (in the case of the red liquid), church candle (in the case of the solidified wax), or tree (in the case of the palm leaf)? I then reminded the group of the Soviet theories concerning a "bioplasmic body." Perhaps this was the matrix for the "teleportation." An item could simply vanish from one spot and travel through the healee's "bioplasmic body," extended by the action of the "healer" several feet or several miles into space.

I further suggested that the "bioplasmic body" may interact with the person's acupuncture points and meridians, found by the Soviet researchers to be areas of high electrical conductivity. This might explain why Taylo's healees winced in pain when the ring made from diamond chips was brought near to their acupuncture points. It could have been the case that either their bodily fields or "psychic energies" or both were out of balance.

Tom Valentine, in his book, had quoted Dr. Motoyama regarding Juan Blance's scratching of the skin from a distance: "He accomplished a depletion at a viscera-cutaneous reflex point, which is a kind of treatment often done in acupuncture." Therefore, I was not the first one to see a connection between the Philippine "healing" process and acupuncture. Nor was I the first to suspect some sort of "teleportation" as a mechanism; Dr. Lee Sannella, of the Academy of Parapsychology and Medicine, reached a similar opinion following his visit to the Philippines earlier in 1974, as did G.W. Meek after an earlier visit.

In addition to the "healers'" ability to affect their healees' "bioplasmic bodies," I observed considerable knowledge of "healing" itself; if one believes that a certain procedure will help one get well, that person is already on the road to recovery. The Filipino "healers" appeared to speak in terms of their healees' belief systems, especially in regard to "spirits," even though Bustamante and Taylo had made side remarks to me that were more understandable in terms of a traditional Western belief system.

For example, Blance's healees suffered from a number of ailments which usually have strong psychosomatic components: indigestion, asthma, and respiration difficulties. Even warts, which Blance was often called upon to remove, have been known to disappear through hypnosis. Perhaps all that some of the healees needed from Blance was assurance, through his attempts at psychokinesis, that he had "healing power." Thus they allowed their own "self-healing" capacities to begin functioning. In the reported "healing" of infants and animals, this explanation would not suffice by itself. However, I suspected that "self-healing" was a very important part of the Philippine phenomena.

Shrewd application of psychological principles also played a part. I remembered the old woman who, upon coming into "Merciful Endeavors," could not identify her relatives. Her memory returned after Taylo massaged her limbs, and after her relatives paid her some attention, perhaps after years of ignoring her.

Harold Sherman had written, in *"Wonder" Healers of the Philippines,* that the "psychic surgeon" often "makes incisions, does whatever surgery is required, and then closes the openings he has made in the bodies. . . ." Further, Sherman quoted Henry Belk as stating, in reference to Agpaoa:

> He will begin to knead this part of the flesh as though he is mixing dough. The next thing you know, blood begins to come out. . . . The flesh rolls back. He sloshes around with the guts. . . . When he locates the tumor, *bam,* out it

comes, still no knife! Then he sloshes around again and. . . , instantaneously, *bam,* the stomach is healed back up. . . .

The Filipino "healers," such as Juan Blance, who could not produce this "opening" and "closing" effect were considered, by implication, inferior to Agpaoa. For example, Sherman quoted his associate, Nelson Decker, a chiropractor, as reporting:

> Blance just held his finger about eight to ten inches above this woman's body, and moved it horizontally through the air and her body opened up. . . . Blance can open this way, but he can't close. He has to let nature help out when he brings the flesh together again. Some "psychic healers" can do one thing, some another.

Krippner, on the other hand never saw an "opening" of the body with the exception of the small slit produced once by Blance. He noted:

Even if this phenomenon does occur, I would not rate it as being any more "advanced" than the procedures I observed. In fact, the "opening" may not be in the physical body at all, but in the "bioplasmic body," allowing the viewer to see the bioplasmic counterparts of the physical organs. A change in the "bioplasmic body" might well affect a change in the physical body; therefore, this procedure could be extremely useful in certain cases.

If, indeed, the physical body is "opened," Harold Sherman has given a possible explanation of this occurrence. The hypothesis states that cell structures can be separated and then reunited by the electromagnetic power of the "healer."

Another theory has been discussed by G L. Playfair in

The Unknown Power. Playfair, who based his ideas on the "biological organizing models" (or BOM) proposed by Hernani Andrade, has written:

> Psychic surgeons act as intermediaries or mediums for a force unknown to man but apparently known to certain plants and animals, which enables diseased tissues to heal themselves. They operate on human beings by merely bringing the force to them, often visibly disrupting the cell structure in the process, though this may not be necessary and is done for the patient's benefit. The so-called healing is effected by the biological organizing model that has programmed our bodies and has been attached to us ever since our embryonic bodies were animated by a living . . . psi component or spirit. In order to explain what they do to the general public, psychic surgeons find it convenient to give credit for their powers to discarnate spirits, which they sincerely believe to be responsible for their skills. Psychic surgeons discover their abilities by a combination of accident and good intentions, and are able to link up with the four-dimensional BOM by purely non-physical methods which have not yet been established. . . .
>
> A drastically simplified version of this hypothesis can be compared to the experiment . . . where you put iron filings on a piece of paper and place a magnet underneath, so that the filings instantly jump into place according to the shape of the magnet's field. Now, if you put another magnet over the filings, reversing the polarity so that north is opposite south and vice versa, you will break up the field and the filings will be free to move around. Take the second magnet away again, and they jump back into place at once.
>
> In psychic surgery, the lower magnet is the BOM, the iron filings are the molecules of the human body cells, and the top magnet is the medium's hand, causing what we might call an anti-biomagnetic field. The psychic surgeon does not really do anything except just be there, serving as a disrupting influence on the bodily cell structure. The body itself, with its built-in BOM, does the rest.

It can be seen that there are any number of theories to explain "psychic surgery." It is also apparent that the term "psychic surgery" is a poor one to describe what is transpiring. Even if any given phenomenon is paranormal in nature, it is not "surgery" in the conventional sense of the term. It would be better to speak of a "psychic intervention"; in this way, these phenomena could be explored in their own right.

Princess Orduha

Krippner was giving additional thought to these issues as he and Ramos drove to Baguio City in their final foray with the Philippine's Spiritist "healers." Krippner reported:

Ramos and I had driven to Baguio City to see Antonio Agpaoa's "healing" center, "Dominican Hill." However, we were informed that the center, largely financed by West German funds, was in legal difficulty and that a lawsuit had already been served against Agpaoa's wife. Clearly, this was not the best time to visit "Dominican Hill." Instead, we drove to the small hamlet of Villasis in the province of Pangasinan. Dr. Fox, the anthropologist, had told me that more of the Filipino "healers" were from this province than from any other. The most recommended of the Pangasinanian "healers" was Josephina Sison.

Leaving the main highway, we drove a few miles down a dirt road to the home of Josephina Sison, her husband, and her two children. We entered the small concrete chapel which served as the "Orduha" branch of the Spiritists' Union, and Sison appeared. Because of heavy rains the usual flood of healees had not yet arrived, so we had a chance to visit and ask questions.

Born on All-Saints' Day in 1941, Sison told me that she

had her first visitation with "spirits" when she was 13 years of age. She recalled, "My parents thought that I was crazy," but at the age of 22 Sison began her "holy work" or "psychic healing." She remarked that she was guided to move in this direction by the "Holy Spirit" which manifests itself in the form of St. Michael, the archangel. "Sometimes," she recalled, "St. Michael takes me on a white horse to other planets. And he gives me precious stones which are very beautiful but which don't last very long."

Sison and her husband have had two children. St. Michael told her that she would need to have a physican's help for the delivery of her first child. So Sison went to the hospital and it developed that a Caesarean birth was necessary. When she again found herself pregnant, Sison was told by the physicians she should have another Caesarean. St. Michael told her otherwise and she had her baby by natural childbirth. Then she decided that she wanted no more children and St. Michael instituted a "spiritual birth control program" for her. Since that time, she has had sexual intercourse but no children, merely by praying to her patron before making love.

When I asked her about the "healing" process itself, she said, "There is much about it I do not understand." However, she was of the opinion that the blood which appears during her work "carries disease out of the body" and that often she removes foreign materials from the body that "have been placed there by witchcraft." I asked if any people have come for "healing" who are skeptical about her ability; Sison replied, "It is easier to 'heal' if they believe, but if they are doubters I swallow my pride and 'heal' them anyway."

As I looked around the center, I noticed a sign stating, "God does the work and I am only his instrument; please pray," and another, "This is our chapel; please keep her clean." On a banner, the name of the center had been sewn. Sison told me that St. Michael himself had suggested "Orduha" as the name of her center; I discovered later

Stanley Krippner with Josephina Sison. (Courtesy S. Krippner.)

Inside of Sison's healing chapel showing her banner as well as a sign saying, "God does the work and I am only HIS instrument. Please pray." (Courtesy S. Krippner.)

that Orduha was the name of a legendary princess who, according to Islamic tradition, lived in the Far East. Attached to the banner were pieces of paper bearing names of healees being treated in other countries and in distant parts of the Philippines.

Sison told me that she would like very much to go to a foreign country but that St. Michael has advised against it. He has let her accept invitations to appear in Manila but only if the "healing" is done inside a sanctuary. One time, Sison had been asked to demonstrate in Manila along with three other "healers." At the last minute, St. Michael warned against it—and with good cause. The other three "healers" were later reported to have been discredited when sleight of hand was observed during their demonstrations.

I observed two tables, one wooden and one plastic. Sison told me that the plastic table was brought from the United States by the Academy of Parapsychology and Medicine early in 1974 when several of their members filmed her at work. The transparent property of the plastic would have disclosed any hidden objects. Sison said, "At first the table gave off a strange vibration, but then I performed a ritual of consecration and found that I could work quite well with it."

Sison noted that she could do her "holy work" for hours without becoming fatigued. However, heavy manual work in the garden would sometimes exhaust her and St. Michael would tell her to rest or the labor might diminish her "healing" ability. She has disobeyed St. Michael when overly eager to finish a task of manual labor only to be stung by an insect, bitten by an animal, or cut by a garden implement in a self-inflicted accident. Sison admitted that sometimes she disobeys on purpose, "just to test St. Michael and make sure he still knows what he is talking about; after all, sometimes I have a hard time believing all of this myself!"

Sison agreed to perform a "psychic intervention" on Krippner.* He then was invited to observe the subsequent "healings." Krippner reported:

I stood by Sison's table as an elderly man was placed on his back. He was blind in both eyes. As Sison rubbed the right eye, red fluid poured down the side of his face. She repeated the procedure with his left eye then thrust a wad of oil soaked cotton in his left ear. As she poked it in his ear, it appeared to disappear completely. Moving her hands, she seemed to pull a wad of cotton from his right ear. The cotton had the same shape and size as the wad which had apparently entered the left ear; the oil could not be seen and there were red streaks on the cotton. Sison predicted that sight would begin to return to his left eye in three weeks.

Another healee was a young man complaining of a stomach problem. As he bared his abdomen, I could see a gastrectomy scar. Sison rubbed his abdomen until the red fluid appeared, then had him turn over. She appeared to poke cotton into a carefully selected spot on the man's back until it disappeared. After a short period of time, she seemed to withdraw it from a point on the opposite side of his back.

By this time, several more healees had arrived. Their names were written down by Sison's brother, Romeo Escandor, along with their complaints. Escandor called out each name in turn, as well as the stated ailment. He told me that his sister only did a complex diagnosis if the healee did not know what was wrong, or if there was a suspicion of witchcraft being responsible for the disease.

The next name to be called was that of an elderly man who complained of a chronic cough. Sison had him lie down on his stomach and moved her hands toward his

---

*This episode is described in Chapter One.

neck. Almost immediately, the red fluid flowed down his head; in this case it was thicker and darker than what I had previously observed. She then moved to the left shoulder blade, and then the right; the dark red fluid flowed copiously in both cases. She then went to his left and right heels; there was so much of the fluid in evidence that it stained the cuffs of the man's trousers. However, there never seemed to be as much red fluid on the cotton–or the healee's clothes–as I observed on the body before it was wiped away.*

Sison then reached for the cotton and discovered the box was empty. Her brother used a towel to wipe up the red fluid, and Sison called her father who said he would drive the horse cart to Villasis and buy another supply.

While waiting for the cotton, I asked Sison about her treatment of opiate addiction and alcoholism. She told me that she uses the cotton technique to "clean the blood," but that at least three visits are necessary. For alcoholism, she has prescribed a special herbal tea. Sison mentioned that she had frequently used herbs in her work and gave me a bundle of twigs from the Zepa rosebush which she recommended as a healthful tonic to prevent disease.

As it appeared that we might run into rain if we waited too long, we decided to leave Sison's center. She told us that sometimes St. Michael predicts rain. On one occasion, she was about to irrigate the garden, but St. Michael told her that rain was imminent. By the end of two days, Sison had nearly lost her patience–and then the rains started. As

---

*This phenomenon was also noted by Mary Jane Ledyard, a psychologist whose visit to Sison was mentioned in Chapter One. After obtaining the permission of the healee, Dr. Ledyard placed her right index finger on the healee's body, right in the middle of some red fluid. She told one of the authors (S. K.) that as she brought her finger to her face to smell and taste the fluid, it seemed to disappear. Dr. Ledyard attempted this procedure a second time; again the fluid appeared to vanish from the fingertip. If this account is accurate, it could substantiate the notion that the fluid is "teleported." It could also indicate that the red fluid is produced by legerdemain and contains a high percentage of ether—a substance which would make most of the colored fluid appear to evaporate.

our car left the dirt road we saw Sison's father driving his horse cart, smiling, and holding a box of cotton.

Could Sison's effects have been the result of legerdemain? For this position to be defended, one would have to conjecture that small capsules of red fluid had been "palmed" by Sison before she touched a healee's skin. But I saw no empty capsules anywhere in the building.

Another possibility would have been that the coconut oil which she used contained one chemical. A second chemical could have been placed in the water she used to rinse her hands. When these two chemicals combined, the red fluid could have been produced. However, sometimes Sison did not use the coconut oil. Sometimes she did not rinse her hands. Yet the red fluid invariably appeared.

The cotton phenomenon would also be difficult to ascribe to sleight of hand as I was observing the session in good light, standing quite close to the "healer" and healee.

The only other alternative explanation to the Filipino phenomena would have been an enlistment of several Filipino "stooges" who came to the three centers I visited with objects already hidden on their bodies, or flesh-colored tape (or a thin overlay of animal skin) from which objects could be removed or suddenly appear. Why anyone would have wanted to go to the expense of hoaxing me is a question for which I found no sensible answer. But whatever validity this conjecture might have is destroyed by the fact that I was a participant in a session myself and with no plastic coating over my abdomen.

However, if Sison's phenomena were genuine, how would they fit into the hypothesis I outlined at Caliraya? The red bloodlike liquid could have been "teleported" from a dye factory, painting shop, hospital, or butcher shop. But the disappearing cotton needed to be explained somewhat differently. One could conjecture that the cotton may have entered the "bioplasmic body," at one point and emerged from the "bioplasmic body" at another point.

A Psychic Placebo Effect

Whether or not Josephina Sison and the Spiritist "healers"
of the Philippines employ paranormal skills, they still de-
serve attention. If none of their visitors found relief from
pain and illness, they would not have the constant stream of
healees that they do. Krippner concluded:

*The paranormal phenomena involved in the Spiritists' ses-
sions may be only indirectly involved with the "healing"
itself. It is my suspicion that much of the "healing" that
occurs is "self-healing," inspired by the "healer's"
pyrotechnical displays. Therefore, medicine could learn a
great deal from what was going on in the Spiritists' centers,
even if they remained skeptical about the psychic nature of
the incidents themselves. I guessed that even fraudulent
"healers" could bring about "healing" in much the same
way that a physician administers a sugar pill when the patient's complaint appears to be psychosomatic. In other
words, the "placebo effect," which accounts for a sizeable
proportion of "cures" in Western medicine, may also apply
to both psychic and pseudopsychic "healing."*

*Lessons applicable to psychotherapy also emerged from
a number of specific practices that I observed. Taylo had
spoken to an ailing boy's mother of a "hex," but had told
us that the young man's swollen testicles could have been
the result of anger or resentment "that he was unable to
express." This may have been a case of "psychic healing"
which also involved the emotions; it would have been interesting to follow up the case to see if the swelling of the
boy's testicles went down as he began to deal with his feelings more directly.*

*While at "Merciful Endeavors," I also observed Bus-
tamante at work with a young boy who was losing hair. As
medical treatment had been ineffective, and as skull X-rays
had been inconclusive, one could certainly posit a psycho-*

somatic reason for his disturbance. Bustamante dropped melted candle wax into a bowl of water, telling the boy and his mother that the shapes of the solidified wax would resemble the "spirits" who were causing his trouble. Once the three blobs of wax had solidified, Bustamante told the mother that they should be placed under the boy's pillow at night and that incense should be burned during the day. In an aside to me, Bustamante noted that the shapes "represented things the boy is afraid of" and that his advice, if taken, would "help him overcome his fears."

I interpreted the waxen shapes as serving a projective function similar to that of Rorschach inkblots. The act of placing them under his pillow would force the boy to confront his fears; the burning of incense would force him to attend to this task by day either consciously or unconsciously. Thus, a resolution of his fears was entirely possible through these procedures; once his fears were worked through, his hair might even start to grow back.

Psychology is another field which could benefit from studying the Filipino phenomena, whether or not any paranormal phenomena are found to occur. Why does each "healer" engage in slightly different procedures? The explanation might rest in the "healer's" psychodynamics and personal history. Blance, for example, had a record of violence in his personal history which included throwing rocks at the Spiritists when he was a boy. Perhaps this aggression was sublimated in his purported "laser beam" scratch which did destroy some tissue but to the healee's greater benefit. One of the authors (S. K.) made some further suggestions:

In the case of Sison, cotton and a bloodlike substance appeared to be the trademarks of her "healing" procedures. On a hunch, I asked her when she began to menstruate, and she recalled the age as 16. Ramos told me that the average Filipino girl begins to menstruate at the age of 12. Sison, it will be recalled, first came into contact with the "spirit world" when she was 13. Perhaps she unconsciously postponed menstruation, directing her attention to Spiritism instead. Once she did begin to menstruate, the blood and cotton associated with menstruation became integrated into a larger belief system, fully manifesting themselves when she began to see healees at the age of 22.

Although I did not know enough about Bustamante's and Taylo's earlier lives to conjecture how their psychodynamics related to their "healing" processes, there were several correspondences between their healees' histories and the foreign objects which seemed to surface at "Merciful Endeavors." In the case of a gardener, it was pebbles and clay that emerged. In the case of an 83-year-old man, a withered brown palm leaf appeared. Perhaps the presumptively "teleported" objects related to the psychodynamics of the healee, the "healer," or both.

Sociology could benefit from a study of the Filipino phenomena. I agreed with Dr. Fox that the "healers" were clever social psychologists. I could see that uneasy interpersonal relations and even community stresses could be alleviated by the "healing" process which might well restore an equilibrium.

As for anthropology, the investigation of "healing" in the remote areas would be worthwhile, covering an area typically omitted in much scientific research. For example, anthropology books which discuss native "healing" in the Philippines never mention the "psychic healers." Nevertheless, many of the investigative techniques in these books could be used in anthropological field studies of the "healers" living in remote areas. Fox's assertion that the "healing" ceremonies date back at least 2,000 years deserves investigation.

For the suggested scientific investigations to proceed properly, some misconceptions would have to be laid aside. For example, I was warned that the "healers" would be wary of a scientist and would not deviate from their set patterns on behalf of scientific research. On the contrary. I found that I could inspect anything in the room, stand as close to the healee as I liked, make any simple requests, and even assist in the procedures, thus affording me a closer look.

I had also been told that the Filipinos were too modest to allow much of their skin to be exposed; hence it would be difficult to check for trickery. However, the "healers" I observed removed much more clothing from the healees than did the "healers" in the films I had seen previously. It was not unusual for a woman to be completely nude from the waist up. When the removal of this much clothing was required, the healees could request that a cloth be held between her and the other people in the room, a request I only observed on one occasion. Exposure of the pubic area was more unusual, for both men and women, but it was often necessary to pull down the pants or skirt to expose as much of the abdominal area as possible.

Another misconception involves the impression that no adequately trained scientists, physicians, or magicians have felt the Filipino phenomena to be genuine. While in Manila, I was given a long list of professional people who had visited the "healers." It is true that many of them observed blatant examples of fraud and chicanery. However, a number of "healers" including those I observed had elicited bewilderment from some magicians who admitted they could see no sign of trickery.

Special attention must be paid to the comments by Rogo and Bayless in the British Society of Psychical Research journal. Both persons are extremely astute observers whose statements need to be taken seriously. As their comments were directed only to one of the Filipino "healers," they do not necessarily apply to the "healers" I witnessed. For example, Rogo and Bayless wrote of a "hidden sponge" and tissue wrapped around a finger; I observed neither of these attempts at subterfuge, having had a chance to inspect the process very closely. Rogo and Bayless talked of the tendency to choose "obese" persons for the "operations"—a procedure that I did not observe. As for the animal tissue and insect pupa emerging from the healee, neither item characterized my observations. The presence of pebbles, palm leaves, etc., if not due to trickery, could be explained in terms of "teleportation." Thus, the Rogo and Bayless letter contains several excellent points, but their critique misses the mark when directed toward the "healers" with whom I had contact.

Among the experiments I suggested were one in which a radioactive isotope would be placed in the cotton; in that way, its path could be traced once it appeared to leave Sison's hand. Or a drop of vegetable dye could be placed on the cotton to assure that the piece appearing to "go in" was the same as the piece appearing to "come out." Yes, the entire series of phenomena could have been tricks. If so, they were the cleverest examples of legerdemain I had ever witnessed. Therefore, even on that ground they deserved to be studied by professional magicians!

How to be a "Psychic Surgeon"

It is critically important that any investigator planning to observe "psychic surgery" have some knowledge of sleight of hand. For any serious research to take place, it would be important for the team of investigators to include a magician. In his book, *Mediums, Mystics and the Occult*, the well-known magician, Milbourne Christopher, tells of a trick he learned as a boy:

> With a sharp knife I slashed my left thumb, just below the knuckle, from side to side. The bloody cut extended almost an inch. Rubbing the wound with the fingertips of my right hand, I then healed the incision in seconds, or so it appeared.
>
> Actually, I made only a small nick on the left side of my thumb. As I seemed to cut across the skin, I forced a drop of blood up through the nick and spread it with the end of

the knife along the deepest wrinkle from left to right. This thin crimson line looked exactly like an open wound. I "healed" it by wiping away the blood with the secretly moistened fingertips of my right hand.

There are additional techniques* which individuals can learn if they want to become a "psychic surgeon" the easy way:

1. Hold two small cellophane bags in the palms of your hands, one containing chicken blood and the other pure ether. You slap the hand with blood in it onto the patient's stomach, making a terrible mess, and start prodding away with your fingers, perhaps even making a "cut" beforehand with a knife so as to leave a red line on the skin. Then, when you have finished "operating," you burst the ether bag in your other hand and mop up the blood, most of which will appear to evaporate, helped perhaps by your assistant's casual dabs with damp cotton wool.

2. A simpler procedure is to claim that you are only going to operate on the "perispirit." Then all you have to do is to wave your hands in the air above the body, manipulate invisible scissors, knives, and other implements, muttering instructions to your unseen helpers.

3. Following either procedure, write out a prescription for your patient. Write it out for anything you like, preferably something totally harmless! Assure your patient that the "spirits" will slip something into the prescription to make it work better. You will find that some of the sick people you see will actually improve.

4. If the patient does not get better and returns to complain, you can always consult the "spirits" and reply, "Your problem is one of Karma. In your past incarnation you were a prison guard in Siberia, and before that you were one of the assistants who threw Christians to

---

*Some of these appear in *The Unknown Power* by G. L. Playfair.

the lions in Rome. Before that you were a mass mur-
derer in Atlantis, and in the Mesolithic Age you were a
child rapist. In this lifetime, you have been given a great
chance to pay off all your past debts at once. Next
patient please."

5. Above all, would-be "psychic surgeons" must remember the cardinal rules of conjuring: do not tell your
audiences what you are going to do, and never try the
same trick twice on the same evening. Only perform at
night, in poor light. If a serious investigator shows up,
announce that the "spirits" are taking the evening off
and do likewise yourself.

There are many opportunities for sleight of hand in
"psychic surgery." And many "healers" see nothing
wrong with using it either infrequently or constantly.
Ronald Rose, observing an Australian aboriginal shaman,
noticed he used sleight of hand. When queried by Rose as
to why he did this, the shaman replied, "Because it
works." In the shamanic tradition, legerdemain is often
utilized. Furthermore, many of the adults in the tribe
realize that trickery is being used. However, they are not
upset but accept it as part of the ritual.

Many tourists who seek help from a "psychic surgeon"
in another culture display an inordinate amount of interest
in whether or not the "magic" is real. This is a legitimate
question for the parapsychologist. But for a healee, this
attitude may obstruct the "healing" process. Alan Watts,
in *Psychotherapy East and West*, speaks to this issue:

> It has been said that the good doctor is one who keeps the
> patient amused while nature works the cure. This is not
> always true, but is a sound general principle. It is easier to
> wait for a natural change when one is given the impression
> that something is being done to bring it about. What is being
> done is the trick; the relaxed and rested waiting is the actual
> cure, but the anxiety which attends a disease makes direct
> and deliberate relaxation almost impossible.

Furthermore, in *The Natural Mind*, Andrew Weil describes the role of witch doctors in tribal societies as that of inducing an altered state of consciousness which replaces the anxiety of those in some form of distress. Anxiety can be seen to be as much of an obstruction to "healing" as any infectious substance remaining in a physical wound.

It is just barely possible that a "psychic surgeon" removes diseased tissue during a psychic intervention. This could be determined by the use of before-and-after X-rays and biopsies, signed by the examining physician and notarized. But it is more likely that the "healer" is attempting to stimulate "self-healing" by strengthening the healee's belief system and, in Watts' words, keeping "the patient amused while nature works the cure."

A related question raised by some healees concerns the state of the "healer's" health. If a "healer" is observed to be ill, the query is made, "How can someone who is sick pretend to be able to cure other people?" Milbourne Christopher, for example, discussed the purported "psychic dentistry" of the Reverend Willard Fuller who supposedly treats cavities by paranormal methods. However, Christopher wrote that he "lost interest in holy dentistry when I learned that Willard Fuller . . . wears a set of dentures."

As a matter of fact, in the shamanic tradition the "healing" of other people is often seen as part of a process of "self-healing." The psychologist W. E. Henry has written that the shaman "would appear to be one who has found a *cure*, via personal experiences in socially specialized routes," a personal solution that makes manageable and useful his or her personal distress.

Shamans and other "healers" sometimes appear to be ill much of the time, but it is from these illnesses that they supposedly learn how to treat others. Rolling Thunder has stated that he is best able to cure a disease if he has had it—or a similar ailment—first. And during a prayer service, one of Rolling Thunder's young sons brashly said, "I pray that my father will be able to cure all sicknesses known to our people." Rolling Thunder was horrified because he knew that, if this prayer was answered, he would be sick much of the time.

Observation Before Experimentation

There is no more controversial area in parapsychology than that of "psychic surgery." Many psychical researchers do not take it seriously at all. Others suspect there might be something to it, but that it should neither be discussed nor investigated because the fraud involved in the phenomena is sure to sully the reputation of the investigators and discredit the field. A few parapsychologists, on the other hand, feel that much current research in the field is trivial and redundant, but that the science of parapsychology is now advanced and sophisticated enough to tackle even the most complex processes.

The authors have collected a number of observations of "psychic surgeons" in action and have proposed both theories and experiments to help parapsychologists plan research strategies. The cited observations are from skeptics, believers, and others who simply wrote down what they recalled. One cannot make a definitive judgment about "psychic surgery" on the basis of observations alone. However, sound advice was presented in *The Psychology of Science*, by A. H. Maslow. He stated that observation should precede experimentation in the social sciences, despite the fact that most psychology students are "taught to use the controlled experiment as the model way of acquiring knowledge." Maslow wrote:

> Slowly and painfully we psychologists have had to learn to become good clinical or naturalistic observers, to wait and watch and listen patiently, to keep our hands off, to refrain from being too active and brusque, too interfering and controlling, and to keep our mouths shut and our eyes and ears wide open.

This is different from the model way in which we approach physical objects, i.e., manipulating them, poking at them . . . , taking them apart, etc. If you do this to human beings, you *won't* get to know them . . . . Our interfering makes knowledge less likely, at least at the beginning. Only when we already know a great deal can we become more active, more probing, more demanding—in a word, more experimental.

Chapter Seven

How "Healing" Happens

When scientists confront a new item of knowledge, they check it out against the paradigms they share with their colleagues. These paradigms are beliefs and concepts that solve puzzles posed by new bits of data. If, someday, a puzzle comes along which cannot be solved by the prevailing paradigms, scientists have a choice. They can ignore the new piece of information, they can deny that it exists, or they can wait until additional information is available. If, eventually, new information keeps coming into the picture that challenges the paradigms, it is obvious that the old paradigms must be discarded or modified and that a new paradigm must be provided.

The laboratory and clinical data that have been gathered on "psychic healing" are becoming more widely known. Traditional Western science has no paradigm that would solve the puzzle posed by many of the claims and reports from "healers" and healees. Most scientists simply ignore the data. Others reject it, stating that all the reports they have heard about are due to fraud, wishful thinking, coincidence, or the placebo effects and psychosomatic processes which are well known occurrences in medicine.

Some scientists, however, have suspended judgment and are waiting for more information to accumulate. These scientists have observed that something undoubtedly happens in "psychic healing" and are not so sure that they can explain all of the phenomena with traditional paradigms.

Of course there are a few scientists who have accepted the reality of "psychic healing" as well as radically new paradigms that would explain it. However, the authors of this book would urge a more cautious approach at this time, given the very preliminary nature of the laboratory experiments in this field as well as the poor documentation that accompanies almost all of the dramatic clinical reports they have examined.

Orthodox Assumptions

The scientific paradigms that have emerged in the last few centuries reflect a mechanistic interpretation of nature that negates the role of consciousness in cause-and-effect relationships. To some extent, these paradigms were reactions to religious doctrines which insisted that all scientific discoveries adhere to the paradigms set down by Christian theologians. Unfortunately for the church, several scientific discoveries could not be explained by the old paradigms; data supporting the idea that the earth rotated around the sun violated the geocentric paradigm that the earth was the center of the solar system. Eventually, a heliocentric paradigm emerged, placing the sun at the solar system's center. Gradually, the church lost its credibility and most Western scientists began to express skepticism regarding anything that seemed to involve consciousness, the "spirit," or the paranormal.

Mechanistic paradigms about the nature of the universe have acquired, for many scientists, the same dogmatic status which once characterized the paradigms set forth by church theologians. These paradigms reflect a world-view which, in many respects, is in sharp contrast to certain aspects of the world-views held by most "psychic healers." One might say that "psychic healers" operate under their own set of paradigms and that when a "psychic healer"confronts an orthodox Western scientist there is a "paradigm clash" resembling those described by Thomas Kuhn in his book, *Structure of Scientific Revolutions.*

For example, the orthodox Western scientist assumes that the universe was created accidentally and that there is no "purpose" for its existence. The universe is basically "dead"; life is an infinitesimal, insignificant part of the universe.

"Psychic healers," on the other hand, typically see the universe as a "living" entity created by some sort of deity or "higher consciousness." The universe itself is seen as having a "purpose"—that of evolving toward a higher level of "consciousness." Rolling Thunder, for instance, speaks of the "spirits" he communicates with in rocks and rivers, as well as in plants and animals. The Brazilian and Filipino Spiritists argue that "spirits" are everywhere and that their presence permeates the universe.

Another aspect of orthodox scientific paradigms is that anything that is "real" can be perceived by the senses or by a physical instrument which assists the senses. "Psychic healers," on the other hand, often speak of "spirits" which most people cannot see and which are not detectable through contemporary technology. Further, such "healers" as doña Pachita, Rolling Thunder, Fausto Valle, Olga Worrall, and the Brazilian Spiritists often depend on the healee's "aura" to give them clues in regard to diagnosis. These rays of "light" which purportedly surround a living object cannot be seen by most other people and cannot be detected by any known physical instrument.* The "healers" maintain that "non-physical" things—such as the

*Although many questions remain unresolved concerning Kirlian photography, no serious investigator supports the notion that the corona seen on electrophotographs coincides with the so-called human "aura."

"aura"—are just as "real" as physical things; their "reality" is not to be judged by whether or not they can be perceived by other people or detected by a physical instrument.

Another assumption underlying mechanistic paradigms is that people are their physical bodies and nothing more. Most of the "healers," on the other hand, speak of "nonphysical," "spirit," or "etheric" bodies. These "nonphysical" bodies provide the vehicle for the "out-of-body" experiences reported by shamans. They are "treated" in Spiritist "healing ceremonies" because, it is held, what happens to the "spirit" body is reflected in what happens to the "physical" body. The Brazilian medium dona Regina claimed she was able to bring sick peoples' "spirit" bodies to "healing" séances, then reunite them with their physical bodies.

Most Western scientists also make the assumption that each person starts life "fresh," except for limitations set by his or her genetic inheritance and environment. However, Hernani Andrade, doña Pachita, Rolling Thunder, Fausto Valle, and Josef Zezulka all speak of previous incarnations. They would hold that a person starts life with an inheritance, both favorable and unfavorable, from his or her experiences in previous lives. Thus, individuals often "choose" which parents to have in order to fulfill some mission or purpose in their current incarnations.

Orthodox Western science holds that all events are ultimately reducible to lawful interactions of matter and energy. Psychological energy is completely derived from physical energy, as expressed in the body's physiological processes. One may modify the efficiency of energy metabolism within the body by drugs and diet, but there are definite limits to what a human being can attain, these limits being not too far above the ordinary. "Psychic healers," on the other hand, admit to the importance of food intake as being an essential source of energy for human beings; many of them stress diet in their work with healees and a few of them occasionally use mind-altering drugs as part of their own self-development.

But the "healers" claim that there are other types of "energy" which can be tapped; Rolling Thunder, Olga Worrall, and Josef Zezulka pay special attention to these "life energies" and their manipulation by the "psychic healer." It is held that these "life energies," if turned off, would cause disease or death; it is their presence which keeps human beings alive and in good health.

The mechanistic world-view assumes that death is the inevitable end of human life. Medical science may postpone death, but it will catch up with everyone eventually. "Psychic healers," of course, generally believe in the immortality of the "spirit." Olga Worrall is not attracted to the idea of reincarnation, as are many other "healers," but still conceives of a life which transcends physical death. In addition, the esoteric tradition maintains that a few individuals have been able to attain life spans of hundreds of years by practicing certain rituals and by consciously controlling life processes.

Orthodox Western science sees consciousness as something produced by nervous system activity. Many scientists do not like to use the word "consciousness"; those who do, typically see it as dependent upon physical activity. This leads to the further assumption that human beings are ultimately alone in the world since consciousness is a function of nervous system activity and the nervous systems are not connected. "Psychic healers," on the other hand, typically treat the brain and other parts of the nervous system as "instruments" of consciousness—something which is just as "real" as its physical "instruments." As a result, all human consciousness is connected; people are not alone but are linked together in ways that become apparent during telepathic experiences as well as in "psychic healing."*

---

*These assumptions of orthodox Western science, as well as several others, are developed by Charles T. Tart in his book, *Transpersonal Psychologies*.

The Importance of Replication

In the face of this "paradigm clash," what is someone to do who has both an interest in "psychic healing" and a respect for the scientific method? The simplest courses of action would be either to accept the world-view of the "healers," abandoning mechanistic science, or to support current scientific paradigms and dismiss the evidence that something really happens in at least some instances of "psychic healing." In so doing, either a basically "psychic" model of the universe will be accepted or one that is basically "physical."

The authors of this book would like to propose a third path—one which is more difficult, but one which would subject the assumptions of both the Western scientist and the "psychic healer" to scientific scrutiny. Psychic and physical models would both be considered, but so would psychological models which often are ignored by extremists of the opposing world-views. This process would use methods that would be acceptable to most members of the scientific community, but would also take seriously the claims made by "psychic healers" and investigate them with open minds, keeping in mind William Wordsworth's warning:

> Sweet is the lore which Nature brings;
> Our meddling intellect
> Mis-shapes the beauteous forms of things
> We murder to dissect.

Scientific method is based upon four principles: accurate observation, the repeatable nature of observation, the necessity to therorize logically, and the testing of theory against predicted, observable consequences.

There is certainly a need for accurate observation in "paranormal healing" research. Bernard Grad has worked with seeds and wounded mice, M. Justa Smith with damaged enzymes, Dolores Krieger with human hemoglobin, Douglas Dean with hydrogen bonding in water, Graham and Anita Watkins with anesthetized mice, and Joyce Goodrich with the reactions of healees to "healers" working at a distance. In addition, some preliminary work has been done with Kirlian photography, gashed leaves, and cloud chambers. However, each investigation has studied "psychic healing" from a different vantage point. "Psychic healing" research can only move to the level of repeatable observations when a variety of investigators repeat the work that the pioneers have started.

Replication by outside experimenters is necessary for a variety of reasons. The most obvious is that of fraud. In 1973, W. J. Levy, Jr., was named director of the Institute for Parapsychology, a division of the Foundation for Research on the Nature of Man. Levy had made his mark in the field by testing the psychokinetic ability of rats. In one of his experiments, for example, Levy had implanted electrodes in the brains of rats in a zone where stimulation gave the rats intense pleasure. The rats were stimulated at random intervals by a computer. Ordinarily, the computer would stimulate the rats' pleasure zones 50 per cent of the time. If the rats could influence the computer by PK to deviate from randomness, their pleasure score would exceed 50 per cent.

Early in 1974, Levy had reported a significant 54 per cent pleasure score. Then one of Levy's assistants became suspicious, noticing Levy loitering needlessly about the equipment. With two colleagues, the assistant decided to check his intuition. From a hiding place, one of them observed while the others helped Levy run a test. The observer saw Levy tamper with a recorder, causing the scores to run above 50 per cent. Another set of instruments had been installed without Levy's knowledge—and recorded the expected 50 per cent score. The three assistants reported the situation; Levy was confronted with the evidence and resigned.

A second reason for replication is that of unconscious experimenter bias. This bias is sometimes called the "Rosenthal effect" because Robert Rosenthal, a psychologist, has conducted many experiments which demonstrated that the expectations of the experimenter often influence the outcomes of an experiment. For example, Rosenthal once trained assistant experimenters to administer subjects a picture-rating test. This involved a series of photographs, originally selected to be quite neutral in terms of how "successful-looking" the persons appeared who were on the photographs. Subjects were asked to rate how successful each subject looked on a 20-point rating scale. The training of all assistant experimenters was identical except that for one group of them, Rosenthal offhandedly remarked that subjects generally scored about 15 on the rating scale. The assistant experimenters never said anything explicitly like this to the subjects; they administered identical, written instructions that they read to all the subjects. But the assistant experimenters who had been biased were more likely to have subjects whose scores conformed to that bias than did the other experimenters. One does not have to explain these results in terms of telepathy; it is likely that the experimenters gave non-verbal clues—such as gestures and smiles—to influence the subjects' behavior. However, in "psychic healing" research, experimenters also could unconsciously allow their bias to influence test results. Replication by other experimenters is one way to counter this possibility.*

A third reason why replication studies are needed centers around the issue of an observation's accuracy. There are many experimenters who are honest and unbiased whose

---

*Possible experimenter effects have also been explored in psi experiments. One of them, designed by Charles Honorton, involved 36 subjects, half of whom were assigned to an experimenter who had a friendly discussion with them before the psi task began. The other subjects were oriented toward the ESP test by the experimenter in an unfriendly way. The subjects experiencing the friendly interaction with the experimenter scored significantly better than those whose interaction was abrupt and formal.

work cannot be trusted because they are careless. In a "psychic healing" experiment, it would be easy to mix up the experimental water with the control water, to miscount the number of seeds which have sprouted, to make an error when adding the number of healees who have responded to treatment, or to use statistics which are not appropriate to evaluate certain types of data. Further, a careless experimenter who also suffers from bias can harm the development of "psychic healing" research by reporting results which are not valid and which do not "fit in" with other experimental studies. Eventually, it will be observed that no one else can repeat that particular study and its significance will diminish. In the meantime, however, confusion results which will slow up the development of the field.

Clinical studies of "psychic healers" are also needed. If a "healer" is alleged to have "cured" a "spiritual malaise," no adequate study can be made because instruments are not available to measure "spiritual illnesses." There are psychological tests to evaluate changes at the psychological level, although these are hardly as precise as those which exist to measure physical changes.

Ideally, a potential healee should have adequate documentation of his or her ailment before seeing a "healer." This documentation, for example, could be a series of X-rays, a biopsy report, or a neurological examination. Preferably, the documentation should be notarized so that there is no doubt as to date and examiner. Following the "healing," an identical set of documents should be obtained and notarized. There may still be disagreement as to whether the observed change was due to psychic intervention rather than to physical or psychological mechanisms, but at least there would be no reasonable doubt that a broken bone had mended, a tumor had disappeared, or a hearing loss had vanished.

Again replication is important. These documents conceivably could be produced by fraud. Just possibly a technician who knew the purpose of the examination could produce distorted information due to bias. Once again, human error could result in spurious data. But if a set of standard procedures were used for documentation purposes by several researchers and if similar information were forthcoming, any charges of trickery, bias, and carelessness would be taken less seriously.

Theory Building

In the physical sciences, one can expect replicability of results most of the time. Mixing two elements together should always produce the same compound, a liquid should have the identical boiling point whenever heat is applied, and conductive material should transmit similar amounts of electricity if the conditions are standardized. In the behavioral sciences, however, more variables come into play. Even simple experiments on animal learning rates will not produce identical results each time they are conducted; the strain of the animal species used may differ, the animals' diet may have changed, the time of year and the physical environment may be factors, not to mention the varied personalities of the experimenters themselves.

Parapsychologists conduct experiments that probably involve more variables than have even been identified. Therefore it is unlikely that an ESP or PK experiment, in the near future at least, will be repeatable each time it is attempted. A former president of the Parapsychological Association, K. Ramakrishna Rao, has sadly concluded that "there are far too many variables influencing the subject's ESP performance to be adequately dealt with by the experimenter." J. G. Pratt, another psychical researcher, has conjectured that psi might represent "an area of nature in which nonpredictability and nonrepeatability are the rule." A third parapsychologist, Emilio Servadio, has stated that attempts to circumscribe psi within one's customary reality "could be compared to the efforts of a natural scientist who should want by hook or by crook" to study fish only be taking them systematically out of the water, to establish the "reality" of fish within the boundaries of a world without water.

In the meantime, parapsychologists are pleased if an experimental design *usually* produces significant results. Gertrude Schmeidler and her associates have found that individuals who "believe" in ESP make higher scores in ESP experiments than skeptical subjects. These results have been duplicated by some—but not all—of the experimenters who have replicated the studies. Experiments conducted at Maimonides Medical Center in Brooklyn indicated that sleeping subjects were able to incorporate, in their dreams, pictures concentrated upon by a person in a distant room. When other researchers attempted to do similar studies the results were usually—but not always—statistically significant. These are examples of some of the most productive lines of research in parapsychology. Even these do not warrant the description of "repeatable," and the "psychic healing" experiments are in a far less reputable position.

Furthermore, those observers who fail to see any evidence of psi in "psychic healing" generally agree that something happens to a healee at least some of the time. In *Healing: A Doctor in Search of a Miracle*, William A. Nolen has concluded that he could not find a single case of a "miraculous" cure. Nevertheless, he admitted that

> . . . half the patients who go to the office of a general practitioner have diseases or complaints that are self-limited, e.g., the common cold. No matter what anyone does for these people, they are going to get better. So the healers are going to achieve at least a 50 per cent cure rate, even if they do nothing. Add to that 50 per cent those patients whom the healers cure of functional disabilities—tension headaches, for example—and they are going to achieve an overall cure rate of 70 per cent. We may as well admit this; it's a fact.

In other words, we need theories to explain how "healing" happens even if it eventually turns out that psi plays a limited role—or no part at all—in the process. These theories should be open-ended enough so that they can be adapted to "psychic healing" phenomena if they ever reach the level of repeatable observations.

The Physical Model

Theories cannot explain "psychic healing" adequately unless they are multidimensional. They must integrate material emerging from both physical and psychological models of "healing" and leave room for the psychic model as well.

From the vantage point of a physical model, we can inspect the role played by the human nervous system in "healing." Neurologists divide it into the "voluntary" and the "autonomic" nervous systems. The voluntary nervous system is composed of the spinal cord, most of the brain, and the nerves which run from the spinal cord to the arm, leg, facial, and abdominal muscles—all those areas where muscle movement is ordinarily under voluntary control. Voluntary acts such as speaking, walking, and writing, depend upon messages which pass from the brain along the spinal cord to the appropriate muscles. If these messages are interrupted by an injury or a disease, voluntary control over one or more of these functions is lost. Brain damage, an injured spinal cord, or a severed nerve will hamper the voluntary nervous system's ability to function.

The autonomic nervous system includes some small portions of the brain and a network of nerves usually subdivided into the sympathetic and parasympathetic systems. The sympathetic system may cause a blood vessel to contract, the parasympathetic system may cause it to relax. The sympathetic system is often activated by threats, emergencies, or other emotionally-toned incidents while the parasympathetic system is more active when the environment is safe, non-threatening, and peaceful. Under ordinary circumstances, people have little control over the autonomic system; few people can dilate or contract the pupils of their eyes, increase or decrease their heart rates, or alter the functioning of their sweat glands, their digestive system, and the temperature control system of their body.

Dysfunctions of the voluntary nervous system bring about many obvious symptoms, usually reflected in faulty or uncoordinated muscle movement. But dysfunctions of the autonomic nervous system can also cause problems. Asthma, duodenal ulcers, colitis, constipation, impotence, high blood pressure, irregular heartbeats, many types of headaches, skin rashes, and menstrual disorders are wholly or partially caused by a poorly functioning autonomic nervous system.

Anxiety and tension are often involved in autonomic nervous system malfunctioning. Therefore, a physician might prescribe sedative drugs. If the damage has already been done—as in the case of an ulcer which has perforated the wall of the duodenum—surgery may be necessary. The proclivity of many Western physicians to rely on "the pill and the knife" stems from the frequency with which the autonomic nervous system is involved with disease.

Using a physical model alone, how would the effects of "psychic healing" on the autonomic nervous system be explained? There are several ways that most "psychic healing" sessions could alleviate tension and anxiety, either on a short-term or long-term basis:

1. The healee is usually in a relaxed position during the "healing" session. For some active healees, the session represents one of the rare occasions during which they are physically relaxed. Stress is absent, allowing the autonomic nervous system to function in an improved manner, at least for a short period. Meditation may help to de-stress people in much the same way. The authors of the best-selling book *TM* claim that the success of transcendental meditation lies in "creating psychological and physiological conditions which op-

timize the natural tendency of the nervous system to stabilize itself."

2. Frequently, a "laying-on" of hands will be an indispensible part of the "healing" session. Body contact is rarely used in Western medicine, but the Nigerian *babalawo* and the Mexican *curandero* massage the healee's body extensively and, in Bali, the *balian* devotes half of the "healing" session to rubbing medicinal oils into the body. Body contact is an integral part of the Umbanda "healing" ceremonies in Brazil and the "laying-on" of hands practiced by such intuitive "healers" as Olga Worrall and Josef Zezulka sometimes lasts for several minutes. All of these practices allow for bodily relaxation to replace tension and anxiety.

3. The "healer" will often prescribe physical activities that induce relaxation. A frequent comment made by "healers" is, "Do not leave right now; sit quietly and allow the 'healing powers' to permeate your body." Doña Pachita had beds in her quarters where healees could rest following a "healing" session; Rolling Thunder often sent his healees to bed following a session, claiming they would sometimes sleep around the clock.

4. "Psychic healers" frequently prescribe medicinal herbs for their healees; sometimes these substances have sedative qualities that enhance relaxation. Rauwolfia root has been used by "healers" in India and West Africa for centuries as a tranquilizer. The Nigerian *babalawo* often uses it to produce prolonged sleep for the healee. Other drugs used by "healers" in primitive societies include kava-kava and marijuana. In Yemen, the *mori* often uses opium to treat depression. Not all the substances used are sedatives; the *nele* of Panama's San Blas Islands uses a drug which pro-

duces convulsions. Several Andean tribes have a tradition of using psychedelic cacti to encourage healees to express their inner thoughts, under the guidance of a shaman. The emergence of repressed material often has salutary effect upon the healee's health. Outsiders often criticize "healers" for using these substances but E. M. Schimmel reported a study in the *Annals of Internal Medicine* in which he had surveyed about 1,000 patients in an American medical center. Some 20 per cent of the patients suffered from complications, usually due to drugs. Over half of these complications were rated moderately severe or very severe; in 16 cases they caused or contributed to the patient's death. It is doubtful that "healers" have a higher casualty rate than found in that particular hospital!

The autonomic nervous system, of course, is not the only portion of a person's physiology that plays an important part in the maintenance of health. One's biochemical status is also vital to well-being, especially the hormones secreted by the endocrine glands and the collection of internal processes often referred to as the body's "immunological system." This bodily system involves the production (and circulation) of lymphocytes and blood antibodies as well as the regulation of histamine, cortisone, and epinephrin in the body. Studies with rats reported by Robert Ader and Nicholas Cohen in 1975 have demonstrated that it is possible to train responses of the immunological system to respond to external stimulation.* It is theoretically possible, therefore, that something in the behavior of a "psychic

---

*In a 1976 issue of *Science* Marvin Stein and his associates reviewed research data which led them to conclude, "It has been shown experimentally that psychosocial processes influence the susceptibility to some infections . . . and to some aspects of humoral and cell-mediated immune responses . . . . Various processes may participate, including the autonomic nervous system and neuroendocrine activity."

healer" could enhance the functioning of the body's antibodies as well as increasing production of the chemicals that ward off disease and suppressing those that make one vulnerable to illness. If the voice, touch, or manner of a "healer" has this effect, it would be possible to use this variable in the further treatment of that healee and others with whom the same link might be created. Experiments could be designed in which blood chemistry is examined before, during, and after "healing" to determine the optimal time for the intervention of a "psychic healer."

Jack Schwarz' reputation as a "psychic sensitive" with remarkable control over his immunological and autonomic systems brought him to the attention of Elmer and Alyce Green at the Menninger Foundation. Under laboratory conditions, Schwarz stuck an unsterilized six-inch knitting needle through his biceps. There was no bleeding, no subsequent infection, and the wound began healing visibly within minutes after the needle was withdrawn. Schwarz stated that this feat and others were accomplished by taking a detached attitude toward the pain and by using visualization—picturing himself as being whole and well in the "mind's eye." Green and Green's report on Schwarz read, in part, "He has highly developed control of his body functions. Other people can also learn to control these functions and thus be relatively free of disease." It is thus quite likely that any number of "cures" attributed to "psychic healers" are due to individuals temporarily developing some of the abilities which characterize such people as Schwarz.

In *The Well Body Book*, Mike Samuels and Hal Bennett stress the importance of self-healing. They note, "The things your body does to heal a simple cut are so complex that only the most advanced medical scientists are beginning to understand them." Albert Szent-Györgyi, in *Electronic Biology and Cancer,* notes, "If I cut myself, my life is in danger as long as the wound stays open. The cut makes my cells proliferate, fill the gap, and heal the wound. My cells form a system which is activated by the cut, and corrects the damage. This reflects the basic principle of defense. The damage is made to correct itself by activating a dormant mechanism . . . . The question is: How was this system kept in an inactive state before it was activated by the cut, when the damage had to be corrected?" The answers to questions of this nature will be important in the search for the role that "psychic healing" may play in accelerating the body's self-repairing mechanisms.

Another area of interest to observers operating with physical models of "healing" would be the allegation that some sort of "energy" is involved in the process. This "energy" has defied measurement, but there are ways in which the phenomenon can be explained in some instances:

1. Sometimes a "healer" will do a ritualistic dance before "laying hands" on a healee. This gives the "healer" an opportunity to build up an electrostatic charge, if the surface of the floor is made from appropriate material. As soon as the "healer" touches the healee, a mild shock is experienced which is often interpreted as "energy." Perhaps some "healers," because of unique properties of their skin electricity, are better able than others to facilitate this electrostatic effect. In fact, when government officials in the U.S.S.R. organized a commission to study the "psychic healer" Alexei Krivorotov, electrical discharges were sometimes observed coming from his hands as he touched a healee. This often correlated with the healee's experiences of "warmth" and "energy." The commission eventually concluded that Krivorotov was often successful, and he was later called upon to treat government officials and scientists.

2. Mexican *curanderos* often surprise the healees by throwing water in their faces during a "healing"

session. This produces a mild shock often interpreted as "energy." Other "healers" produce
similar results by slapping a healee or using
frightening masks or incantations. Still others are
able to produce sensations of "warmth" when
they touch a healee because of unique properties
of their blood circulation. In addition, the "healer"
may stimulate acupuncture points that in some way
produce an experience of "energy."

3. Electric eels and catfish have been used by "healers" in primitive cultures. The Navaho Indians
use a sweat-bath; Rolling Thunder often precedes
a "healing" session with a trip to the sweat lodge,
and steam is used by the *alfa* in Sierra Leone. All
of these procedures are likely to produce bodily
sensations easily interpreted as "energy."

One of America's most celebrated "psychic sensitives,"
Edgar Cayce, gained renown and stimulated controversy
for his attempts at paranormal diagnosis of disease. Once
Cayce had closed his eyes and entered an altered state of
consciousness, he would be given the name and location of
a subject. Within a few minutes, Cayce would give a detailed diagnosis of the ailment and suggest a treatment. One
physician, Wesley Ketchum, gave Cayce 180 names and, in
1910, announced the results before a meeting of the Boston
Clinical Research Society. Ketchum reported that Cayce
had made only two errors in diagnosis.*

Cayce's suggested treatment procedures emphasized
herbs and diet. He remarked "Healing is allowing the life
force to flow through, and its action is to stimulate and
arouse each cell of the body to its proper activities." He
also spoke of "body energies" and in some cases suggested
running a weak electric current through the body to aug-

---

*An excellent resource book for material on Cayce is Thomas Sugrue's *There
is a River*. Additional information may be obtained from the Association for
Research and Enlightenment, P.O. Box 595, Virginia Beach, Virginia 23451.

ment these "energies." Several years later, Robert O. Becker and his associates at the Veterans Administration Hospital in Syracuse, New York, began to apply electricity to broken bones. Becker found that when bones were unable to heal properly, stimulating them with an electrical current often assisted the body's own self-repair mechanisms, some of which are basically electrical in nature.

Some "psychic healers" take credit for cures which would have occurred anyway. For example, Becker has described three types of ways in which bone and tissue heal:

1. Scarring, in which cells produce scar tissue that binds together the edges of the injured tissue. In human beings, the heart, skeletal muscle, and nerve tissue including the brain heal by scarring.

2. Tissue replacement, in which the cells of some tissues produce more of their own kind to replace missing portions. In humans, this process heals skin and part of the gastrointestinal tract.

3. Regeneration, in which a single tissue or a complex multi-tissue portion of the body is restored. The salamander can regenerate an amputated leg, but in the human being only bone heals by regeneration. The control and self-repair systems that regulate healing become less efficient as animals proceed up the evolutionary scale.

Becker has used electricity to regenerate an amputated frog's leg, something a frog cannot do under ordinary circumstances. It is his conviction that eventually procedures utilizing electric current will be discovered to regenerate limbs and organs in human beings. If so, this will demonstrate that primitive "healers" and "psychic sensitives" who used electricity to stimulate "body energies" were using concepts that correlated with a contemporary physical model of the "healing" process.

The Psychological Model

Most observers who use a psychological model to explain "psychic healing" would accept everything offered by proponents of the physical model. However, they would point out that an understanding of the healee's motivations and needs, as well as the "healer"-healee relationship, can explain many more "healing" phenomena than can the physical model by itself.

The personal qualities of a "psychic healer" may play a role in the healee's response regardless of what procedure is used for "healing." Positive statements concerning Andrade, Pachita, Rolling Thunder, Sison, Valle, Worrall, and Zezulka were frequently made by healees interviewed by the authors. If the "healer" possesses personal qualities that in themselves are more therapeutic than those characterizing the healee's physician, a chronic ailment might respond—especially if it is psychosomatic. The research with psychotherapists, pioneered by Carl Rogers, an eminent psychologist, demonstrates that "accurate empathy, nonpossessive warmth, and genuineness" are of crucial importance in producing effective psychotherapy. These traits appear to be more important than the specific techniques used by the therapists or than the type of training they have had. Rogers has commented, "Intellectual training and the acquiring of information has, I believe, many valuable results—but becoming a therapist is not one of those results."

It also seems to be important for the "healer" and healee—or the physician and the patient—to share a similar world-view. The anthropologist, Claude Lévi-Strauss, has noted that the very process of naming an ailment is an important factor in its amelioration. The use of words as symbols for what is wrong is effective not only because of the knowledge that the words convey but, according to Lévi-Strauss, "because this knowledge makes possible a specific experience, in the course of which conflicts materialize in an order and on a level permitting their free development

and leading to their resolution.'' When a physician names
what is wrong, the patient realizes that someone understands and that there is a way to get well. And in discussing
the process by which mental illness was handled by a shaman he observed, Lévi-Strauss wrote:

> The shaman provides the sick woman with a *language* by
> means of which unexpressed, and otherwise inexpressible,
> psychic states can be immediately expressed. And it is the
> transition to this verbal expression . . . which induces the
> release of the psychological process, that is, the reorganiza-
> tion in a favorable direction of the process to which the sick
> woman is subjected.

On the other hand, a psychiatrist who tells an illiterate African warrior that his phobia is related to oral deprivation in
infancy or a witch doctor who tells an American tourist that
her phobia is related to possession by an ancestral "spirit,"
will probably be met by equally blank stares. This may be
one reason why tourists who show an initial improvement
following psychic intervention by doña Pachita or the
Filipino Spiritists sometimes regress when they return to
their homes; their temporary acceptance of the "healer's"
belief system falls apart under scrutiny by their relatives
and neighbors—and so do the benefits they attained.

Patient expectation is another important variable in
"healing" and is strengthened by the "healers'" personal
attributes and their culturally determined "healing role."
The efficacy of physicians as well as of "healers" is based,
in part, on their ability to mobilize the hope of sick people
and raise their expectations of getting well. In *Persuasion
and Healing*, Jerome D. Frank concluded, "The apparent
success of healing methods based on all sorts of ideologies
and methods, compels the conclusion that the healing
power of faith resides in the patient's state of mind, not in
the validity of its object." Studies of placebos provide
further evidence for the importance of patient expectations;
some of the prescriptions (crocodile dung, swine teeth, etc.)
given to healees by "healers" over the years have no

known medical value but they often worked because people expected them to work. And sometimes voodoo ceremonies practiced by the outlawed Brazilian Quimbanda sect and other groups around the world often result in the death of victims who seriously believe that they have received a fatal "hex."

E. F. Torrey has discussed the psychological components of "healing" in his book, *The Mind Game: Witchdoctors and Psychiatrists*. He has cited evidence that witch doctors obtain about the same therapeutic results that psychiatrists do, observing:

> A witchdoctor who does not share a world-view with his patient, does not have personal qualities deemed therapeutic in his culture, cannot raise patient expectations, or has no command over therapeutic techniques will be equally as ineffective as a psychiatrist with similar inadequacies.

Stressing similar factors as those cited by Torrey, Jerome D. Frank has used the Roman Catholic shrine at Lourdes to demonstrate the important aspects of psychological components in "healing." When Bernadette Soubirous reported her famous visions in the 1850s, nothing was said to her about the "healing powers" that would eventually be attributed to the shrine she founded and to the spring waters which she located by following the instructions purportedly given to her by the apparition of the Virgin Mary. Nevertheless, over two million pilgrims visit Lourdes every year, many of whom yearn for a "healing." Frank has observed:

> The world-view supporting Lourdes, like those on which religious healing in primitive tribes is based, is all-inclusive and is shared by almost all the pilgrims to the shrine. While cures are regarded as validating it, failures cannot shake it. Those who seek help at Lourdes have usually been sick a long time and have failed to respond to medical remedies. Like the primitives who undergo a healing ritual, most are close to despair.

The decision to make the pilgrimage to Lourdes changes all this. Collecting funds for the journey, arranging for medical examinations, and making the travel plans requires the cooperative effort of members of the pilgrim's family and the wider community. Prayers are offered for the sick person; often pilgrims from many communities will travel together and conduct religious ceremonies en route. Frank has noted:

> It is interesting in this connection that, except for the original cures, Lourdes has failed to heal those who live in its vicinity. This suggests that the emotional excitement connected with this preparatory period and journey to the shrine may be essential for healing to occur.

Upon arriving in Lourdes, the pilgrim's expectation of help is further strengthened; accounts of previous cures are on every tongue and the ailing person sees the piles of discarded crutches of those who have been healed. Frank continues:

> Thus the ritual may be said to begin with a validation of the shrine's power, analogous to the shaman's review of his cures in primitive healing rites . . . . The pilgrims' days are filled with religious services and trips to the Grotto, where they are immersed in the ice-cold spring . . . . The great majority of the sick do not experience a cure. However, most of the pilgrims seem to derive some psychological benefit from the experience. Like participation in healing rituals in primitive societies, the pilgrimage is regarded as conferring merit in itself . . . . Therefore, the words attributed to an old pilgrim may be very largely true: "Of the uncured none despair. All go away filled with hope and a new feeling of strength. The trip to Lourdes is never made in vain."

In the first century of the shrine's existence, less than a hundred cures passed the stringent tests leading the Roman Catholic Church to declare them "miraculous." And in a study of the eleven "cures" pronounced "miraculous" at

Lourdes between 1946 and 1956, the psychiatrist and parapsychologist D. J. West concluded that although the "cures" themselves were well-documented, a lack of adequate medical investigation made a complete appraisal of most of the cases impossible. Jerome D. Frank has noted that the processes by which "cures at Lourdes occur do not seem to differ in kind from those involved in ordinary healing, although they appear to be strengthened and accelerated."

> Careful reading of the reports reveals that healing is not instantaneous, as is often claimed, but that, like normal healing, it requires time. It is true that the consciousness of cure is often (not always) sudden and may be accompanied by immediate improvement in function—the paralyzed walk, the blind see, and those who had been unable to retain food suddenly regain their appetites. But actual tissue healing takes hours, days, or weeks, and persons who have lost much weight require the usual time to regain it, as would be expected if healing occurred by the usual processes. Moreover, gaps of specialized tissues such as skin are not restored but are filled by scar formation as in normal healing. No one has regrown an amputated limb at Lourdes.

Frank's comments not only describe the psychological components of "healing" but illuminate how these components can facilitate "healing" as described from a physical model. The immersion in the Grotto's cold water may produce a mild shock which could stimulate "healing." The scarring and tissue replacement mechanisms may be enhanced by the healee's expectations, as well as minor bone regeneration. However, no limb has regenerated at Lourdes, which is what one would expect from the scientific study of the human body's self-repair systems and their limitations.

In re-examining the voluntary nervous system, the autonomic nervous system, and the immunological system, all of which are critically important in maintaining and restoring health, one can see further examples of the interface between physical and psychological factors.*

1. The voluntary nervous system's functions have been enhanced by psychologists and other therapists working with a variety of body movement exercises. Such voluntary functions as walking, speaking, and writing have been restored or improved among some individuals whose cases were considered "hopeless" by traditional medical examiners. These individuals, both children and adults, had suffered strokes, infectious disease, or accidents resulting in severe damage to the brain, spinal cord, or nerves. Among the originators of these body movement exercises (many of which differ greatly from each other) have been F. M. Alexander, Jean Ayres, Gertrude Enelow, Moshe Feldenkrais, and Ida Rolf. The Rolf method, for example, is a deep, intensive massage which purports to use the force of gravity to restructure the body. Dr. Rolf claims that the basic structural change following several weeks of this treatment can change the chemistry of the body. Apparently, it can also improve functioning in some individuals with damage to the voluntary nervous system. Similar results are sometimes obtained from the other programs of body exercise as well, many of which involve breathing coordination, visualization, and relaxation techniques. By combining psychological and physical activities, the voluntary nervous system can be affected in ways similar to those claimed by some "psychic healers."

2. The autonomic nervous system has been found to be more responsive to voluntary control than most

*Even though these examples will be discussed under three headings, there is considerable overlap and the categories are not mutually exclusive.

psychologists once conceived. The claims made by yogis of controlling their heart rate and skin temperature have been verified by biofeedback training. Biofeedback is a process by which a particular bodily response is "fed back" to a person electronically. For example, an individual suffering from headaches could have electrodes attached to the muscles which often are tense during headaches. During a training session, that individual would watch a screen, when a red light goes on, the muscles are tense. The individual's task, then, is to become aware of the internal feeling that keeps the red light off. Once this internal feeling has been detected, many people are able to shift into that feeling state when a headache begins; in so doing, they can often stop the headache before it starts. Sometimes a sound is used instead of a light. Among the autonomic nervous system functions which have been altered by biofeedback training are heart rate, blood flow, skin temperature, brain waves, and various obstacles to relaxation. Two of the pioneers in biofeedback research, Elmer and Alyce Green, have stated, "one of the most interesting and potentially useful areas is control of the autonomic nervous system, through which most psychosomatic (mind-body) diseases are developed. Physicians believe that from 50 to 80 per cent of human diseases are psychosomatic, that is, they result from the body's unconscious reaction to psychological stress. Thus, it is possible, in theory, to train patients to control 50 to 80 per cent of their diseases, to handle other psychosomatic problems, and, hopefully, to decrease their dependence on drugs." For individuals who object to the machines used in biofeedback training there are the alternatives of yoga, meditation, and a sophisticated procedure developed by J. H.

Schultz and Wolfgang Luthe called "autogenic training" which provides a step-by-step approach to controlling autonomic functions. Again, these procedures can produce similar results to those claimed by many "psychic healers."

3. The immunological system is directly related to recovery from many diseases, especially those said to respond to "psychic healing." Like the voluntary and autonomic nervous systems, its malfunction can produce bodily pain; a restoration of function often decreases pain and brings about testimonials of "cures." In addition, many psychotherapists suspect that cancer may be caused—in part—by psychological factors which affect the immunological system. E. P. Pendergrass, a past president of the American Cancer Society, has stated that there is solid evidence that the course of cancer is often affected by emotional distress. A variety of psychological procedures have been developed to treat cancer both physiologically and psychologically; one of them is the outgrowth of work initiated by O. C. Simonton, a radiologist. Dr. Simonton was puzzled by cases of "spontaneous remissions"—people who recovered from cancer for no apparent reason— and by other cases in which patients correctly stated that they would not die "until my son graduates" or "until I see my first grandchild." Concluding that psychological factors could have an influence on the immunological system, Simonton developed a system in which patients would visualize the cancer cells or tumors, picturing them in the "mind's eye." They would then picture the immunological mechanisms at work, visualizing an army of white blood cells swarming over the cancer, and carrying off the malignant cells that had been weakened or killed by previous radiation treatment with a cobalt machine. One

woman reported seeing the white blood cells as a vacuum cleaner sucking the cancerous cells away; a young boy saw cowboys using lassos made of white blood cells capturing the bandit cancer cells and destroying them. Simonton has educated his patients in the general principles of immune mechanisms so as to aid a correct visualization of the processes at work. Noting Lawrence LeShan's findings that cancer patients typically have an emotional trauma six to eighteen months prior to the disease, Simonton has put his patients in touch with that event to change their lives accordingly. In studying 152 patients he saw over a two-year period, Simonton found that response to the treatment was directly related to having a positive attitude and practicing the visualization regularly. Again, these findings relate to cases in which "psychic healing" was said to have helped healees suffering from cancer.

These examples of how psychological factors can enhance the body's protective systems demonstrate the folly of dividing "body" and "mind" in discussing health and illness. As Nikolaas Tinbergen stated, in accepting the 1973 Nobel Prize for Physiology and Medicine, "The more that is being discovered about psychosomatic diseases, and in general about the extremely complex two-way traffic between the brain and the rest of the body, the more obvious it has become that too rigid a distinction between mind and body is of only limited use to medical science . . . . " Tinberger concluded that if this division is maintained by medicine, it "can be a hindrance to its advance."

This point is also apparent when one studies the literature on hypnosis. Franz Anton Mesmer, who lived in the eighteenth century, is often regarded as the originator of hypnotic procedures but actually his theory and therapy were minor variants on the teachings of various "psychic healers" throughout history. His therapy combined "laying-on" of hands with a thinly disguised "exorcism" of evil forces. His theory combined esoteric teachings such as astrology with the notion of an "electric fluid" that permeated the universe. This "fluid" needed to be balanced in the human body if health was to be maintained. Mesmer thought he was transmitting some of his own "fluid" into ill people who came to him; this transfer would typically create a convulsive seizure or "crisis" after which equilibrium would become restored. As long as both Mesmer and his healees shared the belief that the "crisis" would restore a balance, many health problems were ameliorated.

One of Mesmer's followers, the Marquis de Puységur, shifted treatment away from the "crisis" to a relaxed state in which "healing" seemed to occur. Puységur also believed that a curative "fluid" provided the mechanism of the "cure," but a nineteenth century surgeon, James Braid, rejected the notion of a "fluid," insisting that the relaxed state was produced by psychological means. (The notion of a "fluid" reappeared in the United States in the mid 1800s when Phineas Quimby claimed to use "animal magnetism" in his healing sessions. One of his healees was Mary Baker Eddy who later founded Christian Science, establishing her own method of "healing.") In the twentieth century, Milton H. Erickson stressed the relationship between hypnotist and subject as the key to medical hypnosis and emphasized its pragmatic usefulness in treating a variety of ailments, producing relief from pain, and assisting the psychotherapeutic process. Some "psychic healers," without realizing it, use suggestions which produce effects similar to those in hypnosis—with many of the same psychotherapeutic outcomes. Reports exist in which warts have been removed and even in which congenital *ichthyosifurm emythroderma* (crocodile skin) has disappeared—not through "psychic healing" but by hypnosis.

In 1972, a book edited by Erika Fromm and R. E. Shor was published named *Hypnosis: Research Developments and Perspectives*. Some of the studies on hypnosis reported in this book resemble effects produced during "psychic healing" sessions. In one experiment, five subjects were hypnotized who were highly allergic to leaves of the Japanese wax tree. They were blindfolded and told that their arms were going to be touched by a chestnut tree leaf; none of the subjects showed any allergic reaction even though they had actually been touched by a wax tree leaf. Then they were told that their opposite arms would be touched by a wax tree leaf. In reality, a chestnut leaf was used but four of the subjects developed reactions. In other studies, subjects learned how to significantly alter localized skin temperatures, heart rates, and even the content of nighttime dreams through hypnosis. The fact must be stressed that scientists do not understand all the mechanisms of hypnosis (or of the placebo effect, biofeedback, therapeutic visualization, etc.); however, it is apparent that one should be reluctant to ascribe a "cure" to "psychic healing" until the utility of psychical and psychological models has been exhausted.

Hypnosis can reveal another dimension which is important for people studying "psychic healers." In addition to his work in medical hypnosis, Milton H. Erickson demonstrated how hypnotic techniques could alter a person's perceptions of reality. The Erickson technique involves pacing—adopting the subject's bodily position, breathing rate, gestures, speech tempo, and tonality. By *matching* the subject's subjective experience so closely, it is possible for the hypnotist to *lead* the subject's experience and eventually suggest a shift in perception that the subject will accept. Erickson also developed a number of "confusion" techniques in which he used paradoxical language; once the subject became confused, it was easier for Erickson to make a statement that would resolve the confusion while at the same time altering the subject's perception of reality. In some cases, Erickson used these techniques to produce visual hallucinations—and occasionally he would use these techniques without telling the subjects that they were being hypnotized. This is the reason that a certain amount of skepticism must be employed when evaluating firsthand reports of especially dramatic cases of "psychic healing" (especially "psychic surgery")*; there is always the possibility that the "healer" was using hypnotic techniques to alter the healee's perceptions of reality.

The factor played by suggestion is also a part of the effectiveness produced by charms, amulets, rings, talismans, religious objects, effigies, and magical formulae given a healee by a "healer." Sometimes these objects are even used to prevent illness from occurring. In addition, the special costumes worn by "healers" can add to the impact of what is done—as can the ritual itself. The daily procession at Lourdes, as described in *Persuasion and Healing* by Jerome D. Frank, serves as an example of the impact a ceremony can have upon healees:

> At four the bells begin to peal—the Procession begins to form. The priests in their varied robes assemble at the Grotto . . . . The loudspeakers open up. A great hymn rolls out, the huge crowd joining in unison magnificently. The Procession begins its long, impressive way . . . . First the Children of Mary, young girls in blue capes, white veils . . .then forty or fifty priests in white surplices . . .then come the Bishops in purple . . . and finally the officiating Archbishop in his white and gold robes under the golden canopy. Bringing up the rear large numbers of men and women of the different pilgrimages, Sisters, nurses, members of various religious organizations, last of all the doctors . . . . Hymns, prayers, fervent, unceasing. In the Square the sick line up in two rows . . . the Sacred host is raised above each sick one. The great crowd falls to its knees. All arms are outstretched in one vast cry to heaven.

---

*One of the authors (S. K.) attended a parapsychological meeting where two different researchers—Hans Bender and Ernest Naegeli—gave varied reports of a Filipino "healer" at work despite the fact that both were there at the same time. For some reason, they perceived reality quite differently on that occasion.

Is it any wonder that many of the pilgrims benefit from this experience?

Transcendental meditation has demonstrated its effectiveness in lowering the blood pressure of many people, as well as slowing rate of breathing, lowering the concentration of lactate acid in the blood, improving perceptual ability, quickening reaction time, and enhancing motor coordination. However, in his book, *The Relaxation Response*, Herbert Benson presents a simple twice-a-day procedure to obtain similar results. It involves assuming a comfortable position, repeating the word "one" over and over for 20 minutes, and concentrating on one's breathing. Despite the effectiveness of Benson's technique, some individuals prefer paying for lessons in transcendental meditation because of the "private mantra" or sound given each initiate, the interesting ritual with fruits and flowers, and the reassuring teacher who guides them through the program. These ritualistic factors appear to be quite necessary for certain people to obtain full benefit from a "healing" procedure.

The Psychic Model

At the end of the nineteenth century, a person named D. D. Palmer attempted a new "healing" technique with a deaf man and the patient's hearing returned. Palmer, who "adjusted" the man's spine, was not a "psychic healer," but the founder of chiropractic. Despite the American Medical Association's claim that chiropractic is "an unscientific cult whose practitioners lack the training and background to diagnose and treat human disease," chiropractors see about five million patients per year in the United States. Michael Goldstein, a sociologist at the University of California in Los Angeles, and his colleague, Gregory Firman, a psychiatrist, have stated that chiropractors actually serve a vital purpose for medicine by providing an outlet for many potentially time-consuming and trouble-making patients whom physicians cannot serve well. They noted that chiropractic fills a need not met by traditional medicine by offering a simple theory of disease (misalignment of the spine) that is easily understood by poorer patients and those living in rural areas. Chiropractic also legitimizes the sickness of patients whose problems physicians dismiss as "just nerves"; therefore, chiropractors often succeed where physicians fail.

Much the same evaluation could be made of "psychic healing." For a variety of reasons it sometimes succeeds where orthodox medicine fails; the only danger is that seriously ill patients will go to a "healer" *instead of* of a physician rather than to a "healer" *as well as* a physician.

It is apparent that most of the claimed effects of "psychic healing" can be adequately explained by using a physical model, a psychological model, or both. But can everything be explained without recourse to a psychic model? Not quite. First, there are the laboratory experiments. If such studies as that done by Watkins and Watkins regarding distant effects on mice are valid, a psychic model would be needed to explain the phenomena. Second, there are the purported effects of "healers" which lie outside what physical or psychological intervention is known to do.

It might be thought that the mediums who "incorporate" "spirits" present another phenomenon not easily explained. To the contrary, many of those researchers who have studied these individuals have proposed explanations which usually fall into a psychological model.

Eileen J. Garrett is generally considered the most remarkable medium of the twentieth century. She would enter an altered state of consciousness and a variety of voices would speak which purported to be "spirit entities." Always cooperative with scientists, Garrett once went to Ira Progoff, a Jungian psychoanalyst, asking the nature and meaning of the voices which appeared to speak through her. During Progoff's interviews, a voice would speak purporting to be Ouvani, an Arabian soldier who died in battle during the thirteenth century, or Abdul Latif, a Persian physician of the seventeenth century, or others. Progoff concluded that Garrett was in psychological conflict—her psyche required a strong and active role in a world run by men. To resolve this conflict, according to Progoff, Garrett's psyche "worked out its necessary arrangement with exceptional ingenuity." The voices "made it possible for her to live efficiently in the midst of a psychic tension that would otherwise have made life untenable."

However, Progoff noted that "a psychological interpretation of the phenomena involved . . . cannot by any means exhaust the implications of the subject." He observed that the voices "seemed to have access to information that Garrett was not familiar with and they had clairvoyant perceptions which she did not have without their presence." Thus, a combination of psychological and psychic models may be needed to understand the mediumship of Garrett—and, perhaps, of the Brazilian and Filipino Spiritist "healers" as well.

A seven-year research study on "spirit possession" was reported in a 1975 issue of the *Archives of General Psychiatry*. The author, Carlos A. León, a Colombian psychiatrist, interviewed all members of the twelve families studied, conducted psychological testing, and took brain wave recordings of many of the individuals. He reported that all the "possessed" individuals "presented symptoms compatible with mental disorders." Dr. León identified five cases of hysteria, four of epilepsy, two of chronic anxiety and one of latent schizophrenia.

The "possessed" individuals reported that they had been hit, scratched, bit, stabbed, whipped, and slashed by the "spirits." In addition the "spirits" were said to have broken furniture, burned household objects, thrown rocks, and hurled crockery. They purportedly rapped, knocked, spilled food, soiled clothes, stole possessions, cursed God, and destroyed religious artifacts. One woman claimed that a "spirit" raped her. Others asserted that rooms became ice cold, objects flew around corners, and people levitated. Exorcisms by Roman Catholic priests were not effective, but Spiritists were able to expel the "spirits" in eight out of the twelve cases.

León concluded that evil "spirits" often become scapegoats to which all a person's destructive and aggressive impulses are ascribed. The pattern of "possession" is determined by the culture and reinforced by group beliefs. León suggested that reports of flying objects and levitation could be "the purely imagined products of dissociated minds coupled with group psychology or hypnosis" or that the "possessed" people emit a psychokinetic force involving "various alternative explanations, including the type supplied by parapsychologists . . . ."

León's study is an excellent example of one done by a investigator who has taken a psychic-psychophysiological approach to "possession" and evil "spirits." He considered physical factors in his brain wave studies, finding four cases of epilepsy. He was able to reach tentative conclusions that stressed psychological explanations, but did not rule out the possibility of psychic components in some of the phenomena.

Supporters of the notion that "spirit entities" actually do speak through mediums, at least part of the time, can cite some interesting research to support their position. Frederic Myers and Edmund Gurney, early members of the Society for Psychical Research, said that after their deaths they would try to communicate through various mediums. Indeed, for 30 years afterwards, a dozen different mediums reported receiving messages, typically literary puzzles that would make sense only when statements from different mediums were put together.*

---

*These studies, referred to as "cross-correspondences," are summarized by Gardner Murphy in *The Challenge of Psychical Research*.

In addition, there is some evidence to support the concept of reincarnation. The psychiatrist Ian Stevenson has investigated over 500 cases "suggestive" of reincarnation. Stevenson has travelled all over the world to interview subjects for this study, often taking them back to the town of their purported earlier life. One case involved the Lorenz family in southern Brazil. A close friend of Ida Lorenz died in 1917, telling Ida on her deathbed that she would come back as her daughter. Less than a year later, Ida had a daughter, Marta, who spontaneously began to describe a former life when she was two years of age. Marta not only described the farm where she "used to live," but gave the correct name and nickname of Ida's dead friend, and described incidents from her "previous life." Dr. Stevenson checked out 28 pieces of evidence provided by Marta, interviewing nine different witnesses in the process. Six of these items proved to be unknown to any member of the Lorenz family other than Marta herself.

Hernani Andrade has also collected a number of cases "suggestive" of reincarnation. However, even if the cases are scrupulously investigated, and all information which would be based on conscious or unconscious clues is discarded, it is still impossible to conclude that reincarnation has been established. There is always the possibility that clairvoyance or some other form of ESP is at work supplying the information. The same interpretation can be made of the Myers and Gurney material; perhaps the mediums used their own ESP to obtain the vital information.

Sir Oliver Lodge once told his friend Charles Richet that even if he were to find himself on the "spirit plane" after death, he would have a difficult time trying to prove his survival. Could he have a medium cite his experiments? They would be well-known already. Could he correctly predict an event? This would be regarded as a "coincidence." Could he have the medium read poetry in French? This would be the medium's clairvoyant ability. If he produced raps, "ectoplasm," and other phenomena, the medium would be accused of fraud, or would be regarded as adept in psychokinesis. In other words, science must continue to explore the questions of survival and reincarnation, but it will not be an easy task.*

In the meantime, there are other phenomena which may be simpler to document and which—if verified—would need to be explained using some sort of psychic model. Joan Fitz Herbert, a psychoanalyst, reported two such cases—both of which were observed following a "healing service" in Great Britain. One was an instantaneous disappearance of an inoperable goiter and the other the instantaneous development of a sizeable piece of new bone. Special attention should also be paid to reported cases in which infants and animals have been "healed." In neither case could the conventional psychological causes be easily applied unless the "healer" soothed the infant or animal by "laying-on" of hands or changed the behavior of the baby's parents or the animal's owner in some beneficial manner.

In directing attention to these cases, science must first of all integrate the physical and the psychological models. The material that has been presented by the authors throughout this book demonstrates that neither model is complete by itself. Physical and psychological are two sides of the same coin; together they comprise the "psychophysiological system." A "system" is an indivisible whole, one that loses its coherence when taken apart. When science studies the "healing process," it will find that coherence is lost if only

---

*Preliminary work attempting to discern "spirit" influences on plant reactions and tape-recorded sounds has been presented in *Future Science*, edited by John White and Stanley Krippner. In *Mysteries of the Far North*, A. R. G. Owen describes how the Toronto Society for Psychical Research "manufactured" a "spirit," allegedly through group psychokinesis. This "spirit" reportedly was capable of producing strange rapping sounds, tilting a table, and bending a key which nobody was touching at the time. If this experiment is valid, it suggests that many or all "spirit" phenomena actually represent unrealized psi potentials of living human beings, expressed unconsciously or during altered states of consciousness.

the physical *or* the psychological data are examined. After all, nature and the world are not organized the way science is subdivided.

J. Z. Young, in *An Introduction to the Study of Man* has noted that "We learn to arrange our whole store of information around a 'model' in the brain that makes useful forecasts." A psychophysiological model will explain more phenomena and make more useful forecasts than either a physical or a psychological model.

The next question is whether the psychic model needs to be integrated with the other two? Can science learn even more about the realms of healing if it adopts a psychic-psychophysiological model?

Consciousness and the Cosmos

Science aims not merely to classify and describe phenomena but also to explain and predict them. Thus science organizes its phenomena in such a way that it will assist explanation of past events and prediction of future events. However, phenomena in the psychological world change more quickly than phenomena in the physical world, thus they are not as amenable to prediction and control. This is one factor which has prevented many scientists from adopting a psychophysiological model of reality. One can imagine the resistance that will be met if a psychic dimension is proposed; even those investigators who accept the reality of psi processes admit their unpredictability and rapid rate of fluctuation.

A number of directions could be taken by workers in parapsychology who are eager to see the psychic model of reality accepted and integrated with psychophysiology. Some researchers have proposed bold ideas that, if accepted, would unite the psychic and the psychophysiological, leading to the "paradigm shift" that Thomas Kuhn

wrote about in his book on scientific revolutions. Inyushin's "biological plasma"—the proposed new state of
matter—would be an example of a new paradigm. Another
would be Andrade's "biological organizing model."

Other writers are more cautious, saying we are not yet
ready for this step. In the *Journal of Parapsychology*, R.
H. Thouless has commented:

> It would . . . . be a misunderstanding . . . of Kuhn's ideas
> to infer that our task now is to think out a new paradigm. It
> is not thus that scientific revolutions have taken place in the
> past. The call is rather to more detailed and more precise
> research. As we know more about the psi phenomena and as
> our knowledge becomes more exact, the shape of the future
> paradigm will gradually become clear.

And in an article in the *Journal of the American Society for
Psychical Research*, J. G. Pratt noted that "No theory has
yet been adequately confirmed in the field because of its
logical consistency and strength." Pratt argues for further
research that will ultimately provide material for a paradigm constructed by "the future Einstein of parapsychology."

While some parapsychologists continue to search for a
"repeatable experiment" that would lead to prediction and
control of psi, others say this is only necessary *after* the
need for a new paradigm is obvious. Charles T. Tart has
reflected, "Replication is more important in a science when
it is in a paradigmatic stage. At the present level in parapsychology, we might just as well stumble along hoping we'll
run into something with a greater yield."

Those who have begun to speculate on how psi processes
would interface with psychophysiology typically turn their
attention to human consciousness. In so doing, their efforts run counter to those scientists who object to using the
term "consciousness" because it cannot easily be measured or defined in terms of external activity or behavior.

This extreme position has been ridiculed by Irving L. Child in his book *Humanistic Psychology and the Research Tradition:*

> . . . The purist might have wished to dispense with the concept of a star, since at most only the radiant energy reaching the earth could be known—and for most stars only the marks produced on a photographic plate through lengthy exposure to very weak energy.

The eminent philosopher Karl Popper, has met this problem head on by speaking of three "worlds." One "world" represents the total of all matter and energy in the cosmos, the second "world" represents the total of all consciousness, and Popper's third "world" represents humanity's models, ideas, concepts, and theories about matter, energy, and consciousness. It is one of the tasks of the third "world" to propose how the first two interact. At least three points of view have been proposed by those who have studied this issue:

1. Consciousness is a property of the brain and other forms of matter, just as hardness is a property of metal and warmth is a property of fire. Without matter there can be no such thing as consciousness.

2. Consciousness and matter are separate. Sometimes their functions overlap, but it is quite easy for them to exist independently of each other. Thus it is possible for "spirits" to exist without a physical body.

3. Consciousness and matter can exist separately but typically they interact. For science to study consciousness properly, this interaction must be understood.

While in Copenhagen, one of the authors (A.V.) had the opportunity to discuss with the Danish physicist R. D. Mattuck the quantum mechanical theories of Evan Harris Walker, a noted physicist and mathematician. Dr. Walker has presented a concept of consciousness which many people believe allows it to be studied from an interactionist point of view. Quantum theory lies at the foundation of modern physics. Quite in distinction from the older, classical physics based on the laws of motion set down by Isaac Newton, quantum theory is based on two totally distinct equations.

The first equation describes not only what is going to happen but all the infinity of events that can happen, all the events that are possible in literally any situation. But that first equation does not tell what *will* happen. Of course, when one checks up, or observes, what is going on, one will always find that one event is happening. The other possibilities, then, did not occur.

The second equation simply makes formal this statement that when an investigator looks, that person finds that only one event happened. In addition, the second equation outlines a procedure for determining the likelihood that one possibility will occur rather than another possibility.

This concept may be difficult for a person to conceive at first because most events occur on an atomic level. In addition, Western culture is accustomed to very simple notions of cause and effect. The idea of cause and effect tells us that a given cause leads to a result, a single effect. If one drops a ball, it falls. If one hits a baseball in a particular way, it flies away in a given direction. All understanding of physics before the turn of the century was based on this concept. But the new physics—quantum mechanics—points out that this picture is too simple.

This new picture can be illustrated by a common, if artificial, example—the example of a dead tree that falls far from anyone who can see or hear it. People used to ask the question that if no one heard the tree fall, was there any sound. But this is merely a semantic question. In quantum theory, the question is whether the tree has fallen or if it is still standing. Both are possible. Thus the first equation of quantum theory says something that seems like nonsense: the tree is standing *and* the tree has fallen. The second equation states that if investigators go and look they will only observe one of these two possibilities—and that possibility will become the reality.

The statement that both conditions exist is not just due to a lack of knowledge as to whether or not the tree has fallen. This is one of the remarkable aspects of quantum theory. There are many experiments that can be carried out to show that both must really be considered to have a kind of partial reality, a potentiality. There are cases that can be tested in which the possibility of the existence of one case actually affects the character of the other case. These instances exist in almost every problem studied in quantum mechanics.

The first of these two basic equations of physics is called the "Schrödinger equation."* It is actually deterministic and describes the objective world, but as an overview of all the possible things that can happen. The second equation that formalizes and embodies the so-called "Copenhagen interpretation" is not deterministic but probabilistic. It describes what happens when we observe the physical world and thus incorporates processes that are more than simply part of the objective world. This process is probabilistic. The equation does not say what will be observed but simply that only one event will be observed. What happens appears to be kind of a game of chance!

Such unreliable behavior in nature was found abhorrent by many of the great physicists. Albert Einstein, for example, insisted that God did not play dice with the universe. One thing happened—the tree fell or it did not fall, whether anyone knew it or not. This discontent in physics arose from a desire on the part of physicists to return to an earlier day of certainty—the certainty of classical physics, the cause and effect of Newtonian mechanics. But in that earlier mechanics, there was no place for the concept of consciousness, and no conception of the human being as other than a mechanism just like any other mechanism.

The discontent with quantum theory gave rise in the 1950s to the proposal by David Bohm of "hidden vari-

---

*Even though the "Heisenberg formulation" was developed about the same time, the "Schrödinger formulation" is closer to the more fundamental character of the phenomenon.

ables.'' Bohm originally thought these "hidden variables" were some subatomic machinery that would soon be discovered to show that cause and effect held ironclad even on the atomic level. It has now come to be realized that these variables must go undetected escaping observation in any ordinary experiment. These variables, which were discussed by such innovative theorists in physics as Werner Heisenberg, link the deterministic and indeterministic worlds together but in a way quite unsuspected until recently.

Heisenberg formulated the "uncertainty principle" in which he demonstrated that if the position of a particle (such as an electron) was very precisely known, an observer could know its velocity only very imprecisely. On the other hand, if the observer had a very precise knowledge of the particle's velocity, its position would become very imprecise. In other words, one of the variables would always remain "uncertain."

Because there is this "uncertainty" or "fuzziness" about a particle's position and velocity, when a particle of known velocity is drawn, it can only be depicted as being more or less near a particular place. That is, one can only specify the *probability* of the particle being at a particular position. This "fuzzy" picture of the particle is referred to as a "wave packet." For example, one can only say that it is most probable that the particle is at a position of 2.0 centimeter (cm.)—but it could also be at 1.9 or 2.2 cm. (In reality, of course, the position of subatomic particles would be even smaller—one ten-millionth of a centimeter or less.)

Imagine that someone measures the position of a particle and finds that the first measurement yields 2.1 cm. Yet the next time it is measured, with all other factors remaining the same, one finds it is at 1.9 cm., and the third time at 2.0 cm. This fact that the "fuzzy" particle acquires a *precise* position in each *individual* measurement is called the "collapse of the wave packet." There is a tendency when first encountering these facts about the fuzzy nature of position to ascribe this imprecision simply to errors that occur in

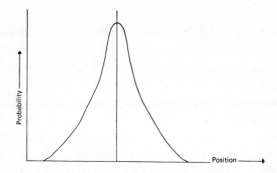

Probability distribution for the position of the particle (wave-packet).

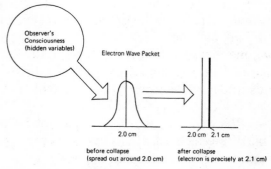

Interaction between the consciousness of the observer and the electron determine the exact location of the particle through collapse of the electron wave packet.

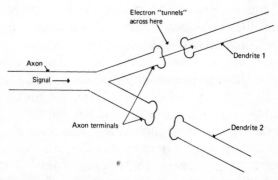

Electron "tunnelling" from one axon to the correct dendrite.

measuring the particle's position. Heisenberg's uncertainty relations do derive from simply calculating the magnitude of errors produced as an effect during measurement. But if this were all there was to it, quantum mechanics would be reduced to just a few rules on accuracy in physical calculations. It is not that way, however. The Heisenberg formulations describe not a limit on our knowledge as much as a limit on the reality of position as something exact. The idea that a body is located in one place at a given time moving with an exact speed is false. The position of a body and its motion must be represented in a much more complex fashion.

Feeling that there must be some undetected influence acting upon this particle which would cause its position to differ from one measurement to the next, a few physicists have elaborated on the notion of "hidden variables." In other words, the particle, aside from having the qualities of position and velocity, would have something else accompanying it—a "hidden variable." This cannot be detected directly, but the effects of it can be measured. When the particle is measured to be located at 2.0 cm., it is because there is a "hidden variable" associated with the particle which caused the wave packet to "collapse" at 2.0 cm.

If the experiment is conducted again, and a measurement of 2.1 is obtained, it is because the "hidden variable" had another value associated with it on that occasion. So while the effect of these "hidden variables" can be observed, the "variables" themselves have yet to be identified.

Perhaps, thought Walker, "hidden variables" are the mechanisms through which consciousness interacts with the particles in the physical world. Walker went on to describe consciousness in terms of "hidden variables" which can have different values, and which determine the exact position of a particle at any moment of time.

The interactions between the consciousness of the observer and the physical world, by means of the "hidden variables," do not occur in the form of a force or energy field, but through what might be called an "information field." The "hidden variables" supply information to the systems, so that the "collapse" of the electron wave packet occurs at a specific point in space. Then, to move the electron to the right—for example—by PK, one causes the wave packet to "collapse" to the right of its original position. In other words, it produces an ordering of the brain's information processing, selecting one stream of consciousness from the myriad of possibilities permitted for quantum mechanical processes in the brain.

The situation is similar to that of expecting a visit from a friend on either Sunday, Monday, or Tuesday; the probability of the friend's coming is 0.33 for each of those days. But when the friend telephones and pinpoints Tuesday as the day of arrival, the probability distribution is suddenly narrowed to 1.0 for Tuesday and 0.0 for Sunday and Monday. The probability distribution—or wave packet—of the friend's arrival has "collapsed" to the value of Tuesday. Or other friends could announce their arrival on Tuesday at either the bus station, railroad station, or airport. When they call again and say they are flying in, the probability distribution has "collapsed" to the value of the airport. In one instance the "collapse" is in time, in the other it is in space. In both, the wave packet "collapses" to a specific point as new information is supplied.

Walker's first application of this theory was in constructing a quantum mechanical model of the brain. He attempted to explain how electrical impulses in the form of electrons which would otherwise move in a largely random fashion in the brain, were made to move coherently from one nerve cell to another along a particular brain pathway. The process by which an electron moves from one nerve cell to another was referred to as "quantum mechanical tunnelling" by Walker.

The act of standing up, for example, would involve transmitting the information "I want to stand up" by means of "hidden variables" to cause the electron wave packets to "collapse" at precise points so that the electrical nerve impulses would travel along the correct "pathway" in the brain. Eventually, appropriate information is received by the motor center corresponding to the muscles used in standing up.

The brain contains billions of nerve cells, each having a transmitting fiber, or axon, and at least one receiving fiber or dendrite. The "hidden variables," acting in the form of an "information field," have to regulate the exact timing of the "collapse" of electron wave packets, so that the nerve signal that is leaving one axon makes the "jump" to the correct dendrite in its prescribed pathway. As the nerve impulse "tunnels" in this way, its "pathway" is prescribed by consciousness. Walker has estimated that if only chance were operating in the path and a nerve impulse were to go through ten nerve cells, the odds that a person could—for example—pick up a pencil would be nearly one out of ten million. Something is operating in "tunnelling" and the "hidden variables" appear to be consciousness.

In this way, Walker accounts for information "directed outward" from the brain in such acts as picking up a pencil or standing upright. However, consciousness also processes information entering the brain. Thus, the "hidden variables" must also adjust themselves to the positions of electrons in the brain. When we "see" the image of a tree several feet high, the "hidden variables" adjust themselves to the pattern of electron movements in the brain which "correspond" to the image of the tree. Thus consciousness is continuously aware of "information fields" and electron movements in the brain.

Walker has described consciousness in terms of its information content. He has estimated the rate at which information is processed by what he has called the "will" function of the brain—as when people "will" to stand up, choose one piece of food over another, etc. Walker has estimated that the "will" can supply information to the brain at the rate of 10^4 "bits" per second,* a "bit" being a

---

*10^4 is a monumental amount of "bits"; it stands for 10 multiplied times itself four times.

measure of information equal to one unit of data, one "yes-or-no" choice. This would suggest that consciousness can be associated with an output of 10^4 "bits" of data per second, "tunnelling" through the proper collapse of wave packets in the brain.

In addition, the brain is constantly being bombarded with information from the external world, as well as from the organism itself. Visual impressions, sounds, and other external sensory data as well as metabolism, respiration, and other internal functions flood the brain. This input material is processed by the brain's unconscious computer-like functions, according to Walker, at a rate of approximately 10^8 "bits" of information per second. He refers to this as the total "conscious data rate." Walker estimates the "unconscious data rate" as 10^{12} "bits" per second.

Ordinarily, the data rate of the "will" is smaller than the total "conscious data rate." However, according to Walker, under certain conditions—such as altered states of consciousness—this rate can increase 10,000 times to the total "conscious data rate" of 10^8 "bits" per second. In this case, one's total conscious activity would involve the faculty of "will."

If Walker's theory is correct, a PK process occurs constantly in the brain. Consciousness influences the physical world by directing electrons in their "tunnelling" process through the brain. Consciousness moves an electron from one nerve cell to another via the continuous flow of information contained by the "hidden variables" which "determine the collapse" of the electron wave packets.

If PK can affect one electron, why can it not affect several electrons? If it can affect electrons inside the brain why can it not affect electrons outside the brain? Quantum physicists claim to have demonstrated that "hidden variables" have a property referred to as "non-locality"; they have no fixed position in space or in time. They coordinate events throughout space and time regardless of where these events are to be found or when they occur. If this is so, consciousness, as Walker sees it, would have the quality of being non-local in space and time, yet to connected the events in one brain; the consciousness of others, and to the events influencing other people. For this reason, consciousness may well extend beyond the limits of the body and the brain, although it is only in certain instances and with certain people that PK on a noticeable scale is easily observed. For example, Walker has calculated that Nina Kulagina's* reported ability to psychokinetically move a small object across a table would require 10^4 "bits" of information per second—a feat within the range of what is possible by the "will." Walker has further conjectured that the distance an object can be moved by PK is not as dependent on the object's weight as it is on the degree that the subject can focus his or her "will."

It should be recalled that many "psychic healers" operate in altered states of consciousness, temporarily inactivating their ordinary personality roles. Many of them claim to be turning their own "wills" over to a "will" higher than their own—to El Hermanito or Saint Michael or the Old Black Ones. The "healers" then become "vehicles" for a benevolent "spirit" who purportedly works through them to "heal" afflicted persons.

If Walker is right, it would be possible, in certain altered states of consciousness, for a "healer" to employ the full "conscious data rate" of 10^8 "bits" of information per second. If a rate of 10^4 could move a small object across a table, what act of "healing" could not be carried out by a rate of 10^8?

Even the form of "psychic surgery" which purportedly involves "pulling apart" and "rejoining" skin and tissue would be theoretically possible. It would, of course, be infinitely complicated to alter molecular bonds and, later, re-structure them. There would have to be a successive

---

*Kulagina is a psychic sensitive in Leningrad whose reported PK abilities have been studied by scientists from six nations.

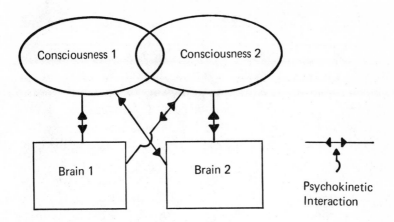

Psychokinetic
Interaction

Diagram of consciousness interacting with its own and with another brain. (Note that because of non-locality, consciousnesses must overlap each other to some extent.)

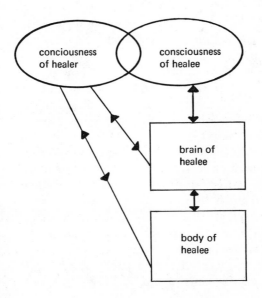

Diagram of "healer" interacting with healee causing "healer" to rise to a higher degree of order.

"collapse" of wave packets by the billions in the skin and tissue.

Complicated though this may seem, there are analogs for it. When a person "sees" a tree or an animal or a building, considerable "tunnelling" is going on. In "psychic photography," an image is purportedly produced on photographic film through PK;* if legitimate, this effect represents an effect in the same order of complexity as "psychic surgery."

What of the other types of purported "psychic surgery"—the alteration of the "bioplasmic body" of a healee, the "teleportation" of distant objects to the healee's skin, the "materialization" of objects from free-floating atoms in the cosmos? Human "will," according to Walker's theory, may be able to account for all of these phenomena, but by using explanations which are quite amenable to investigation.

In an interview and exchange of letters with one of the authors (A. V.), Dr. Walker discussed the implications of his theory for people investigating "psychic healing":

> There is the important question of how the consciousness knows how to rearrange the atoms, etc., to achieve "healing." The answer to this question is so simple that it is hard to understand. It is simply that the consciousness does not need to know the "path" from the sick condition to the healthy condition. All that is required is that (1) there exists an allowed or possible "path" from the sick to the healthy condition no matter how improbable—including the possibility that the atoms suddenly "tunnel" to the proper positions; (2) that the consciousness can recognize the healthy (and of course the sick) condition so that the proper state, if allowed by quantum mechanics, can be selected, and (3) that the psychic's channel capacity (which I have designated $W\psi$) be sufficiently high so that the selection of the desired

---

*Examples of images allegedly produced psychokinetically on film by Nina Kulagina appear in *The Energies of Consciousness,* edited by Stanley Krippner and Daniel Rubin.

state can be carried out—in other words, that the state can be found.

The difficulty many people have in understanding this process is that one is too accustomed to the customary mode of thought in which the observer stands outside the physical process looking in—describing the "path" from one state, some initial condition, to a subsequent state. But the consciousness (including the "will") *is* the mechanism that selects states! And in this *action* on the physical system of selecting from the quantum mechanically allowed states, there is a "reaction" (to borrow Isaac Newton's term) which is the conscious experience in which state selection is felt.

Although most of one's conscious experience is tied to the present state of one's brain at any instant, the $W\psi$ (psychic's capacity) channel is the link with the overall quantum mechanical system that extends beyond the body and beyond the present moment. We usually do not realize this because the $W\psi$ channel is so much less in magnitude than the consciousness data rate.

But because the $W\psi$ channel transcends time and space, it is intimately tied to the future state to be selected. Thus the psychic *feels*, at the moment he attempts to "heal," the "healed condition" as though he were there in the future to see it—and to some extent he is. There is really no paradox here nor much real difficulty in understanding how this happens. The consciousness simply selects the appropriate state. The unwanted states are sluffed off as dead skin that does not feel good.

The reason all this appears as a paradox comes from the development of scientific thought. In Newton's day this explanation would have seemed simpler than the explanation that Newton gave. Newton did not explain "why" but described "how." Indeed, "why" has no meaning when applied to the inanimate. The physicist does not explain "why" one magnet attracts another, but describes the fundamental properties of matter that give properties of matter that give rise to the phenomenon. But such a description of "free will" in terms of mechanics would equally be an inappropriate mode of explanation, for there is no outside machinery that dictates the selection of the "will."

This is easier to understand for simpler selected states of consciousness. Suppose you want to call the toss of a coin. If your call is correct, you will be very happy. The toss is made and while the coin is in the air a small part of your consciousness is already linked to the experience of the fall of the coin and the choice of your call being heads. If that channel were perfect, your feeling now would tie in the correct call linking together the call of heads with the fall of heads. But only one part in ten thousand of your consciousness is linked. The feelings will be mixed, your choice will come from some clue in the present and your call will probably be by chance. However, the psychic has simply learned to feel more precisely.

The importance of understanding these processes is practical as well as theoretical. Recently, I was visited by a 41 year old man who underwent brain surgery as an adolescent. The operation was performed because he had had three epileptic attacks. To cure this minor dysfunction, the man was robbed of nearly half the capacity of his brain. Here we see all the absurd gall of a plumber working on a computer with a fire ax. Many surgeons, psychologists, and psychiatrists with no knowledge whatever of what the mind is have become the pillars of our medical world. In contrast, the "psychic healer" does not always succeed, but does begin by asking "Is the plug in? Is the power on?"

The "Will" in "Healing"

Walker's theory is not accepted by all physicists or parapsychologists. When he presented it at the Twenty-Third International Conference of the Parapsychology Foundation, some of the participants referred to it as "nonsense." Even many of those who are impressed with Walker's theory would feel that it cannot be extended to explain some of the incredible stories involved in "psychic healing." For example, how could a "healer" diagnose an illness without knowing a great deal about anatomy and physiology? However, this information *is* present at some level, such as in an altered state of consciousness where a data rate of 10^8 is possible.

Perhaps the "healer" in an altered state focuses on his or her knowledge of one's own molecular structure, projects this onto the healee, and compares it with the more familiar data of one's own anatomy and physiology, until the disease is diagnosed. If the "will" can diagnose, the "will" could also "heal." It is only one step from understanding the healee's psychological and physiological states to being able to alter them—or to influence the "will" of a healee so that "self-healing" can take place.

Many psychotherapists emphasize the "will" as well, most notably the practitioners of psychosynthesis. Roberto Assagioli, the founder of psychosynthesis, wrote, in *Act of Will*, that psychotherapy involves movement toward a goal (the patient's recovery) that is facilitated by a genuine volitional act—willed, decided, and executed in active volition between the patient and therapist, in which each participates in a specific manner. Precisely the same type of interaction appears to occur in "psychic healing" and Walker may have given science a clue as to the underlying subatomic mechanisms which allow "healing" to happen.

In applying Walker's ideas to illness, one could say that an organism in ill health has a high degree of bodily disorder. There are an unlimited number of ways of being unhealthy but relatively few ways of being healthy. So if we consider the organism, in a figurative way, as a wave function with a high probability of unhealthy states, one of the effects of a "healer" may be to supply information to the sick person's system. This causes the "collapse" of the wave function to occur at another point—namely, that of health. This point would be characterized by a high degree of order. In effect, the consciousness of the "healer" may be providing information through its "hidden variables" to the healee. At the same time, the healee responds by stimulating the body's natural self-repair mechanisms.

In other words, Walker has used quantum theory to explain psi phenomena. And the authors of this book have demonstrated how Walker's theory can explain "psychic healing" phenomena without resorting either to "spirits" or to undiscovered forms of "energy."

Walker attempted to summarize his theory for Willis Kinnear in a book of readings on psychical research. Walker wrote:

> Consciousness refers to the immediate inner experiences—sensory, emotional, intellectual . . . . Despite the fundamental reality of . . . our own conscious reality, it has not been incorporated into prior physical concepts . . . .
>
> A new tack has been taken in which consciousness has been treated as something having innate reality with its own characteristics distinct from those of purely material bodies . . . . In this new understanding, consciousness exists as a distinct entity *associated* with certain physical processes occurring in the brain of our body . . . .
>
> At the same time that the brain is processing sensory data, a separate process is going on interconnecting a small part of the brain's competing functions. About one ten-thousandth of all this computing is tied directly together by means of a process called quantum mechanical tunnelling . . . .
>
> . . . This mechanism is not entirely physical and is not deterministic. But how can one talk about something like that and call it science? . . . . The remarkable fact is that not only can it be done, it has turned out to be necessary to introduce such ideas into physics.
>
> . . . We can show that arising from our conscious experience there exists a distinct entity identifiable with the concept of *will* . . . that determines from moment to moment the state of our consciousness-brain association.
>
> This flow amounts to only one ten-thousandth of our total conscious experience, one part in a hundred million of all the data processing carried out by the brain subconsciously, but it is exceptional in that it is at the same time linked to

other conscious entities in the universe. This connecting link provides the basis for understanding in detail paranormal phenomena, including an understanding of psychokinesis . . . .

J. Z. Young, in *An Introduction to the Study of Man*, has written that the attempt to find general schemes to include particular things or events is evidently a rather common human tendency. Every human society has its ways of "understanding" particular natural events as "caused by" some member of a "spirit world." Attempts of this sort usually fail for lack of economy and efficiency rather than of consistency or generality. The Walker theory is economic and efficient as well as consistent and general. Time will tell if this theory will explain the unusual events of "psychic healing."

Research Possibilities

Science is not a body of knowledge but a way of knowing. The task of scientists is to present the facts of human life that interest them in such a way as to relate these facts to a scheme that is as general as possible, with a maximum of explanatory and predictive powers.

One way that science proceeds is from inquiry to observation, to a controlled observation, to a controlled experiment, to a replicated experiment. In "psychic healing" there are numerous observations, and a few controlled observations which have led to controlled experiments. Replicated experiments are needed, and will then be followed by theories which will suggest hypotheses for further experiments.

One hypothesis for the future, for example, would state that "healers" who do well on PK tests can also "heal" people effectively. It has been taken for granted that a "psychic healer" can also help seeds to sprout and change the hydrogen bonding in water. But most experiments of this sort were done with only two "healers," Oskar Estabany and Olga Worrall. It could very well be that "healing" and laboratory PK are very different abilities which are not as closely associated as some parapsychologists would like to think.

In her use of damaged enzymes, M. Justa Smith utilized test materials which were closely related to healing processes. When additional work with enzymes is done, it should be remembered that enzyme molecules, which readily change their shape and properties, may be sensitive detectors of psi. Enzymes are known to catalyze reactions in living cells and to be of considerable importance to the organism. Benson Herbert, director of the Paraphysical Laboratory in Downton, England, has conjectured that if a "healer" can influence enzymes, perhaps a psychic sensitive could clairvoyantly detect which of several test tubes contains an enzyme. Herbert has proposed that, in such a case, the enzyme may be "influencing the brain of the clairvoyant, perhaps by a form of radiation enhanced by resonance."

Herbert has also proposed that both the left and the right hemispheres of the brain are involved in psi ability, at least in the case of Nina Kulagina, a psychic sensitive with whom Herbert has conducted various PK experiments. Writing in the *Parapsychology Review*, Herbert noted:

> . . . Kulagina prefers to perform PK upon tall vertical objects such as erect cigar cases, which, being parallel to the sagittal plane of symmetry dividing the hemispheres, suggests that both hemispheres are involved. Similarly and conversely we have found that a tube containing hemoglobin is more readily located in directions perpendicular to the sagittal plane; that is to say, it is easier to guess how far it is to the left or right of the subject than to guess how far it is away from him. This directional propensity clearly suggests that both hemispheres are involved.

Science is the search for an explanation of a naturally occurring phenomenon using the scientific method. There are various scientific procedures to the study of "healers," among them linguistic procedures. Languages have evolved to convey the effects that each society requires. The use of words for scientific reasoning, therefore, cannot be divorced from their daily use. Methods of thinking and criteria of truth differ, for example, between Western European and Asiatic cultures. Nevertheless, it is possible to reach some degree of agreement as to the classification of the modes of reasoning that provide sure conclusions.

Donald Bahr and his colleagues have studied the shamans of the Piman Indian tribe from the viewpoint of linguistic analysis; their findings are reported in *Piman Shamanism and Staying Sickness*. After investigating the language structure used to explain how "healing" is effected, they concluded that the shamanistic system is fully as complex and sophisticated as that of Western medicine. These studies are important on a descriptive basis as they provide a clear picture of the shamans' world-view and the model used in their "healing" sessions.

Bahr's group reported how the shamans would "stay sickness" and prevent disease by concentrating on the healee's condition; "spirits" may help "but only as the ultimate means for solving the problem within the patient." Their rituals, once thought impossible to describe in English, actually yield to an interesting and meaningful accounting. Whatever private experiences may be, there can be no scientific advantage in describing them by a sort of special private language. The language we have is by its nature a very public one, used for describing, among other things, the states of ourselves. If shamanistic "out-of-body" experiences can be described, so can Spiritist "incorporations" and the initiation rituals of esoteric "healers." All of these approaches are useful in determining how "healing" happens. They would also be helpful in developing the "state-specific sciences" proposed by Charles T.

Tart. One can imagine a group of anthropologists, for example, undergoing training with a shaman, entering altered states of consciousness with the shaman, and conducting research into the new aspects of reality thus opened up to them.

The importance of altered states of consciousness to a study of "psychic healing" emerges from a careful reading of such books as *Magic, Faith, and Healing*, edited by Ari Kiev. Many of the contributors to Kiev's book viewed primitive "healers" from the standpoint of their own culturally conditioned state of consciousness. Thus, it was simple to note that "folk psychiatry" uses "primary process thinking" and the "exploitation of emotions" rather than "objectivity" and "secondary process thinking" which allegedly characterizes modern medicine. Tribes using these techniques are often labelled "hysteric," while sorcery practices are analyzed to be "institutionalized instruments of covert aggression." A view from the "inside," based on shared states of consciousness might lend greater depth to these studies.

Carlos Castaneda, as a graduate student in anthropology, wrote four books concerning the teachings of "don Juan Matus," a name given by Castaneda to a Yaqui Indian *brujo* supposedly living in Mexico. Castaneda claimed to have studied with "don Juan," ingesting mind-altering substances, confronting "spirits" and "allies," having "out-of-body" experiences, and eventually becoming a *brujo*, or sorcerer, himself. Three pilot studies were carried out with Castaneda by Douglass Price-Williams, an anthropologist at the University of California, Los Angeles.

The most complex of these studies was initiated in 1975 and resembled the experiments in ESP and dreams conducted by one of the authors (S. K.) at Maimonides Medical Center. However, Castaneda's task was more difficult as he was not given the names of the seven subjects. Nor were the subjects told that they were participating in the study. Price-Williams had selected seven individuals he knew personally, and recorded their names in the presence of his wife, who served as a witness to the events.

During the following week, Price-Williams contacted the subjects and asked them if they had recalled any interesting dreams. The responses are summarized below:

Subject 1,   a research psychologist dreamed about Castaneda and a "swarm of fish" flying in the sky. He stated, "The fish resembled the kind of carp one sees in Hawaii."

Subject 2,   a graduate student dreamed of a chimpanzee which was eating "a bunch of tiny light colored monkey babies—the size of tiny mice." On the following night, the student dreamed that he was to meet a mutual friend of himself and Castaneda. Instead, a pack of dogs attacked him. One of the dogs was the "size of a small rat or mouse."

Subject 3,   was an anthropologist. He dreamed that Price-Williams had acquired a "carp farm in Hawaii" and was looking for someone to manage it.

Subject 4,   an architect, dreamed of insects, bumblebees, and rodents. The creatures were not perceived as threatening but were "coming to see me" and buzzed around his head. The dream was so out of character for the architect that he told his wife about it as well as a friend.

Subject 5,   was a physical scientist. He had a dream or waking reverie about a strange animal, "larger than a cat, slightly repulsive." It was gray and "could have been a rat with long legs."

Subject 6,   a parapsychologist, dreamed about a toilet bowl "in which there are two rodent-like fish, or fish-like rodents." Although not aggressive, "there is something disgusting about them. They look half cartoon-like, with pink bodies, black ears, and long black tails."

Subject 7,   was another graduate student. His dream was
               of a small cat "that had the breasts of a
               woman." The creature rubbed against the
               dreamer's leg.

It is surprising that all seven people remembered dreams
without being told they were part of a dream experiment. It
is also remarkable that the dreams centered around animals, principally cats, fish, and rodents. What had Castaneda been doing? He had been going through a ritual by
which images of several of his "allies" would appear in the
dreams of the seven subjects—individuals of whose iden-
tities he was unaware. Price-Williams has not claimed his
studies are conclusive, and there are certain methodological
shortcomings that need to be tightened up in future experiments. Nevertheless, his work shows how science can investigate even the most unusual phenomena if the sorcerer,
shaman, or "healer" is cooperative.

Possible Applications

Scientific method involves collecting information, making
hypotheses about future events, testing them by experiments, and reporting the results in a form that allows others
to verify these data and ultimately to apply them in people's
lives. It is still too early to make definite statements about
applied parapsychology, especially "psychic healing."
However, the Spiritists, shamans, esoteric "healers," and
intuitive "healers" of the world are plying their trade without waiting for the data to come in. As has already been
demonstrated, there are a number of reasons why their
healees will get well or improve, sing the "healers'"
praises, and insure a continuation of the various traditions.

It is interesting that "psychic healing" is no longer confined to primitive areas or to the poor. Toshio Yamamoto,
director of the 800-bed Tenrskyo Hospital in Japan, has 80

"healers" available for the hospital's patients. Dr. Yamamoto has claimed that many patients for whom all hope had been abandoned have been cured by the "healers." In addition, the British National Federation of Spiritual Healers has obtained permission from the Minister of Health for its members to see patients in some 1,500 hospitals throughout the country. A patient can ask hospital authorities to telephone the Federation which will then obtain the services of a "healer." And in 1975, the World Federation of Healing was organized at a conference held at London University. Its members announced that one of their goals was to make "healers" available to hospital patients all over the world on the same basis as has been practiced in Great Britain.

Volume 19 of the official *Great Soviet Encyclopedia* describes "paradiagnostics" as "medical diagnosis without contact with the patient, based on clairvoyance." Any number of physicians have begun to use psychic specialists who claim an expertise in this skill. For example, Norman Shealy, director of the Pain Rehabilitation Clinic in La Crosse, Wisconsin, has used the services of Henry Rucker, a psychic sensitive, to diagnose illness. In tests involving some 350 patients, Dr. Shealy claimed that Rucker was 80 per cent accurate. According to Shealy, in his book, *Occult Medicine Can Save Your Life*, a similar accuracy rate was reported by Thomas Becker, a physician at the University of Tennessee College of Medicine. Usually, Rucker is described as seeing the patient during diagnosis, so the possibility of sensory cues cannot be ruled out.*

There are applications and implications of "psychic healing" that may affect even more people who are infirm. Many contemporary physicians have claimed that virtually all the medications of the past were "nothing but

---

*A highly sophisticated form of purported diagnosis, "radionics," is related to dowsing and uses a pendulum, forked stick, or other types of equipment which move in a way that gives a positive or negative response to questions of a person's health when the equipment is held by the "psychic diagnostician."

placebos.'' However, the snake root prescribed by ancient Indian folk medicine turned out to be a potent tranquilizer known today by its brand name, Serpasil. Paracelsus, the esoteric physician of the middle ages, used quicksilver and laudanum successfully. The use of hot dates prescribed in the Old Testament as a cure for boils may have been an effective remedy, as was mold when applied to combat infection—if the mold was of the variety containing what today is called penicillin. Therefore, it would be wise to investigate the herbs and salves used by "psychic healers" to see if these substances could be of more general value.

Jan Ehrenwald, a psychiatrist, has seen the importance of integrating psi effects into the psychophysiological variables involved in orthodox healing. In an article in the *Parapsychology Review*, Ehrenwald told the story of Sir Kenelm Digby, a seventeenth century seafarer who claimed to own a powerful remedy, the "Powder of Sympathy," imported from the "mysterious East." The main ingredient of this remedy was copper sulphate prepared according to secret alchemical and astrological formulas. Sir Kenelm demonstrated its most spectacular curative effect in a courtly setting in England when his friend, James Howell, was wounded while intervening in a duel. The wound bled profusely, though friends tried to stop the bleeding with the wounded man's garter. He survived, but gangrene set in and the king's court surgeon feared for the patient's life. However, Digby's "Powder of Sympathy" is said to have come to his rescue. Sir Kenelm asked for Howell's blood-drenched garter and soaked it in a basin containing the "Powder." Howell, at the other side of the room, suddenly remarked that his pain was gone. Later, Digby took the garter out of the basin and placed it beside a fire to dry. Soon, Howell's servant came running to report that his master had felt a sudden burning of the affected limb. Digby sent the servent back with a reassuring message and put the garter back in the copper solution. The servant returned to find Howell free of pain. Within six days the wound was completely healed. The incident reportedly was corroborated by several witnesses and noted among the observations of Sir Frances Bacon.

The "Powder of Sympathy" is often used by psychiatrists as an example of psychological effects in healing— shared belief, suggestion, the placebo effect, etc. However, Ehrenwald argues that the story—if true—also indicates that the "Powder" apparently served as a vehicle for telepathy from the practitioner to the patient. Laying aside the issue of the tale's validity, its recounting by contemporary psychotherapists usually omits the psi factor entirely. Yet, without including ESP in the solution, certain parts of the account remain unexplained.

In addition, the psi factor may be helpful in explaining why some medicines seem to lose their effectiveness over the years. Some preparations are hailed by physicians after passing stringent double-blind research tests and laboratory analyses. But eventually, they fade into near-obscurity to be replaced by another enthusiastically-touted substance. Jan Ehrenwald has suggested that:

> There is circumstantial evidence to suggest that one of the flies in the ointment is an effect of parapsychological origin . . . .
> . . . The first wave of high hope and expectancy, and its attending telepathic reverberations, may well sweep across the boundaries of the most tightly controlled double-blind situation. It may spread from the investigator to the nursing personnel, to the medical profession, to patients and the public at large. If so, it may account for some of the striking but elusive and ultimately shortlived effects of a new product or curative procedure, followed by the failure of its attempted replication in other laboratories.

Perhaps it is only the test of time that will enable medical researchers to determine whether or not a new drug or other type of treatment needs a psychic component—as well as a more easily explained psychological component—to be effective. In the meantime, Ehrenwald sees nothing wrong in using a substance as long as it works, even though a "psychic placebo effect" is one of the factors involved in its success.

Finally, a model of healing that integrates physical, psychological, and psychical factors could be of potential use in the treatment of mentally ill persons. Ehrenwald has written:

> Intercessionary prayers and alleged healing at a distance are cases in point . . . . In such a scenario we would have to assume that it is the healer's mental state—particularly his therapeutic motivations dovetailing with the patient's hopes to be cured—which introduces the psi factor into the therapeutic equation.

Can science ever eliminate the "healer" from the psi equation? John Taylor, in his book *Superminds*, suggests that if a "healer" does emit a radiation, and if this radiation is ever identified, equipment could be devised to simulate the "healer's" action. This "healing machine" could emit the same type of radiation associated with the "healer," thus benefiting more people.

There is a slight possibility that such a machine already exists. In the laboratory of Antoine Priore, work has been proceeding for several years on a machine which Priore has described as emitting "radiation in an electromagnetic field." A report from France's Institute for Cancer Research notes that cancerous rats, when treated with an earlier version of Priore's device, survived while an untreated group died. A researcher from the University of Bordeaux carried out an experiment with infected rabbits. Those treated with the Priore device survived; indeed, many appeared to develop immunity to further infection. The untreated rabbits, however, deteriorated.

Priore was accused of falsifying the experimental results by substituting animals. So in 1969, a prestigious committee of scientists performed an experiment involving 60 infected mice. Of the 30 treated with Priore's apparatus, 29 survived. Of the 30 untreated mice, 26 were dead within five days. A third group of 30 uninfected and untreated mice all survived.

In the meantime, the World Health Organization has given Priore a grant for further research and he has said only that he built it intuitively from "feeling." And there the matter rests until the apparatus can be closely examined and tested by outside investigators.

A Rendezvous with Doña Rosita

The authors discussed the realms of "healing" at the Sixth International Conference on Humanistic Psychology held in Cuernavaca, Mexico, in December, 1975. One of them (A. V.) attempted to locate doña Pachita, but she had gone into hiding, again being persecuted by the police for "practicing medicine without a license." However, he did locate another "healer," doña Rosita, and brought her from Mexico City to hear several addresses being given at the conference.

Later that day, Rosita discussed her "healing" abilities with several conference participants. In 1970, doña Rosita became ill and her physician is said to have diagnosed an "untreatable" heart condition. Allegedly, Rosita was given less than a year to live. Her mother, a "healer," said that she would teach Rosita how to "heal" herself. A few months later the heart condition had disappeared. This procedure resembles the cycle of "self-healing"/"healing"-of-others found among shamans and other paranormal "healers."

The basic procedure taught to Rosita by her mother involved "cleansing" the "aura" with a fresh egg. At the same time, she would "incorporate" an Indian "spirit" who would guide the "healing process." This procedure places doña Rosita in the Spiritist tradition. And like many

Spiritists, she also venerates the Roman Catholic saints, praying to them during "healing sessions." When asked to "heal" someone, doña Rosita motioned toward one of the authors (S. K.), saying she would like to work with him. Rosita had stated she would require a raw egg for her work and Villoldo had brought several. She expressed disappointment because they were brown rather than white, but decided to try anyway. Krippner reported:

Doña Rosita stood directly in front of me, passing the egg over my entire body–sometimes touching the body with it. All the while she was praying–praising God, the saints, the Indian "spirits," and finally Christ. She also told the evil "spirits" to leave my body alone and stop causing trouble. She then broke the egg into a glass; the white formed a dome over the yoke. A small twig-like object could be observed in the egg white. Rosita claimed that the egg white formed a dome-like structure to symbolize the protection I have been given by loved ones over the years. The twig, however, represented the "evil influence" that a "witch" had cast on me. We removed the twig, inspected it, then flushed it down the toilet after which Rosita performed a special blessing on the bathroom. The twig-like object was so small, it could have been placed in the glass by sleight of hand. Or it could have been an impurity or discolored portion of the egg yolk. To Rosita, however, it was a symbol of the disease she had removed from my body. She claimed it would have been larger had a white egg rather than a brown one been used.

On the following evening, one of the authors (S. K.) and two of his friends arrived at the home of Eugenio Barbera, a Mexican surgeon. Dr. Barbera attested to doña Rosita's abilities by saying that she had helped his stepdaughter, Andrea, a young ballerina, who had experienced only temporary relief following one of doña Pachita's psychic interventions for a painful ligament in her heel. Rosita had worked with the ballerina in 1975, performing her usual "healing" ritual with an egg. Andrea's pain disappeared and she was able to resume her ballet lessons and performances. A physiological model of the phenomenon would explain this by stating that the ballerina had adjusted to the pain over time or that physical compensation had taken place to alleviate the stress. Those holding to a psychological model could say that the ballerina's desire to perform again had become so strong that she was able to modulate the pain psychologically. From the viewpoint of a psychic model, it could be claimed that the ballerina's faith (or "will") was finally strong enough to allow the "healing" to take place. Of course, there would be no difficulty in combining the three explanations in determining how "healing" occurred in this instance.

Dr. Barbera and his wife Luisa had purchased a dozen white eggs. Krippner and his friends (Joel Hendrick, a videotape technician, and Don Fersh, a graduate student) each selected an egg, taking care to choose eggs on which were easily indentifiable scratches or other marks. This would enable them to be sure that the eggs which Rosita would break were the same eggs used during the "healing" session. Krippner, an amateur magician and a Fellow in the American Society for Clinical Hypnosis, instructed the group how to avoid being deceived by trickery and hypnotic effects while, at the same time, remaining receptive for any "healing" from which they might benefit. Joel Hendrick reported on what transpired when the group kept their rendezvous with Rosita at her home:

> Doña Rosita's apartment was filled with people, both adults and children, as we entered. As we had telephoned Rosita and made an appointment, the five of us were taken directly to a bedroom. The room consisted of a bed, a chair, and a small table on which rested a tumbler half-filled with water, and an old detergent bottle which we later discovered was filled with water which had been blessed in a nearby church. There was a bathroom directly across from the table. We

observed a picture of Jesus on the wall as well as a picture of a figure meditating.

I chose to be "healed" first, so Luisa Barbera translated my name and health concerns to Rosita. One day before, I had suffered from the 24-hour flu. More important, I had a long-standing concern that there were impurities in my blood system.

I stood before Rosita holding my white egg. Her hands were clasped over mine. I had the subjective feeling that Rosita's "energy" was pouring into me. I also experienced complete faith in her ability to "heal." I knew that this faith needed to run deep within me for the session to be the most effective. Closing her eyes, she took the egg from me and began to recite, in Spanish, a long prayer asking her Christian and Indian "spirit guides" to protect me from many harmful forces. She began passing the egg over my chest and making circles over my stomach as the prayer continued.

Rosita's hands encircled my head, then ran down my shoulders and arms to my hands. Next, her hands moved down my entire body. Rosita passed the egg from one of her hands to another as she brought her hands down my legs and over my feet. She then "cast off" the accumulation of "negative energy" by shaking it from her hands. She moved her hands up and repeated this "casting off" of "negative energy" over my chest and stomach area.

At this point, I glanced at the egg to be sure it was mine. The distinctive mark was still there and I was convinced that the egg had not been "switched." However, much to my surprise, I appeared to see the eggshell turning a dark color as if the inside of the egg had turned black.

Rosita then turned me around and passed the egg over my right shoulder and the back side of my head. Rosita dropped her hands over my back and legs purportedly to release the "negative energy." Suddenly, she blew against the back of my neck and I experienced a surge of "energy" rush throughout my body. She ended by turning me around and passing the egg over my body as she had the first time. The entire "healing" session, accompanied by constant praying, had lasted about five minutes.

She then turned to the small table and the glass which was half-filled with a liquid which appeared to be water. Three times she touched the side of the glass with the hand holding the egg. I paid careful attention to this procedure, to be aware of any possible sleight of hand. The other four people in the room were also observing Rosita and the egg from every possible angle. The room was well lit and she did not object to our careful scrutiny. Rosita cracked the egg on the edge of the glass, emptying the contents into the tumbler. Out came the egg white, the egg yolk, as well as a black lumpy substance. The black substance appeared to permeate the entire glass. I wondered if, perhaps, the water in the glass had contained a chemical that would turn black when it came into contact with the natural chemicals in the egg. This possibility was made less likely when I noticed the egg shell. It had been broken in half and the black substance had coated the inside of the shell. It was very difficult for us to conjecture how the inside of the shell could have obtained the black coating through chemical reaction as it never entered the tumbler.

I inspected the shell and observed the mark that convinced me that the same egg had been used during the entire session.

Rosita then plucked a large piece of the black substance from the tumbler. I touched it and noticed the texture was very much like ashes or burned wood. Rosita said that some years ago someone gave me a drink which contained "negative energy." This "poison" had been in my system for some years, and I had suffered from it in various ways. Now, however, she claimed I had been "healed." One aspect of the "healing," according to Rosita, involved the temporary "merging" of her "energy" with mine and the "joining together" of both of our "spirit guides."

I held Rosita's hands and thanked her. She turned and picked up the old detergent bottle filled with blessed water. She poured it over both our hands and continued to pray so as to cast off any remaining "negative energy" from my body. Then Rosita flushed the contents of the tumbler down the toilet and uttered a short prayer. I thanked her again.

Don Fersh and Stanley Krippner underwent the same

process. Stanley told Rosita that Don needed "healing" for a mild case of epilepsy. However, Stanley had not seen Don for six months and did not know that a recent physical examination indicated that the problem was no longer present. Nevertheless, Rosita performed the "healing" ritual. When the egg was broken, no foreign objects appeared. Rosita remarked there had been a health problem at birth but it no longer appeared to be present.

Turning to Stanley, Rosita repeated her procedure. Again, we observed the process very closely. As Rosita broke the egg, I appeared to see several bright red and dark green objects fall from the broken eggshell along with the white and yolk. Rosita and Stanley reached into the tumbler and pulled the objects out, placing them on tissue. There were portions of a plant—buds, seeds, and a flower.

The flower was long and bright red. Rosita allowed Stanley to take it with him, as well as the buds and seeds.* First, however, she poured holy water on them to remove any harmful properties they might have had. She told Stanley that their appearance confirmed her earlier statement that a "witch" intended to harm him, possibly by causing an accident. The red flower symbolized blood; the fact that the flower was beautiful indicated that the "witch" had disguised himself or herself to avoid suspicion. Again, the eggshell was examined and the long scratch could be seen, which served as its mark of identification.

Although Rosita did not ask for any payment, we each gave her 100 pesos before leaving. The next day, Stanley and I left Mexico. On the way to the airport our taxicab plowed into another car. Fortunately the damage was slight and there were no injuries. Could it be that doña Rosita's "healings" had protected us?

The rendezvous with doña Rosita suggested several lines of future research:

1. A session could be filmed or videotaped for further inspection as to the procedures used.

---

*A biologist at U.C.L.A. tentatively identified the plant as crythria, a Mexican wildflower.

There may be common elements in these rituals that are important for "healing" to happen.

2. A professional magician should be brought in as part of the investigation team. For example, the magician might ask Rosita if he or she could break the egg following its use to "cleanse" the healee's body.
3. The contents of the eggs could be collected and examined. Relationships between these substances and the healees' ailments could be investigated.
4. A long-term study could be made of Rosita's healees, the types of complaints they have when they arrive, and—through follow-up—what types of problems respond best to Rosita's ministrations.

Research projects of this nature require attention to the physical and psychological components of "healing" as well as attention to any possible psi effects. This holistic approach indicates that there is a system of "healing"; scientists cannot ignore important portions of that system without risking a misunderstanding of the entire process.

Some individuals may question the scrutiny of purported psi effects for possible sleight of hand. Although it is quite true that shamans and other "healers" often use legerdemain as an integral part of the "healing" process, the scientist needs to know if any type of ESP or PK occurs. Any sophisticated investigator will realize that trickery runs rampant in "psychic healing"; indeed, some primitive traditions do not even differentiate between "real magic" and "artificial magic." But if science is to plumb the entire range of human potential, it simply must know if psi effects occur in "healing" ceremonies, albeit on an irregular basis.

The celebrated magician Milbourne Christopher has referred to "psychic surgery" as "one of the cruelest hoaxes ever perpetrated on a credulous public." Christopher has never made an extensive on-site investigation of this type of psychic intervention; further, the material in his book *Mediums, Mystics and the Occult* indicates that he is unaware of the complexities of shamanic, esoteric, and Spiritist traditions. Nevertheless, Christopher's writings must be required reading for anyone investigating "psychic healers." These investigators must also be very cautious before claiming that they have witnessed paranormal phenomena. If not, they do science a disservice; if deceived, they add weight to Christopher's claims that the clever but fraudulent "psychic sensitive"

> . . . is at his ingenious best in laboratories where he is being observed by scientists who believe he has extraordinary ESP ability and think—without justification—that they have ruled out every possibility of fraud. Unless an expert in deception is present while such tests are being conducted, these experiments are as valid as a four-dollar bill.

The Truth About "Healing"

Albert Szent-Györgyi, the Nobel Prize-winning biologist, noted, in 1971, that the "primary aim of science is to find truth, a new truth." He added, "New truth and knowledge always elevate human life and most usually find practical application."

In surveying the realms of "healing," the authors have searched for one quality above all else—the truth. The authors have emphasized the scientific method because, for all its faults, science is the best procedure that human beings have invented for discovering truth and obtaining agreement about their knowledge of the universe. Its aim is to surmount the foibles of superstition and wishful thinking by a method aimed at discovering facts and relationships that can be known, communicated, and verified by others. A. H. Maslow could have been writing about "paranormal healing" when he stated, in *The Psychology of Science*, that "the first effort to research a new problem is most likely to be inelegant, imprecise, and crude. What one mostly learns from such first efforts is how it should be done better the next time." And in *Humanistic Psychology and the Research Tradition*, Irving L. Child has written:

> Development of scientific knowledge . . . is a long process, with great uncertainty at all stages that we can as yet discern. Neither experimentation nor any other device is likely to eliminate all of the complexities and to supply a perfect and simple understanding. If we truly confined ourselves to knowledge having the clear certainty of experimental findings, avoiding all those extensions, inferences, and generalizations that contaminate their purity, psychology would be a collection of trivia.

The "healing process" is not trivial. Indeed, it can be a matter of life and death. Those who consider themselves "healers" have a grave responsibility to their healees and also to the scientific search for understanding.

In Tantric Buddhism, truth is said to find its most practical expression in terms of "healing." As Western science begins to explore the complexities of the "healing" process, it also may discover that its discipline and structure can lead to the unfolding of awe and flowering of wonder that will enhance the scope of science and vitalize its quest.

Bibliography

Ader, R., and Cohen, N., "Behaviorally Conditioned Immunosuppression," *Psychosomatic Medicine*, 1975, *37*, 333–340.

Andrade, H. G., *Experimental Parapsychology*. São Paulo: Calvario, 1967.

Andrade, H. G., *A Corpuscular Theory of the Spirit*. São Paulo: Privately published, 1968.

Andrade, H. G., *The Psi Matter*. Matão, Brazil: Clarim, 1972.

Andreas, L., *Shamanism: The Beginnings of Art*. New York: McGraw-Hill, 1967.

Assagioli, R., *Act of Will*. New York: Viking, 1973.

Bahr, D.; Gregorio, J; Lopez, D.L.; and Alvarez, A., *Piman Shamanism and Staying Sickness*. Tucson: University of Arizona Press, 1975.

Bailey, A. A., *Esoteric Psychology*. New York: Lucis, 1970.

Bailey, A. A., *Telepathy*. New York: Lucis, 1971.

Bandler, R., and Grinder, J., *Patterns of the Hypnotic Techniques of Milton H. Erickson, M.D.*, Volume I. Cupertino, Cal.: Meta, 1975.

Becker, R. O., "Electromagnetic Forces and Life Processes," *Technology Review*, 1972, *75*, 2–8,

Becker, R. O.; Reichmanis, M.; Marino, A. A.; and Spadaro, J. A., "Electrophysiological Correlates of Acupuncture Points and Meridians," *Psychoenergetic Systems*, 1976, *1*, in press.

Becker, R. O., and Spadaro, J. A., "Electrical Stimulation of Partial Limb Regeneration in Mammals," *Bulletin, New York Academy of Science, 1972, 48*, 627–641.

Benson, H., *The Relaxation Response*. New York: Morrow, 1975.

Bloomfield, H. H.; Cain, M. P.; and Jaffe, D. T., *TM: Discovering Inner Energy and Overcoming Stress*. New York: Delacorte, 1975.

Bohm, D. J., "A Suggested Interpretation of the Quantum Theory in Terms of Hidden Variables, I and II." *Physical Review*, 1952, *85*, 166–179, 180–193.

Boyd, D., *Rolling Thunder*. New York: Random House, 1974.

Bresler, D. E., and Kroening, R. J., "A Three-factor Theory of Acupuncture," *Psychoenergetic Systems*, 1976, *1*, 137–139.

Brown, J. W., "Native American Contributions to Science, Engineering, and Medicine," *Science*, 1975, *189*, 38–40.

Burr, H. S., *The Fields of Life*. New York: Ballantine, 1973.

Castaneda, C., *Tales of Power*. New York: Simon & Schuster, 1974.

Cerutti, E., *Olga Worrall: Mystic with the Healing Hands*. New York: Harper & Row, 1975.

Chaves, J. F., and Barber, T. X., "Acupuncture Analgesia: A Six-Factor Theory," *Psychoenergetic Systems*, 1974, *1*, 11–20.

Child, I. L., *Humanistic Psychology and the Research Tradition*. New York: John Wiley & Sons, 1973.

Christopher, M., *Mediums, Mystics and the Occult*. New York: Thomas Y. Crowell, 1975.

Crowley, A., *The Book of Thoth: Egyptian Tarot*. San Francisco: Level Press, 1974.

Cummings, G., *The Road to Immortality*. London: Psychic Press, 1967.

de Rola, S. K., *Alchemy: The Secret Art*. New York: Bounty, 1973.

de la Ferriere, S. R., *The New Book of Freemasonry*. Mexico City: Diana, 1970.

Dean, D., "The Effects of 'Healers' on Biologically Significant Molecules," *New Horizons*, 1975, *1*, 215–219.

Dean, D., and Brame, E., "Physical Changes in Water by Laying-on-of-Hands," in *Proceedings, Second International Congress on Psychotronic Research*, Paris: Institut Métaphysique International, 1975.

Dennis, W., "Cultural and Developmental Factors in Perception," in *The Proper Study of Man*, edited by J. Fadiman. New York: Macmillan, 1971.

Dodds, E. R., "Telepathy and Clairvoyance in Classical Antiquity," *Journal of Parapsychology*, 1946, *10*, 290–309.

Dooley, A., *Every Wall a Door: Exploring Psychic Surgery and Healing*. London: Abelard Schuman, 1972.

Edwards, H., *Psychic Healing*. London: Spiritualist Press, 1946.

Ehrenwald, J., "Placebo: Ploy, Psi Effect, Research Tool or Psychoactive Agent?" *Parapsychology Review*, September–October, 1974.

Eliade, M., *Shamanism: Archaic Techniques of Ecstasy*. Princeton, N.J.: Princeton University Press, 1964.

Elguin, G. H., and Onetta-Bächler, B., "An Experiment with Psychokinesis and Tumor-Producing Cancer Cells," *Journal of Parapsychology and Borderline Areas of Psychology*, 1967, *10*, 48–61.

Erickson, M. H., "The Confusion Technique in Hypnosis." *American Journal of Clinical Hypnosis*, 1964, *6*, 183–207.

Frankl, V., *Man's Search for Meaning*. New York: Simon & Schuster, 1970.

Fraser, A., and Frey, A., "Electromagnetic Emission at Micron Wavelengths from Active Nerves," *Biophysical Journal*, June, 1968.

Fishbein, M., *Fads and Quackery in Healing*. New York: Covici & Freide, 1932.

FitzHerbert, J., "The Nature of Hypnosis and Paranormal Healing," *Journal of the Society for Psychical Research*, 1971, *46*, 1–14.

Frank, J. D., *Persuasion and Healing*, revised edition. New York: Schocken Books, 1974.

Freud, S., *The Complete Psychological Works of Sigmund Freud*, edited and translated by J. Strachey, Volume 7. London: Hogarth Press Institute of Psychoanalysis, 1953.

Fromm, E., and Shor, R. E., editors, *Hypnosis: Research Developments and Perspectives*. Chicago: Aldine/Atherton, 1972.

Fuller, J. G., *Arigó: Surgeon of the Rusty Knife*. New York: Crowell, 1974.

Garrett, E. J., *Many Voices: The Autobiography of a Medium*. New York: G. P. Putnam's Sons, 1968.

Givry, de G., *Witchcraft, Magic and Alchemy*. New York: Dover, 1971.

Gliedman, L. H.; Nash, E. H., Jr,; Imber, S. D.; Stone, A. R.; and Frank, J. D., "Reduction of Symptoms by Pharmacologically Inert Substances and By Short-Term Psychotherapy," *Archives of Neurology and Psychiatry*, 1958. *79*, 345–351.

Goldstein, M., and Firman, G. Cited in "Chiropractic—the Secrets of Its Success." *Behavior Today*, October 20, 1975.

Goodrich, J., Unpublished doctoral dissertation. Yellow Springs, Ohio: Union Graduate School, 1975.

Govinda, L. A., *Foundations of Tibetan Mysticism*. London: Rider, 1969.

Grad, B., "A Telekinetic Effect on Plant Growth," *International Journal of Parapsychology*, 1963, *5*, 117–133.

Grad, B., "The 'Laying-on' of Hands: Implications for Psychotherapy, Gentling, and the Placebo Effect," *Journal of the American Society for Psychical Research*, 1967, *61*, 286–305.

Green, E., and Green, A., "The Ins and Outs of Mind-Body Energy," in *Science Year, 1974*. Chicago: Field Enterprises, 1973.

Habel, K., "Immunological Determinants of Polyoma Virus Oncogenesis," *Journal of Experimental Medicine*, 1962, *115*, 181–193.

Haich, E., *Initiation*. San Francisco: Seed Center, 1974.

Hanscom, D. H., *Initial Decision in the Matter of Travel King, Inc.*, etc. Filed in Seattle, February 28, 1975.

Harner, M. L., editor, *Hallucinogens and Shamanism*. London: Oxford University Press, 1973.

Heisenberg, W., *Physics and Philosophy*. New York: Harper & Row, 1966.

Heisenberg, W., *Physics and Beyond*. New York: Harper & Row, 1972.

Henry, W. E., "Some Observations on the Lives of Healers," *Human Development*, 1966, *9*, 47–56.

Herbert, B., "Theory and Practice of Psychic Healing," *Parapsychology Review*, November–December, 1975.

Hilgard, E. R., "The Domain of Hypnosis," *American Psychologist*, 1973, *28*, 972–982.

Honorton, C.; Ramsey, M.; and Cabibbo, C., "Experimenter Effects in Extrasensory Perception," *Journal of the American Society for Psychical Research*, 1975, *69*, 135–149.

Inyushin, V. M., "Bioplasma and Interaction of Organisms," in *Symposium of Psychotronics*, edited by Z. Rejdak, et al. Downton, England: Paraphysical Laboratory, 1970.

James, W., "Report on Mrs. Piper's Hodgson-Control," *Proceedings of the Society for Psychical Research*, 1909, no. 23.

Jensen, A. E., *Myth and Cult Among Primitive Peoples*. Chicago: University of Chicago Press, 1963.

Jung, C. G., *Memories, Dreams, Reflections*. New York: Random House, 1961.

Kardec, A., *Spiritualist Initiation*. São Paulo: Lake, 1950.

Kardec, A., *The Medium's Book*. London: Psychic Press, 1971.

Kardec, A., *The Spirits' Book*. São Paulo: Lake, 1972.

Kiev, A., *Curanderismo: Mexican-American Folk Psychiatry*. New York: Free Press, 1968.

Kiev, A., editor, *Magic, Faith and Healing*. New York: Free Press of Glencoe, 1974.

King, T. J., editor, *Developmental Aspects of Carcinogenesis and Immunity: Proceedings of a Symposium, Manhattan, Kansas, June, 1973*. New York: Academic Press, 1974.

Kinnear, W., editor, *Thought as Energy*. Los Angeles: Science of Mind, 1975.

Kirlian, S. D., and Kirlian, V. Kh., "Photography and Visual Observations by Means of High-Frequency Currents," *Journal of Scientific and Applied Photo graphy*, 1961, *6*, 397—403.

Kluckholm, C. K., *Navaho Witchcraft*. Cambridge, Mass.: Harvard University Press, 1944.

Krieger, D., "Healing by the 'Laying-On' of Hands as a Facilitator of Bioenergetic Change: The Response of In-vivo Human Hemoglobin," *Psychoenergetic Systems*, 1976, *1*, 121–130.

Krippner, S., *Song of the Siren: A Parapsychological Odyssey*. New York: Harper & Row, 1975.

Krippner, S., and Rubin, D., editors, *The Kirlian Aura*. New York: Anchor/ Doubleday, 1974.

Krippner, S., and Rubin, D., editors, *The Energies of Consciousness*. New York: Gordon & Breach, 1975.

Krivorotov, V. K.; Krivorotov, A. E.; and Krivorotov, V. K., "Bioenergotherapy and Healing," *Psychoenergetic Systems*, 1974, *1*, 27–30.

Kroger, W. S., "Hypnotism and Acupuncture," *Journal of the American Medical Association*, 1972, *220*, 1012–1013.

Kruger, H., *Other Healers, Other Cures*. Indianapolis: Bobbs-Merrill, 1974.

Kuhn, T., *Structure of Scientific Revolutions*, second edition. Chicago: University of Chicago Press, 1970.

Lachman, S. J., *Psychosomatic Disorders: A Behavioristic Interpretation*. New York: John Wiley & Sons, 1975.

Lamb, B., *Wizard of the Upper Amazon*. Boston: Houghton-Mifflin, 1975.

LeShan, L., "An Emotional Life-History Pattern Associated with Neoplastic Disease," *Annals, New York Academy of Science*, 1966, *125*, 780–793.

LeShan, L., *The Medium, the Mystic, and the Physicist*. New York: Viking, 1974.

León, C. A., "El Duende and Other Incubi," *Archives of General Psychiatry*, 1975, *32*, 155–162.

Levi-Strauss, C., *Structural Anthropology*. New York: Basic Books, 1963.

Liboff, A. R., and Rinaldi, R. A., editors, *Electrically Mediated Growth Mechanisms in Living Systems*. New York: New York Academy of Sciences, 1974.

Lieban, R. W., *Cebano Sorcery*. Berkeley: University of California Press, 1967.

Lok Yee-Kung, "Acupuncture and Moxibustion in Traditional Chinese Medicine," in *The Energies of Consciousness*, edited by S. Krippner and D. Rubin. New York: Gordon & Breach, 1975.

McGarey, W. A., *Acupuncture and Body Energies*. Phoenix: Gabriel Press, 1974.

Man, P. L., and Chen, C. H., "Acupuncture 'Anesthesia'—A New Theory and Clinical Study," *Current Therapeutic Research*, 1972, *14*: 390–394.

Maslow, A. H., *The Psychology of Science: A Reconnaissance*. New York: Harper & Row, 1966.

Masters, R. E. L., "Psychophysical Education: Recovering the Body," *Psychoenergetic Systems*, 1976, *1*, in press.

Meek, G. W., *A Guide to Spiritual and Magnetic Healing and Psychic Surgery in the Philippines*. Privately printed by the author, 1412 Jackson St., Fort Myers, Fla. 33901, 1973.

Melzack, R., *The Puzzle of Pain*. New York: Basic Books, 1973.

Miller, R. N., and Reinhart, P. B., "Measuring Psychic Energy." *Psychic*, May—June, 1975.

Miller, R.N.; Reinhart, P. B.; and Kern, A., "Scientists Register Thought Energy," in *Thought as Energy*, edited by W. Kinnear. Los Angeles: Science of Mind, 1975.

Moss, T., *The Probability of the Impossible*. Los Angeles: J. P. Tarcher, 1974.

Murphy, G., and Ballou, R. O., editors, *William James on Psychical Research*. New York: Viking, 1960.

Murphy, G., with Dale, L., *The Challenge of Psychical Research*. New York: Harper & Row, 1961.

Murphy, G., with Leeds, M., *Outgrowing Self Deception*. New York: Basic Books, 1975.

Murphy, G., and Murphy, L. B., editors, *Asian Psychology*. New York: Basic Books, 1968.

Murphy, J. M., "Psychiatric Labeling in Cross-Cultural Perspective," *Science*, 1976, *191*, 1019–1028.

Nash, J. C., "Medical Parapsychology," *Parapsychology Review*, January—February, 1972.

Nolen, W. A., *Healing: A Doctor in Search of a Miracle*. New York: Random House, 1974.

Owen, A. R. G., *Psychic Mysteries of the North*. New York: Harper & Row, 1975.

Oyle, I., *The Healing Mind*, Millbrae, Cal.: Celestial Arts, 1975.

Panati, C., "Quantum Physics and Parapsychology," *Parapsychology Review*, November–December, 1974.

Patanjali (Woods, J. H., translator), *The Yoga–System of Patanjali*. Cambridge, Mass.: Harvard University Press, 1914.

Pendergrass, E. P., "Host Resistance and other Intangibles in the Treatment of Cancer," *American Journal of Roentgenology*, 1961, *85*, 891–896.

Playfair, G. L., *The Unknown Power*. New York: Pocket Books, 1975.

Poncé, C., *Kabbalah*. San Francisco: Straight Arrow, 1973.

Popper, K. R., *The Logic of Scientific Discovery*. London: Hutchinson, 1949.

Powell, A. E., *The Etheric Double*. Wheaton, Ill.: Theosophical Publishing House, 1969.

Pratt, J. G., "Some Notes for the Future Einstein of Parapsychology," *Journal of the American Society for Psychical Research*, 1974, *68*, 133–155.

Presman, A. S., *Electromagnetic Fields and Life*. New York: Plenum, 1970.

Progoff, I., *The Image of an Oracle*. New York: Helix, 1964.

Price-Williams, D., "Some Field Experiments in Sorcery." A paper presented at the First World Congress of Sorcery, Bogotá, Colombia, 1975.

Rao, K. R., "An Autobiographical Note," *Parapsychology Review*, July–August, 1973.

Rhine, L. E., *PSI: What is it?* New York: Harper & Row, 1975.

Riesen, A. H., "Sensory Deprivation," in *Progress in Physiological Psychology*, Volume I, edited by E. Stellar and J. M. Sprague. New York: Academic Press, 1966.

Robinson, J. W., cited in "Study Explains 'Glow of Life' Photographs," *Christian Science Monitor*, January 7, 1976.

Rogers, C. R. "The Necessary and Sufficient Conditions of Therapeutic Personality Change," *Journal of Consulting Psychology*, 1957, *21*, 95–103.

Rogo, D. S., and Bayless, R., "Psychic Surgery," *Journal of the Society for Psychical Research*, 1968, *44*, 426–428.

Rolf, I. P., *Structural Integration*. Boulder, Colo.: Guild for Structural Integration, 1962.

Rolling Thunder, foreword to *Song of the Siren: A Parapsychological Odyssey* by S. Krippner. New York: Harper & row, 1975.

Rorvik, D. M., "Jack Schwarz Feels No Pain," *Esquire,* December, 1973.

Rorvik, D. M., "Do the French Have a Cure for Cancer?" *Esquire,* July, 1975.

Rose, L., *Faith Healing.* Baltimore: Penguin, 1971.

Rose, R., *Living Magic: The Realities Underlying the Psychical Practices and Beliefs of Australian Aborigines.* New York: Rand McNally, 1956.

Rosenthal, R., *Experimenter Effects in Behavioral Research.* New York: Appleton-Century-Crofts, 1966.

Russell, E. W., *Report on Radionics: Science of the Future.* London: Neville Spearman, 1973.

Samuels, M., and Bennett H., *The Well Body Book.* New York: Random House/Bookworks, 1973.

Schimmel, E. M., "The Hazards of Hospitalization," *Annals of Internal Medicine,* 1964, *60,* 100–110.

Schmeidler, G. R., and McConnell, R. A., *ESP and Personality Patterns.* New Haven, Conn.: Yale University Press, 1958.

Schultz, J. H., and Luthe, W., *Autogenic Training: A Psychophysiologic Approach in Psychotherapy.* New York: Grune & Stratton, 1959.

Schwartz, S., and Bolen, J., "Interview: Ambrose and Olga Worrall." *Psychic,* April, 1972.

Servadio, E., "Comments," *Parapsychology Review,* March–April, 1974.

Shealy, C. N., *Occult Medicine Can Save Your Life.* New York: Dial, 1975.

Sherman, H.,*"Wonder" Healers of the Philippines.* Los Angeles: DeVorss, 1967.

Sherman, M., "The Differentiation of Emotional Responses in Infants." *Journal of Comparative Psychology,* 1927, *7,* 265–284.

Siegler, M., and Osmond, H., *Models of Madness, Models of Medicine.* New York: Macmillan, 1974.

Simonton, O. C., and Simonton, S. S., "Belief Systems and Management of the Emotional Aspects of Malignancy," *Journal of Transpersonal Psychology,* 1975, *7,* 29–47.

Smith, M. J., "Paranormal Effect of Enzyme Activity Through Laying-on of Hands," *Human Dimensions,* Summer, 1972.

Stace, W. T., *Mysticism and Philosophy.* Philadelphia: J. P. Lippincott, 1960.

Stein, M.; Schiavi, R. C.; Camerino, M.; "Influence of Brain and Behavior on the Immune System," *Science,* 1976, *191,* 435–440.

Stevenson, I., "Twenty Cases Suggestive of Reincarnation," *Proceedings, American Society for Psychical Research,* September, 1966.

Stevenson, I., Review of *Healing: A Doctor in Search of a Miracle* in *Journal of the American Society for Psychical Research,* 1976, *70,* 101–108.

Stewart, H., "A Pilot Study of the Afro-American Healer," *Psychoenergetic Systems,* 1976, *1,* 131–134.

Storm, H., *Seven Arrows.* New York: Harper & Row, 1972.

Surgue, T., *There is a River.* New York: Dell, 1970

Szent-Györgyi, A., *Bioenergetics.* New York: Academic Press, 1957.

Szent-Györgyi, A., *Introduction to a Submolecular Biology.* New York: Academic Press, 1960.

Szent-Györgyi, A., *The Crazy Ape.* New York: Grosset & Dunlop, 1971.

Szent-Györgyi, A., *Electronic Biology and Cancer: A New Theory of Cancer.* New York: Marcel Dekker, 1976.

Tart, C. T., editor, *Transpersonal Psychologies.* New York: Harper & Row, 1975.

Taylor, J., *Superminds.* London: Macmillan, 1975.

Tepperman, J., *Metabolic and Endocrine Physiology*, Second Edition. Chicago: Yearbook Publishers, 1968.

Thouless, R. H., "Parapsychology During the Last Quarter of a Century," *Journal of Parapsychology*, 1969, *33*, 283–299.

Tiller, W. A., *Kirlian Photography: Its Scientific Foundations and Future Potentials*. Stanford, Cal.: Stanford University, 1975.

Tinbergen, N., "Ethology and Stress Diseases," *Science*, 1974, *185*, 20–27.

Tinney, S., "Fake Psychic Healers!" *National Enquirer*, April, 1975.

Torrey, E. F., *The Mind Game: Witchdoctors and Psychiatrists*. New York: Bantam, 1973.

Toulmin, S., *Human Understanding*. Princeton, N. J.: Princeton University Press, 1972.

Ullman, M., and Krippner, S., with Vaughan, A., *Dream Telepathy*. New York: Macmillan, 1973.

Valentine, T., *Psychic Surgery*. Chicago: Henry Regnery, 1973.

Van Dusen, W., *The Natural Depth in Man*. New York: Harper & Row, 1972.

Volgyesi, F. A., " 'School for Patients'—Hypnosis-Therapy and Psychoprophylaxis," *British Journal of Medical Hypnosis*, 1954, *5*:8–17.

Walker, E. H., "The Nature of Consciousness," *Mathematical Bio-Sciences*, 1970, *7*, 138–178.

Walker, E. H., "Consciousness as a Hidden Variable," *Physics Today*, 1971, *24*, 39.

Walker, E. H., "Consciousness in the Quantum Theory of Measurement, Part I," *Journal for the Study of Consciousness*, 1972, *5, 46*–63.

Walker, E. H., "Consciousness and Quantum Theory," in *Psychic Exploration: A Challenge for Science*, edited by J. White. New York: Putnam's, 1974.

Walker, E. H., "Science/Consciousness/Religion," in *Thought as Energy*, edited by W. Kinnear. Los Angeles: Science of Mind, 1975.

Watkins, G., and Watkins, A., "Possible PK Influence on the Resuscitation of Anesthetized Mice," *Journal of Parapsychology*, 1971, *35*, 257–272.

Watkins, G. V.; Watkins, A. M.; and Wells, R. A., "Further Studies on the Resuscitation of Anesthetized Mice," in *Research in Parapsychology*, edited by W. G. Roll; R. L. Morris; and J. D. Morris. Metuchen, N. J.: Scarecrow Press, 1973.

Watson, L., *The Romeo Error*. New York: Doubleday, 1974

Watts, A., *Psychotherapy: East and West*. New York: Pantheon, 1961.

Watts, A., *Cloud-Hidden, Whereabouts Unknown*. New York: Pantheon, 1973.

Weil, A., *The Natural Mind*. Boston: Houghton Mifflin, 1972.

Wells, R., and Klein, J., "A Replication of a 'Psychic Healing' Paradigm." *Journal of Parapsychology*, 1972, *36*, 144–149.

West, D. J., *Eleven Lourdes Miracles*. London: Gerald Duckworth, 1957.

Wheeler, J. A.; Misner, C.; and Thoine, K. S., *Gravitation*. San Francisco: W. H. Freeman, 1973.

White, J., and Krippner, S., editors, *Future Science*. New York: Anchor/Doubleday, in press.

Wightman, W. P. D., *The Growth of Scientific Ideas*. New Haven: Yale University Press, 1953.

Winston, S., Unpublished doctoral dissertation. Yellow Springs, Ohio: Union Graduate School, 1975.

Wright, D. F., and Wright, C., "Zap! You're Healed," *Woman's Home Companion*, March 7, 1974.

Worrall, A. A., and Worrall, O. N., *The Gift of Healing*. New York: Harper & Row, 1965.

Worrall, O. N., *Explore Your Psychic World*. New York: Harper & Row, 1970.

Worsley, J. R., *Is Acupuncture for You?* New York: Harper & Row, 1973.
Young, J. Z., *An Introduction to the Study of Man*. Oxford: Clarendon Press, 1971.
Zinn, H., *The Politics of History*. Boston: Houghton Mifflin, 1970.
Zezulka, J., *Matter is Energy, Energy is Vibration*. Prague: Privately produced by the author, Ul. J. Plaglty ZS, 150–00 Prague 5, Czechoslovakia, 1974.
Zezulka, J., "One Healer's Views," in *Proceedings, Second International Congress on Psychotronic Research*. Paris: Institut Métaphysique International, 1975.
Zezulka, J., "Biotronic Healing." *Psychoenergetic Systems*, 1976, *1*, 145–147.
Zorab, G., "From the European Press," *Parapsychology Review*, May–June, 1973.
Zubek, J. P., editor, *Sensory Deprivation*. New York: Appleton-Century-Croft, 1969.

Index

About the Authors

STANLEY KRIPPNER is Program Planning Coordinator of the Humanistic Psychology Institute in San Francisco, and Director of Research for the Churchill School in New York City. After receiving his doctorate from Northwestern University in 1961, he served for three years as Director of the Kent State University Child Study Center and then, for ten years, as Director of the Maimonides Medical Center's Dream Laboratory in Brooklyn. He is the author or co-author of some 300 articles in various professional journals as well as author, co-author, or co-editor of several books dealing with parapsychology and altered states of consciousness. Dr. Krippner served as President of the Association for Humanistic Psychology from 1974 to 1975 and is the Honarary Vice President of the Albert Schweitzer Cultural Association in Mexico City. He has been Visiting Professor at the University of Puerto Rico, the University for Life Sciences in Bogotá, and California State College at Sonoma. He is recipient of the YMCA Service to Youth Award and the Citation of Merit from the National Association for Gifted Children. Dr. Krippner is a Fellow in the American Society for Clinical Hypnosis. In 1971, he gave the first lecture on parapsychology ever presented at the U.S.S.R. Academy of Pedagogical Sciences.

ALBERTO VILLOLDO has traveled extensively through Central and South America conducting field research with psychic healers. After receiving his M. A. in psychology in 1973, he taught at the University of Mexico and California State College, Sonoma, and now lectures to professional groups in the United States and Latin America. He currently directs special education programs in several California pre-schools, is a consulting editor to *Psychoenergetic Systems* and the Freeperson Press, and coordinator of International Development for Latin America with the Association for Humanistic Psychology. Mr. Villoldo carries out parapsychological research in "psychic healing" and other psychokinetic phenomena at a private laboratory in San Francisco, and has authored and co-authored several articles on education,"healing"and altered states of consciousness. He is completing his Ph. D. studies at the Humanistic Psychology Institute in San Francisco.